Out of the New

T0048302

Out of the News

Former Journalists Discuss a Profession in Crisis

CELIA VIGGO WEXLER

McFarland & Company, Inc., Publishers
Jefferson, North Carolina, and London

LIBRARY OF CONGRESS CATALOGUING-IN-PUBLICATION DATA

Wexler, Celia Viggo, 1948–
    Out of the news : former journalists discuss a profession in
crisis / Celia Viggo Wexler.
        p.   cm.
    Includes bibliographical references and index.

    ISBN 978-0-7864-6989-5
    softcover : acid free paper   ∞

    1. Journalism — United States — History — 21st century.
2. Reporters and reporting — United States — History — 21st
century.   3. Television broadcasting of news — United States —
History — 21st century.   I. Title.
PN4867.2.W49 2012
070.92'273 — dc23   2012021929

BRITISH LIBRARY CATALOGUING DATA ARE AVAILABLE

On the cover © 2012 Shutterstock

Manufactured in the United States of America

McFarland & Company, Inc., Publishers
  Box 611, Jefferson, North Carolina 28640
  www.mcfarlandpub.com

To my wonderful and supportive spouse
RICHARD

my daughter
VALERIE

and my late parents
MARY DeSERIO VIGGO and CARL VIGGO

Acknowledgments

It is not often that you get a spouse who also is a terrific journalist and a great editor, as well as a loving supporter of your dreams. So I am particularly fortunate that my spouse is Richard Wexler. Richard wrote his own well-received book, *Wounded Innocents: The Real Victims of the War Against Child Abuse*, so he knew the ropes about publishing. But his contribution was far greater. Richard believed in me, inspired me, and despite his daunting workload, read each and every chapter, never failing to offer suggestions that made this book better. As an alumnus of Columbia University's Graduate School of Journalism, he introduced me to a much wider universe of journalists than I would have known on my own. He also has been my partner in our nearly three-decades-long conversation about journalism and its future.

Through Richard, I met Kathi Paton, who has become the Wexler family agent. I am immensely grateful to Kathi for helping me with a viable book proposal, for sticking by the book and believing that it would find a home with the right publisher.

My daughter, Valerie, helped me put this book together, ensuring that my notes for each chapter were complete, and overseeing the proofreading and formatting of the entire manuscript. She also put up with her Mom's weekends of work and occasional crises of confidence.

I greatly benefited from the wisdom of three seasoned and accomplished journalists—Jim Steele, Bruce Shapiro and James Fallows. They were generous with their time and their invaluable insights.

I interviewed far more journalists than I could profile within these pages. However, their experiences and comments greatly enriched my perspective while writing this book. Thank you to Laura Thompson Osuri, Casey Anderson, Keven Kennedy, and Christopher Schmitt for generously giving me their time and thoughts.

I am a proud member of the National Press Club, and greatly appreciated its Reliable Source bar for providing the relaxed setting for many of these interviews.

Finally, I want to thank my late parents, Mary Elizabeth DeSerio Viggo and Carl Viggo, for always believing in me, and urging me to have big dreams. My mother's storytelling abilities first led me to fall in love with words and to realize their power. My father worked a second job at night, sweeping floors in a local hospital so I could attend a private high school. I know I never thanked him enough.

Table of Contents

Preface

I can see the reason I left journalism. She is 24, brilliant and beautiful, with dark hair and dark eyes, with her father's skepticism and my sense of adventure. She was born in December 1987, and after my three-month maternity leave, I tried valiantly to keep everything together as a reporter. This was true even though I worked for a sympathetic editor, herself the mother of two small girls. But I just couldn't be the mother I wanted to be and the journalist I wanted to be.

I found a different career, trading in 60-hour weeks for 40-hour ones, and a work schedule that allowed for a lot more flexibility. But I also found a different calling, public interest lobbying for the good-government group Common Cause. Common Cause was the premier organization pushing for the reform of campaign finance laws throughout the country and at the national level. It spoke up for reducing the influence of big money on politics, more transparency and more accountability. Who couldn't like that agenda?

There were lots of swings in and out of journalism after that initial career change. When my husband, also a journalist, got a teaching gig at a Penn State University branch campus outside Pittsburgh, I left my job at the state capitol in Albany where I had worked as legislative director of New York Common Cause. When we arrived in Pittsburgh, I pulled together student loans, a fellowship from the American Association for University Women, and a small scholarship from Point Park University, and earned my graduate degree in journalism, while serving as an adjunct professor in Point Park's journalism and communications department. I graduated summa cum laude the same year my daughter successfully completed second grade. I also worked part time as a copy editor for the *Pittsburgh Post-Gazette*.

But the *Post-Gazette* job was only temporary, and my husband was growing restless with teaching. We agreed that the next move would be based on

1

my career choice. I landed us all in Washington, D.C., when I took a job covering federal banking agencies for *American Banker*, a trade daily.

It felt good reporting, but I soon realized I got scant fulfillment from making the world safe for bankers. When Common Cause went looking for a Washington-based writer/lobbyist at its national office, I was eager to switch careers again.

I look at my 12 years at Common Cause, 1996–2003, as giving me the best of both worlds. I was an experiment. The organization was winding down its award-winning magazine, but the Common Cause board did not want to give up on investigative reporting. The board approved hiring a staff person to write a series of studies on corporate welfare, linking unfair benefits granted to large companies to their political donations. That's what I was commissioned to do. I wrote about 50 reports scrutinizing everything from the intense lobbying around the ethanol subsidy to the influence of large pharmaceutical corporations on our trade policy. The last report I wrote before leaving Common Cause was on the subprime mortgage crisis. The report described the intense lobbying by banks that blocked more regulation and more scrutiny. It was, to my mind, the best investigative journalism I had done in my entire life, supported by a team of campaign finance number crunchers with an absolute dedication to accuracy and fairness. My work at Common Cause put me in touch with dozens of journalists across the country who counted on our studies and our research to assist them in their own campaign finance reporting. I rose to the position of vice president for advocacy.

I also grew to love the lobbying half of my job, planning strategy, working with colleagues in the public interest world, framing grassroots messages that resonated, and making our case on Capitol Hill. Indeed, the urge to lobby soon became stronger than the urge to write hard-hitting reports. So when the Union of Concerned Scientists offered me a plate of juicy new issues on which to advocate as Washington representative for the group's Scientific Integrity Program, I was ready to make the transition.

And yet, and yet. I have never quite gotten over being a journalist, or thinking like a journalist. I am a member of Investigative Reporters and Editors, and the Association of Opinion Journalists. I freelanced for *The Washington Post*, *The Nation.com*, the *Post-Gazette*, and the *Columbia Journalism Review*. I read newspapers and watch the evening news with a reporter's eye, keenly aware of the unasked question, the lame cliché, or the lack of balance. I miss the camaraderie of the newsroom, and the wonderful, cynical gallows humor. I miss sludgy black coffee and unhealthy donuts. I miss the excitement of a breaking news story, and the emotional high of seeing your name in print.

I had learned to think about media issues in larger terms. Common Cause lobbied to preserve the independence of the Internet, and it fought against media consolidation. As part of our media reform project, I worked with grassroots groups such as Free Press, joined in the belief that media mergers would harm journalism and impede democratic discourse by an informed citizenry. This lobbying campaign exposed me to the work of media historian and scholar Robert McChesney and media visionary Jeff Chester.

Being a journalist isn't something you get over, I realized. It's a way of thinking about things that is forever a part of who you are.

But in leaving journalism, I had changed. I had developed a healthy skepticism about the accuracy of news reports when doing research and finding that newspapers often differed about the facts of a story. (I instituted a "three-source" rule at Common Cause. We had to find the same fact in three different media accounts from respected news outlets to ensure accuracy.) As I spoke to scores of reporters, I discovered that their level of understanding and competence varied a great deal. Often a quote would not resemble anything I had said. I also experienced situations where reporters used our research without any attribution to Common Cause in their stories. I don't mean the odd fact. I mean nearly the entire story.

But journalism also was changing. Newspapers were shedding jobs, and fact-based journalism was being challenged by bloggers and websites. The Internet was enabling everyone to share and comment on the news, with little editorial intervention. The journalism profession, always on shaky grounds because it required no licensing or certification, felt even shakier.

This, I decided, was a good time to write a book, one that would capture what it was like to be a journalist in the last half of the twentieth century, and the beginning of the twenty-first. This would be a book that profiled the stories of reporters like me, many of whom left the mainstream media at the top of their game, for a variety of reasons.

The stories of these former and transitioning journalists offer a window on some of the most dramatic events of the last 40 years—the fall of communism, the end of apartheid in South Africa, the Watergate scandal, the war in Iraq. But their stories also touch upon some of the issues that continue to dog the profession. In this way, they serve as case studies explaining what went wrong with journalism and offering possible ways to fix it. But since these are the experiences of real people, these profiles also are about resilience and resourcefulness, as individuals find their way in a changing media landscape, looking not only for a livelihood, but a way to make a difference.

Over the course of the nearly two years it's taken to write this book, I have attended many forums, seminars and panel discussions on the future of journalism. Dozens of books have been written about the current state of journalism, and I have read many of them. These books tend either to offer media critiques, or to tell the story of a specific journalist or media institution.

This book is unique: it focuses not on the institutions that disseminate the news, but on the journalism profession itself. Its profiles raise profound questions about the structure of news organizations, and the culture of newsrooms, and the influence of that culture on the quality of journalism. It offers something that much contemporary media criticism does not — the vivid, passionate experience of what it means to be a reporter. This book fills the void between books that address the "macro" challenges facing the news media, and the "micro" memoirs of individual journalists or the insider histories of individual media outlets. This book is media history and media criticism with a human face.

This book also offers hope to aspiring journalists and those who have lost, or fear they will lose, their jobs as journalists. It demonstrates that the skills and experience derived from a career in journalism are fungible. Former journalists were able to craft new careers from what they had learned working in the news media.

I wrote these profiles based in part on in-depth interviews, buttressed by extensive research into each journalist's body of work, including not only their news stories but also the books they have written, and interviews they have given to print and broadcast outlets. For my first and final chapters, I interviewed some of the best thinkers and media critics in the country. Their views also shape this book. My subjects' recollections of the events they covered were checked against the historical record. Each chapter has extensive notes documenting my research.

This book is about three kinds of journalists, those who left the profession altogether, those who left mainstream journalism but returned to nonprofit or alternative journalism, and those whose lives have zigzagged between journalism and other jobs. The structure of the book is roughly chronological, based on the one moment in an individual's life as a journalist that marked a turning point.

It takes years to write and publish a book, so this book attempts to be a snapshot in time, capturing a subject during in-depth interviews and follow-ups. Whenever possible, I've updated information about each subject in a short postscript at the end of each chapter.

Introduction

On September 17, 1982, the *Courier-Express* unit of the Buffalo Newspaper Guild voted to do something no other media outlet in the U.S. had done or would do: it voted to turn down an offer from Rupert Murdoch's News America Publishing Company to buy the failing Buffalo morning daily. The vote meant that Buffalo would be left with one newspaper, *The Buffalo News*. And it meant that the daily paper's 1,100 employees would lose their jobs.[1]

But to the union, being bought by Murdoch was about more than saving their livelihoods. It was about the future of journalism. I was the reporter assigned to cover that vote and the end of my own newspaper. I will never forget the emotionally charged night meeting, or the words of Richard Roth, a *Courier-Express* reporter and Guild international vice president. Roth was a legend at the *Courier*. Big and tough — he'd once threatened a meek city editor with physical violence if he ever changed his copy again — Roth was one of two reporters inside the prison yard in 1971 when Attica prison erupted in a bloody riot[2] which resulted in the deaths of 29 prisoners and 10 hostages.[3] At the tender age of 22, Roth was nominated for a Pulitzer for his work covering the riot and its bloody aftermath.[4]

Murdoch demanded substantial staff cuts in the newsroom, and wanted the power to decide who would go and who would stay. Giving Murdoch that kind of leverage seemed wrong to the vast majority of the 250 guild members who crowded into the Statler Hotel that night to vote on Murdoch's final offer. The guild wanted the rule of "last hired, first fired" to prevail.

It seems almost quaint now, but *Courier* reporters believed that experience should count for something in a newsroom, that there was a value and a dignity to working for a newspaper and learning a beat and a community. They also believed that reporters should have the freedom to write the truth, without fear of reprisal. Journalists, Roth said, needed "to be protected from ruthless publishers who may not want unfavorable things written about them or their friends."[5]

But there was something more leading up to the vote. *Courier* journalists, myself included, had researched Murdoch's U.S. papers at the time and were not impressed. We did not want the *Courier-Express*, whose past editors had included Mark Twain, to be transformed into a sleazy tabloid.[6] We wanted the daily that had existed for well over 100 years to be remembered with dignity.

Fast forward to 2008 and another acquisition by Murdoch, this time the purchase of a jewel in the crown of American journalism, *The Wall Street Journal*. This time there is no newspaper guild to get in Murdoch's way. Journalists may have cringed, but they did not try to fight Murdoch. The little struggle they put up was to write pleading letters to the *Journal* board not to sell.[7] The notion of experience counting for something at a newspaper had died years before, after thousands of reporters and editors had accepted buyouts or been fired at the whim of owners. Murdoch faced no rebellion. Sarah Ellison writes that *Journal* editors "had few options to find jobs outside the newspaper.... This crowd was a captive workforce. At another time they may have faced their new owner with a righteous protest, but that kind of romantic resistance they could no longer afford." When they met the new owner, "they were meek, easily disheartened, and scared. They were auditioning for jobs they already had."[8]

The transformation of the American economy and the demise of unions is not the story of this book. But the story of journalism and journalists at the end of the twentieth century cannot be told without understanding this context.

When I interviewed him in 2010, Roth was senior associate dean for Journalism at Northwestern University's Qatar campus. He had very mixed feelings about that Guild vote. "I lost a lot of sleep about that over the years, in part because a lot of people who were my friends there never did find other jobs," Roth said. He also regretted that with the *Courier's* closing, Buffalo was reduced to one daily newspaper.

Whether the Guild vote was right or wrong for the community and for the paper's staff, it's clear that what happened at the *Courier-Express* nearly 30 years ago likely will never be repeated. And the Murdoch style of media management, with its focus on cost-cutting and keeping journalists on tight leashes, has won. "So many companies are no longer investing their money in newsrooms. They see it not as investing but as a cost center," Roth said.

In the past decade, there have been tectonic shifts in journalism, disrupting the lives of tens of thousands of its practitioners and unsettling those

Americans who care about fact-based news. Any industry that has lost nearly a third of its jobs within the past decade is in trouble.[9]

This is a book of short stories—albeit true—of individuals caught up in a fundamental change in journalism at the end of the twentieth century that has not yet fully transformed itself to meet the challenges and limitations of the twenty-first century.

These stories give us insights into why journalism foundered and what may save it. But they also speak to something more fundamental: how individuals, facing difficulties they didn't expect, adapt, survive and often thrive.

This book features the stories of journalists because I am a former journalist, and these are the people I know best. But it also is about journalists because millions of Americans continue to consume the news and to search out news and information they can trust. Democracy thrives on information, so journalism always has been crucial to participatory government. Its future is linked to ours. When journalism is at risk, so is democracy. Fact-based information about one's community, state, and nation cannot be outsourced.

If you think that social media and citizen journalism can replace what reporters and editors do, ask the citizens of Bell, California, 10 miles from downtown Los Angeles. For years, it paid its city officials outlandish salaries, salaries that dwarfed the average pay in the working-class Hispanic town in Los Angeles County. Ultimately, in July 2010, the *Los Angeles Times* flexed its big-city reporting muscles and unearthed this story.[10] By all accounts, the *Times* reporters deserved the Pulitzer Prize they earned for public service. But if Bell's city hall had been routinely covered by just one enterprising reporter with roots in the community, one wonders how long Bell's citizens would have had to wait. Even the Pulitzer Prize board recognized that the Bell story had been "hiding in plain sight."[11]

Social media best expose evils when people have everything to lose (think Arab Spring) or nothing to lose (think gossip) but not when those involved depend on the very institutions that are failing them. For that reason, even stories of national proportions can get buried, despite the plentitude of blogs, tweets and websites that spew information. Remember the plight of disabled vets at Walter Reed Hospital? In 2007, *The Washington Post* reported the horrific conditions for wounded soldiers who were Walter Reed outpatients, who lived in moldy, rodent-infested buildings. But patients had been enduring these Dickensian living conditions since 2005. Despite the fact that these problems touched hundreds, if not thousands, of patients, and received coverage from a few online media outlets, it was only after *The Washington Post* weighed in that change happened at Walter Reed.[12]

Journalism, at its core, has been and always will be as good as the people who practice it. "The first link in the chain of responsibility is the reporter at the source of the news," observed a blue-ribbon Commission on Freedom of the Press in 1947. "He must be careful and competent. He must estimate correctly which sources are most authoritative. He must prefer firsthand observation to hearsay. He must know what questions to ask, what things to observe, and which items to report."[13] Sixty years later, journalists and media critics Bill Kovach and Tom Rosenstiel made the same point: "In the new century, one of the most profound questions for a democratic society is whether an independent press survives. The answer will depend on whether journalists have the clarity and conviction to articulate what an independent press means and whether, as citizens, the rest of us care."[14]

There have been seemingly endless discussions, congressional hearings, seminars, reports, and conferences about the economic viability of the news media of the future. We hear talk about government subsidies for news, the role of foundations in supporting good reporting, and the possibility of online newspapers achieving enough subscribers to sustain themselves financially. But the survival of the news media will depend first on individuals and their integrity, their powers of observation, and their dedication.

In the mid–1990s, cognitive psychologist Howard Gardner collaborated with two colleagues to tackle the question of "good work"—the work that professionals do and the contributions that work makes to society. It was a time when many professions were changing, often in response to the emergence of new technology and powerful market forces. They chose to compare and contrast the views of two types professionals—one "poised to control the content of our bodies" and the other "with the potential to control the content of our minds." They embarked on a study of journalists and of geneticists. Surveying more than 100 practitioners of varying levels of experience in each profession, they found that journalists were pessimistic about the future, a stark contrast to the geneticists.[15]

"Genetics emerges at the turn of the millennium as a profession in remarkably good shape," Gardner and his colleagues wrote. They found a high level of agreement among leaders and practitioners about the mission of their work, and its fundamental values. Genetics was buoyed by the prospect of new discoveries to prevent and cure disease and prolong life. Geneticists largely were hopeful, and felt that their sense of mission — helping people live longer and more productively — was shared by the public and by the owners and shareholders of biotech firms. Geneticists "look comfortably into their mirrors and are reassured by the identity they behold ... genetics appears to be a beautifully aligned enterprise."[16]

Unlike genetics, where leaders and midlevel practitioners both sang from the same hymnbook, media owners and managers did not share the pessimism of their employees. In contrast, journalists felt besieged. They believed their mission was to serve the public interest, and to provide citizens with the information they needed to govern themselves. News consumers seemed to prefer entertainment news and soft feature stories over in-depth news coverage. The values of journalists also collided with the primary goal of media managers and owners— to maximize profits. The owners and managers "felt more in control ... indeed, some of them may have been energized by journalistic and financial opportunities that have opened up in recent years."[17] Due to the "misalignment" of goals, the profession was "wracked by confusion and doubt" about the future.[18]

Gardner's findings ring true for many in this book who voluntarily left mainstream journalism, often at the top of their game. One of the first reporters to go public with his disillusionment was Bill Walker. Walker left *The Sacramento Bee* in early 1990, and a few months later wrote "Why I Quit" for the alternative weekly, *The San Francisco Bay Guardian.* In that piece, Walker poured his heart out about his experience in changing newsrooms, where it was becoming more and more difficult for a reporter to escape becoming "one of the pack who was chasing around the hot story of the day."[19] His piece, he said, was not meant to be a rant against *The Bee,* but more an elegy for a profession that was increasingly dominated by values that exalted the trivial over the in-depth. The reality, he said, was that "I wasn't the one who was defining the news, the marketplace was defining what was news."

Walker's essay was an elegy because journalism in the twentieth century had for a time spread its wings and encouraged ambitious work, far-ranging coverage, and innovative writing styles. When newspapers and broadcast outlets were competing for audiences in the same community, the first approach was to seek out quality to improve revenues. But as media consolidation became more pronounced, that aspiration died.

For this reason, these stories not only point out the systemic flaws in the way journalists were managed, they also give us a glimpse of what journalists can accomplish. Each chapter offers examples of what it means to be a reporter of excellence. I have liberally used quotes from the stories of my subjects because their stories tell us what journalism can be, and what journalism, under the right conditions, can become again.

A few themes emerge from these stories, but each professional journey is unique. People leave journalism, or transition from mainstream journalism to nonprofit journalism, for reasons that intertwine the personal and professional.

In many cases, the journalists profiled in the following chapters were hamstrung because they wanted to do more and were asked to do less. Some left journalism for the same reason that millions of Americans deserted mainstream media: it wasn't giving them what they needed. Others were pushed out, as media owners tried to stabilize profits. Some are transitioning journalists, still finding their way in a changing media market.

The 11 men and women profiled here took varied paths in and out of journalism. But they all share two attributes: they value the truth and they value journalism. Their lives in journalism pinpoint some of the systemic failings in the structure and culture of their news organizations and their impact on the quality of news coverage, and establish the link between declining quality and the news media's current economic woes. But the paths they've taken also are forging new ways of truth telling and serving the public.

I hope that their stories enrich the conversation about how to revive the profession of journalism, and fundamentally change the structure of news organizations and the culture of newsrooms. This book doesn't presume to offer all the answers but to stimulate a discussion that focuses on what it means to be a journalist in the twenty-first century and how to preserve the core values to which thousands of journalists have aspired: accuracy, fairness and public service.

This book primarily relies on in-depth interviews with former journalists whom I have carefully selected from a network of media contacts built over a 15-year career in journalism followed by a 14-year career as a public interest lobbyist and news source. Since my subjects were successful and productive journalists, their stories also tell the history of some of the more dramatic events of the last 25 years, everything from the fall of communism to the Valerie Plame scandal and South Africa's transition from apartheid to a multiracial democracy. Their careers also remind us of a time, not that long ago, when sexism and racism were pretty common in newsrooms. I have researched their books and articles, and the historic events they covered. Beyond these profiles, I also have interviewed some of the profession's best thinkers and practitioners to include their perspectives on the state of journalism and how it can be revived.

This book is as much about journalism's promise as its pitfalls. What is remarkable about these profiles is what they are not: they are not a litany of complaints about a dying profession. These former and transitioning journalists didn't abandon their journalism training and experience when they moved on. They discovered that the skills they learned as journalists served them well in the second, third or fourth careers they crafted. Their new and evolving lives incorporate many of journalism's highest values and core functions. Each profile constitutes a chapter, and the chapters are structured roughly chronologically, according to the time in each journalist's career that marked a major transition, either leaving the profession altogether or becoming a different sort of journalist.

In these pages you will meet an assortment of journalism professionals:

Bill Walker left *The Sacramento Bee* in April 1990, long before media profits plummeted and layoffs were common. He didn't go quietly. He wrote a scathing criticism of his profession for *The San Francisco Bay Guardian*. His views resonated with many reporters, and he discovered that his critique had been posted on bulletin boards in newsrooms all over the country. Walker transitioned out of journalism by finding all the excitement and romance of his old job as a roving correspondent in a new career as an environmental advocate.

Chuck Lewis left *60 Minutes* in 1988, at a time when the CBS news program was considered the Mount Olympus of journalism. His colleagues doubted his sanity. But Lewis proved them wrong, pioneering a new way to do investigative reporting outside the parameters of mainstream journalism. Even more remarkable, he's one of the few reporters who went toe to toe with the late Don Hewitt, *60 Minutes*'s famously cantankerous founder, and Hewitt blinked. His story explores his growing disillusionment with television news, and his groundbreaking work as founder of the Center for Public Integrity. His achievements won him a MacArthur "genius" fellowship in 1998.

It was only when he left *The Baltimore Sun* in 1995 for what he terms "the fleshpots of Hollywood" that **David Simon** got to write about the city of Baltimore and its problems in a deep and comprehensive way. His HBO series, *The Wire*, focused its final season on a fictional *Baltimore Sun* that hued close to the truth of Simon's experience there and his struggles with editors he felt had abandoned their mission to cover the city in the quest for journalism prizes. Simon's views resonated with the profession, and as a former journalist he finds himself at the center of the conversation about journalism's future.

Paul Taylor was *The Washington Post* reporter whose question to Gary Hart about extramarital affairs forever changed the way political reporters covered the private lives of candidates. But Taylor grew uncomfortable with trends in political reporting that exalted punditry over fact. That growing unease, combined with his experience covering the birth of a multiracial democracy in South Africa, led him to leave *The Post* in 1996 and found a nonprofit focused on improving democratic discourse in his own country.

Joan Connell got her big break in journalism when she discovered a mysterious package in a dumpster in Iowa City, Iowa. That chance discovery helped foster her career, and ultimately Connell was able to travel the world, going beyond breaking news to explore deeper themes, particularly the influence of religion on culture and politics. Ever curious, she went on to become a pioneer in online reporting and audience engagement at MSNBC.com. In 2003, Connell left mainstream journalism, disillusioned by corporate media's failure to critically examine the war on terrorism and the decision to invade

Iraq. She ultimately found a comfortable niche in what she terms "public interest journalism" as online editor at *The Nation*, but her career took a new turn in 2009, when she joined the Dart Center for Journalism and Trauma. The Center's mission is to support journalists covering war and other difficult issues.

Ted Iliff has done it all, having worked for wire services, newspapers, and broadcast news outlets, capping his mainstream media career as executive editor for CNN, holding the cable news network's staff to high standards. When his CNN job was eliminated in 2002, Iliff became his own brand, calling himself a global media consultant willing to "travel anywhere to work in any culture." He's helped nascent media operations in both the Balkans and Afghanistan.

Wayne Dawkins had done everything right. He'd gone to the Graduate School of Journalism at Columbia University, and worked his way up the ladder, reporting and editing. In 1993, his book, *Black Journalists: The NABJ Story*, was published. He rose to associate editor at the *Daily Press* in Hampton Roads, Virginia. But his bosses weren't pleased with him, and the atmosphere at his paper was killing his spirit. In 2003, with his future in journalism in doubt, Dawkins decided to jump ship and find new opportunities. He now prepares the next generation of African-American journalists.

Viveca Novak was for nearly 20 years the consummate "inside the beltway" Washington reporter, comfortable in the world of government policy and agency regulations, while also adept at working "sources," those lawyers and lobbyists who make the wheels turn in the nation's capital. A casual remark to a source who also happened to be Karl Rove's attorney put Novak in the crosshairs of the Valerie Plame investigation. The Plame scandal, and its aftermath, led to a parting of the ways with her employer, *Time Magazine*, and a transition from the mainstream media to nonprofit journalism.

When drapes suddenly hid the naked breasts of the statues in the Great Hall at the Department of Justice during the tenure of Attorney General John Ashcroft, it was ABC News reporter **Beverley Lumpkin** who broke the story. Respected for her in-depth understanding of the agency, Lumpkin often was hamstrung by ABC, where she confronted both sex and age discrimination. Laid off after 23 years at the network, she did brief stints at CBS News and the Associated Press, and then left journalism in 2007. She ultimately returned to the Justice Department as a public affairs officer who works on special projects for both Attorney General Eric Holder and other senior department officials.

A former technical writer who discovered journalism in his mid–20s, **Paul von Zielbauer** knew he'd have to take unconventional steps to get himself hired at *The New York Times*. His career route included a grueling cycling trip from Hanoi to Ho Chi Minh City (formerly known as Saigon) in 1993 that got him the clips he needed to ultimately achieve his goal. When he got to *The Times* in 1999, he felt he'd reached "the promised land." He learned a great deal about journalism and the world at the paper, appreciated the experiences it offered him, and continues to value the friendships he formed there. But his ten-year career at the Gray Lady also was filled with frustrations with a culture he found editor-driven and often inflexible. He left *The Times* and journalism in 2009 to pursue another unconventional goal, starting a travel-adventure-philanthropy company, Roadmonkey.

Solange De Santis could have been an editor at a major wire service, working in some of the glitziest world capitals, and earning a six-figure income. But she turned that opportunity down because her heart was drawn to a different style of reporting, one that focused on people and their stories. Her reporter's instincts ultimately led her inside the gates as an assembly line worker at an auto plant in Toronto that was about to shut down. She wrote about her experience in a well-received book, *Life on the Line: One Woman's Tale of Work, Sweat and Survival.* She discovered that her colleagues in journalism didn't understand working people, and that sense of apartness bled into the media's coverage of blue-collar families. Since then, De Santis's career has taken many turns, including a five-year stint in the Toronto bureau of *The Wall Street Journal.* When her position as editor for Episcopal Life Media was eliminated in 2009, she decided to follow her dream and her love for storytelling. She earned a graduate degree in theater education, and has immersed herself in the arts, as a writer, educator and practitioner.

Chapter 1

Burned Out and Pissed Off

Perhaps no journalist has left the profession with a bigger splash than Bill Walker. There he is, his photograph in the feisty alternative weekly *The San Francisco Bay Guardian*, his dark beard emphasizing his radical pose as he takes a lighter to his press passes. Below in huge headlines, is his story, "Why I Quit." In slightly smaller type, "Confessions of a burned-out, fed-up, pissed-off, smart-ass newspaperman."

What makes this story all the more remarkable is that Walker's departure was in 1990, a time when the news media remained profitable, and journalism was still thriving.

But Walker saw changes coming that troubled him. Interviewed nearly 30 years after he wrote his critique, Walker says the piece really was an elegy of sorts. "It was a lament for a way of life that I thought was passing." The practice of journalism as he had known it had been "both a great thing for me and I also think fairly important for the country and democracy and it's going away."

The piece opens with an anecdote about Walker being sent to a plane crash in Sioux City, Iowa. The Sioux City airport was closed. He had to drive 100 miles to the site. The crush of media meant there were no hotel rooms available. His allergies kicked up, he had to sleep in his car, and he woke up the next morning with a terrible migraine, nauseated and vomiting. He phoned his desk at *The Sacramento Bee* to say he was ill and couldn't work the event and had to go home. The city editor was sympathetic but "just incredulous" that he was not filing. And as he sat in the airport lounge, looking terrible, a television reporter approached him. "Are you a survivor?" the reporter asked. Walker's first instinct was to explain that he was a journalist, and what had happened to him, and complain about his editor not understanding how sick he was. But instead, he just said, "No, I'm not." Then the realization came to him, as a gaggle of reporters hurried to a press conference

15

with an official from the Federal Aviation Administration: "I'm not one of those guys anymore. And I don't want to be."[1]

During his 13 years at *The Bee*, *The Denver Post* and the *Fort Worth Star-Telegram*, he was a type of reporter that has become essentially extinct in print media, and pretty rare even in broadcast outlets, except for the three major networks and dominant cable news operations. Walker was a roving correspondent, who often "parachuted" into news events, but also did more serious reporting, not constrained by geography. If there was a local or regional link, he could pursue it.

He practiced his craft at a time when many regional newspapers developed ambitions—they wanted to become better papers, better written with broader scope. They often took on these approaches when they were battling another daily paper in a circulation war. But after a few years, these regional outlets would decide that improving a paper's quality and breadth wasn't winning the war. Then the paper's management would decide to rein in its ambitions.

At the same time, television news was redefining what ought to be covered. Reporters increasingly were asked to write the human-interest story that would make a reader or viewer tear up, the show-business gossip story, or a disaster. Adding to the pressure was the fact that newspapers were consolidating, and media companies, even those owned by families, became publicly traded corporations with shareholders clamoring for higher returns. That made selling news as a product to consumers a larger and larger concern to editors.

In the meantime, Walker had changed, too. Growing up in Hooks, Texas, a tiny town of about 2,500 near the Texas-Arkansas border, he longed for big-city life and adventure. He was shy, but being a reporter was freeing. "When I had a notebook and pen in my hand, it was my shield, and that was my license to go up and talk to anybody from the mayor to the governor to Jesse Jackson." The chance to travel, to go to major news events, to mingle with reporters from big media outlets, all appealed to him. But as he became a better reporter, he wanted to do more thoughtful pieces. "It was becoming impossible, at least for me, to feel like I was doing anything like independent inquiry. I was going from one journalism mob scene to another." He saw news turning increasingly to covering celebrities and more trivial subjects. "At that point I wanted to write about more serious things, whether it was politics or the environment or ideas."

Walker concedes that there were many dimensions to his decision to leave, which also was influenced by his growing interest in and commitment to the environmental movement. After he left *The Sacramento Bee*, he started doing communications work for the international environmental group,

Greenpeace. And when he would call newsrooms to pitch a story to reporters, he was struck by how many of them knew who he was. "From Miami to Seattle, I'd be on the phone ... and they would say, 'Oh you're the guy that wrote that piece.' ... That piece had ended up on the [newsroom] bulletin boards around the country."

His former editors and The McClatchy Company, the owner of the paper, however, were greatly offended by the piece. They felt it was an attack on the paper, and tried to discredit it. Things got so heated that Walker turned down a request from *Harper's Magazine* to excerpt his op-ed. He just didn't want any more controversy.

But Walker's elegy lived on. Eighteen months after it was published, *American Journalism Review* did a story, "Anger in the Newsroom," which quoted Walker and described his op-ed in great detail. "I don't want to sound egotistical, but I sense that a lot of people are excited to talk to me," Walker told the publication. "They want to find out whether there is life outside newsrooms. And a lot of them are excited to find out there is."[2]

Walker never went to journalism school, and didn't work on any student newspapers in high school or college. He wasn't exposed to a major metropolitan daily. Growing up in rural east Texas, he says, "there weren't a lot of intellectual jobs. Teaching was one of the few things you did if you didn't work with your hands. My whole family, and all my cousins and uncles ... were teachers, and I didn't want to become a teacher." But he discovered early on in life that he could write. And in community college, as he learned more about the work of journalists, he realized that the profession could be "a ticket to learn things and go places and see things."

After attending Texarkana College, he went on to the University of Houston, thinking he'd study broadcast journalism, but discovered that what really held him was the writing. He moved from Houston to the Forth Worth, Texas area to be near a girlfriend, whom he ended up marrying. (They divorced in 1984, and Walker remarried in 1997.)

He entered journalism at its very lowest rung, hired to write promotional copy for a twice-weekly paper at the *Arlington* (Texas) *Citizen-Journal*, owned by the *Fort Worth Star-Telegram*. At that time Arlington was a thriving Fort Worth suburb of about 150,000 people, he recalls. "I was writing fluff business copy ... written as a favor to advertisers," he says. But soon the editor noticed that he could report and write, and asked him to attend the weekly city council meetings. "I excelled at that," he says. He continued to write the puff business copy, but within a few months, Walker also became the paper's "star reporter," covering city hall, police, fire and "everything else that came my way."

Two years later, when there was an opening at the *Star-Telegram's* Arlington bureau, Walker applied for the job and got it. He soon found himself languishing there, trying, with two other reporters, to find enough to fill a zoned weekly section of the newspaper.

A year into the job, however, "I got my big break," Walker says. An editor at the paper's downtown office had noticed his work, called him and asked him how well he spoke Spanish. Walker lied and told his editor that he was pretty fluent. Walker and a photographer traveled to Key West to cover the Cuban boatlift. In 1980, Cuban leader Fidel Castro permitted thousands of discontented Cuban citizens to crowd onto boats headed for the United States. The boats arrived for months, bringing an estimated 125,000 Cuban refugees to Florida.[3]

Walker impressed his editor, filing a feature story every day. He soon found himself promoted to the downtown office. It was an exciting time to be at the paper, he recalls. A number of reporters from the Fort Worth area who had worked in major metropolitan dailies such as the *Philadelphia Inquirer* had been inspired by what newspapers could achieve. They returned to their hometown with the goal of vastly improving the *Star-Telegram*. Just about the time Walker joined the staff, the *Star-Telegram* was trying to be a quality regional paper — going beyond its circulation area and exploring the rest of Texas and the greater Southwest. When a Baptist seminary in Fort Worth sent missionaries to a politically unstable Liberia in 1981, the *Star-Telegram* sent a photographer, whose work won the paper a Pulitzer.[4] The paper sent another team to El Salvador to cover the war there.

"The newspaper was feeling its oats, flexing its muscles," he says. That meant that Walker got a chance to travel. He covered a plane crash in New Orleans that killed more than 150 people, an explosion at a Titan missile site in Arkansas. One of his favorites was a piece about a small town in Oklahoma that banned all dancing. Teens had lobbied to hold a prom, causing an uproar among the townspeople. In the end, the school board voted to permit it.[5] Not only was Walker experiencing the "romance" of travel, filing from hotel rooms, and being in the thick of dramatic events, he also was working alongside reporters from much bigger news outlets. He compared his work with theirs, and realized that he could compete.

Mike Blackman, the *Star-Telegram* editor who had discovered Walker's talent, had returned to the *Inquirer*. Blackman invited Walker to Philadelphia for an interview. The *Inquirer* offered Walker a job. He ended up not taking it, something about which he still has some regrets. But the experience made him feel that, after working for four years at the *Star-Telegram*, he should be shooting for work at a bigger paper.

He was hired at *The Denver Post*, then owned by the Times Mirror chain. *The Post* was battling the *Rocky Mountain News* for market domination, and the push was on to transform *The Post* into a "quality regional paper." He started in 1983, and spent the next three and a half years "having a fantastic time roaming around the 11-state Rocky Mountain region," he recalls. *The Post* was importing talented young reporters from dailies all across the country. "We all were in love with the place, and basically our assignment was to cover the mythic West," he says.

Old-timers at the paper resented them, but they developed their own camaraderie, and competed with one another. "It was very definitely an overt star system," he says.

He vividly remembers one of his assignments, an in-depth examination of the "forced relocation" of Navajo Indians from Hopi land in Arizona. Federal policies and court rulings ultimately resulted in the exodus of thousands of Navajos, "the largest forced relocation of people" in the U.S. since World War II, Walker says. He and a *Post* photographer spent a month traveling and interviewing.

Unfortunately, all this good work did not make much of an impact in *The Post's* war with the *Rocky Mountain News.* "We were losing the battle," he says. Times Mirror brought in new managers who decided it was time to trim the paper's sails, and to concentrate on local coverage. "This new regime" told him, "We don't want you to cover the region anymore. We just want you to cover Colorado. And rather than travel, we think you should do it by phone."

Walker didn't take well to these new limitations. He heard that *The Sacramento Bee* had launched its own ambitious drive to improve the paper's quality and reach. He joined the staff in1986 as a general assignment reporter, but his beat now covered the world.

It is the twentieth anniversary of the assassination of Martin Luther King, Jr.? Send Walker to Memphis, where King was shot, to describe the city's observance of the event. Oral Roberts threatens that God will strike him dead if he doesn't raise $8 million for his church? Dispatch Walker to Tulsa, Oklahoma, to profile the controversial preacher. California's Father Junipero Serra, the Spanish missionary who brought the Catholic faith to California, is beatified, a step to sainthood? Put Walker on a flight to Rome to write about it.

But Walker wasn't confined to breaking news. In nearby San Francisco in the late 1980s, "the AIDS epidemic was just raging," Walker says. Researchers at the University of California, Davis, just a few miles from Sacramento, were in Africa, exploring the potential connection between the AIDS virus in monkeys and in humans.

Walker and a photographer spent a month in Kenya, Uganda and the Central African Republic and produced a six-part series on AIDs in Africa. "All the rules of reporting" that he'd learned in the U.S. "didn't apply in Africa," Walker recalls. "Nobody kept appointments." Government officials would not speak on the record, and they would actively try to prevent a reporter from interviewing AIDs victims.

Walker wrote about the California researchers and their research efforts. But he also found villages where the virus was decimating communities. He made African victims real, and their plight, terrifying. He began one story this way:

> The day after David Kato died, the people of Kiyebe gathered to mourn him. They walked up the hill from the village, to the place where the banana trees parted for a view of Lake Victoria, to the house of mud and thatch where Kato had lived and farmed and died. He was 56. Kato's friends stripped the bark from a mutuba tree, then dried and stretched it to make a strong, long-lasting burial cloth. They built fires and cooked food. They dug the grave. Then they sat down to cry and await another funeral.[6]

Because of the series, Walker was named a finalist in the Mollie Parnis Livingston awards competition, which recognizes quality reporting by journalists aged 35 and under. He calls doing the series "an incredible experience. It was the toughest thing I'd ever done either as a person or a journalist."

But Walker was changing, and so was *The Bee*. "Coming out of northeast Texas, I didn't really have that much of an environmental conscience ... or much of a political conscience," he says. "My politics were just journalism." But Walker's work at *The Denver Post* had exposed him to beautiful places, many of which were threatened by development. "I began to develop both a political and environmental conscience," he says. He also wanted to use the "expertise" he had gained as a reporter over the years to write "more opinionated pieces."

That didn't sit well with his editors. Tensions increased. "I thought that their selection of stories was pedestrian and clichéd, and they thought my selection of stories was too ambitious and highfalutin.' A lot of the traditional stories I'd done as a roving correspondent I began to see as very trivial," he continues. An example of an assignment he chafed at concerned the death of a young heart-transplant patient in a small town near Modesto, California. The paper had written about the young girl when she got the heart transplant. She died three years later. Now, his editors wanted him to write about the reaction of the townspeople to her death.[7] "What does the reaction of the people in this small town in the Central Valley have to do with the issues surrounding heart transplants and medical technology?" he says. "Can't you write that story in your sleep?" He utters the quotes familiar to this type of story: "She was such a sweet girl. So tragic." To him, the assignment was evidence that "we were concentrating on stuff that didn't meet my definition of news anymore." The reality, he adds, was that "I wasn't the one who was defining the news, the marketplace was defining the news."

His editors were increasingly anxious about his working out of San Francisco. They felt he was thinking more like a cosmopolitan San Franciscan, and didn't understand the tastes of the more down-to-earth Sacramento reader. "This climaxed with them saying to me, 'You have to come back to Sacramento. We need to rein you in.'"

The day he got word that he was being transferred, Walker was driving back to his home in the East Bay. It was October 17, 1989, the date of the San Francisco earthquake. He dropped his plans to leave the paper and plunged into earthquake coverage. The Loma Prieta earthquake killed 63, and resulted in thousands of injuries and billions of dollars in damage.[8] "I threw myself into covering the earthquake for the next three or four months. And in the middle of that, I let them know I decided to leave journalism for something else," he says.

The paper agreed not to transfer him back to Sacramento, and he said he would be gone by April 1, 1990. Walker didn't know what he wanted to do, but he did know that he greatly admired environmentalists that he'd met. He thought them courageous and adventurous, but he also felt they did a terrible job telling their stories. So in the back of his mind was the notion that he could help the environmental community do a better job communicating its message. "I didn't see this as being a PR person at all," he says. "I thought of it as being a crusader."

Walker was hosting a barbecue in May 1990 when a friend who had founded the in-your-face environmental group Earth First! got a call. "He went in to answer the phone and when he came back he was white as a sheet," Walker recalls. "Somebody just tried to blow up Darryl and Judi's car," he told the group. Two Earth First! activists had been injured when a pipe bomb under the seat of their car exploded as they were driving in Oakland. Both of them were injured, but "the FBI and local police accused them of blowing up their own car," Walker recalls. There were charges that the activists were eco-terrorists transporting a pipe bomb when it detonated. The couple was arrested.

Walker volunteered to handle Earth First!'s communications for the incident. "I spent most of the summer ... handling the fallout from this big story, trying to refute the FBI and police allegations that they had blown themselves up." (The activists—Judi Bari and Darryl Cherney—were ultimately released by law enforcement authorities for lack of evidence. They sued the FBI and the police for unfairly targeting them as suspects in the bombing. A federal jury voted to award them millions in damages in 2002. By then Bari had died of cancer.)[9]

Since Earth First! lacked an office, Greenpeace, which had a large office in San Francisco, supported their efforts and allowed Walker to use the office fax machine. Getting to know the office staff at Greenpeace led to his accepting a job offer as its West Coast media director.

Not that the shift from journalist to environmental advocate was seamless. Walker says that leaving journalism was "incredibly traumatic. My entire identity for 15 years had been built on being a reporter.... Having entrée to the most important people in the world and having the right to ask them impertinent questions was incredibly important to me. It was a real trauma to leave that behind."

What helped move the transition enormously was his ability to join Greenpeace. "Greenpeace is an international organization with offices in 30 countries and something like 2,000 employees worldwide," he says. Especially at the time he joined, it also was "very much a family." It was known for its "direct actions"—very visual and dramatic statements like "hanging people from a bridge" or "climbing up a tower." Offices often cooperate on these actions, which involve "some danger and intrigue," he says. As in journalism, he traveled frequently for direct actions. "You assemble a team" at the site of the planned action six weeks before. "Doing all this surreptitious scouting and planning, there's an awful lot of romance to that."

He traded the romance of being a reporter for the romance of "being an eco-warrior," he says. If his attachment to journalism is perceived as an addiction, he says, he was able to substitute one addiction for another. "I went from one total-immersion romantic camaraderie experience to another very quickly. I never had to suffer too greatly the pangs of withdrawal."

The goal of direct actions was to draw media attention, and Walker understood the irony. He'd been a reporter who disdained mobs of reporters chasing after the same story of one dramatic event. Now, he was conspiring to create such events for mobs of reporters to chase. "We were exploiting the same values I rejected as a reporter," he says. "What I told myself, and still believe, was that getting coverage of a dramatic Greenpeace action would help draw the mainstream media into raising the visibility of the larger issue." Greenpeace, he says, never does the "dramatic direct action" for its own sake.

When the organization was planning a direct action, it would ask if just one AP photograph comes out of this, "what elements do we want in that photo. What message do we want to send?"

Shortly after he joined Greenpeace, there was a pre-dawn direct action in September 1990 involving about 40 Greenpeace activists. The demonstrators temporarily blocked the repaired oil tanker *Exxon Valdez* from leaving the port of San Diego. The tanker had been responsible for a massive oil spill in Alaska. The *Los Angeles Times* reported that several Greenpeace demonstrators had climbed up the side of the tanker, unfurling a banner that read, "Sane Energy: When?" Other demonstrators, the newspaper reported, "attempted to block the ship's passage by forming a human oil boom in the chilly water." The story went on to note that while the *Exxon Valdez* now had a new name, and was going to the Mideast, not Alaska, the Greenpeace demonstrators wanted to make the connection between oil and the military buildup in the Middle East. Demonstrators had come with a second banner that read, "From Alaska to Iraq, America's Dying for Oil."[10]

"For several hours, I was coordinating media," Walker recalls. "We got NBC Nightly News, I was talking to the Associated Press International," and other reporters. "I wanted to let them know I was one of them, and yet I was in this position all of a sudden of being on the other side. The great advantage I had was that I spoke the language of journalists."

Walker also remembers with pride his role in a series of Greenpeace "direct actions" in Hawaii that prevented extremely toxic soil from U.S. gas stations being transferred to a bridge building site in the Solomon Islands. Greenpeace successfully raised the visibility of the proposed transfer, and that pushed the Solomon government to reject the soil shipment.

But if Walker's journalistic instincts were improving the way Greenpeace dealt with the media, his Greenpeace experience was changing the way he thought about the work of journalists.

While still working in the media, Walker had begun to tussle with the notion of objectivity. As he grew more politically aware and "radicalized" while working for Greenpeace, he says, he realized that often the coverage of its direct actions turned out to be "bland" and "middle-of-the-road."

He continued to respect individual reporters as dedicated and hard-working, but he grew more and more cynical about the "institution of journalism," he says. He began to doubt whether the media could actually speak to a general audience, and he doubted the value of objectivity. Rather than "providing an exhaustive and objective record of what is happening around us, I began to feel that journalism should be more about explaining and interpreting the world."

He came to believe that journalists were being treated not much differently than timber workers, exploited by media corporations just as loggers are exploited by timber companies. "I knew that journalists put their hearts and souls into everything they did ... but increasingly that work was being treated very cavalierly by the corporations that owned them."

Walker worked for Greenpeace for four years, rising to the organization's national media bureau chief based in Washington, D.C. He left the organization as it was undergoing a major financial crisis. In the mid- to late-1990s, "there was a protracted period of time when the organization's budget went into free-fall," Walker recalls. By 1997, Greenpeace USA was facing a deficit of $2.6 million and had moved to cut its budget from $29 million to $21 million. Membership in the U.S. had declined to 400,000 from its 1991 level of 1.2 million, and donations had dropped by nearly half, from about $45 million to about $25 million.[11]

Walker said that donations fell off in part because corporations had successfully convinced many in the public that they were becoming more environmentally aware. "Greenwashing," Walker sniffs. He adds that Greenpeace ultimately was able to rebuild its membership and its financial health.

Walker did some freelancing, and attended to some family matters in Texas, then went back to the San Francisco area and joined the staff of the California League of Conservation Voters, whose aim is to get environmentalists elected to state office. The job meant moving from "a sort of self-professed radical direct action group like Greenpeace" to the "let's get the moderate green to Sacramento" approach of CALCV. "There was some culture shock involved, but I learned a lot about the political process," he says.

Walker says that his transition away from Greenpeace did not reflect a change in his politics. "There was never a conscious decision to say, 'I'm not going to do direct action or be a radical anymore,'" he says. But he acknowledges that as he got older and "started to acquire a family" he needed to make more money. (Walker has three children.) For years, he continued to be active in Greenpeace and belonged to a small group, mostly former employees, who elect its board.

While he was working for the League of Conservation Voters, he was impressed by a new environmental group, the Environmental Working Group (EWG), that had made headlines by matching federal farm subsidy data with zipcodes to uncover many "farmers" receiving government aid who lived in pricey places like the Upper East Side of Manhattan and Beverly Hills. By 1997, he made the switch to EWG, opening up the group's one-person West Coast bureau. Over nearly a dozen years, he built a team of analysts that produced scores of media-friendly reports on issues ranging from toxic chemicals in consumer products to air and water pollution and pesticides.

EWG did reports that took "huge amounts of government data," and analyzed it and did reports on patterns and trends. Walker says he didn't "invent" the EWG report, but he "helped refine it into a form that came closer to journalism." "A journalist would look at [an EWG report] and say, 'Yes, this is a story. I can tell they've got a spin, but here's the data. I can write from this.'" EWG was helping journalists do the things they no longer had the time or staff to do. "We were doing advocacy investigative journalism," he says.

Walker often was the voice of the nonprofit, providing sound bites for coverage of the reports. "As head of the California office, I did everything from fundraising to editing reports to pitching them to reporters," he says.

He is particularly proud of the group's work to warn the public about the dangers of brominated flame retardants, and arsenic in pressure-treated wood. "We also lifted the veil of secrecy" on the wasteful and inequitable way federal water subsidies were distributed in California's Central Valley, he says.

While EWG was often successful in getting media attention, Walker observes that a diverse and fractured media makes reaching the American public much more difficult.

In 1989, Walker recalls, there was the "great Alar episode. I don't call it the Alar scare because, unlike critics of the episode, there was real concern, and NRDC [the Natural Resources Defense Council] was right to raise the flag. NRDC got the [Alar] story on *60 Minutes*, and the next day all those people went out and stopped buying apples."

The segment, viewed by an estimated audience of 40 million, warned that Alar, a pesticide used on apples, had cancer-causing properties and could be particularly harmful to children. Almost immediately, the chemical was pulled from the market, school boards in major cities banned apples and apple juice from cafeterias, and apple sales dropped drastically, costing the industry an estimated $100 million.[12]

"It's really hard for an activist now to do a blockbuster story that gets covered everywhere and really changes things," Walker says. For all activists, pitching stories requires "lowered expectations." In the old days, "if you got a story on the front page of *The New York Times*, you had done the absolute best you could do as an advocate," he says. "That [media attention] practically assured a victory. Today, you might have a story on the front page of *The Times*, although that's rare. People would know about it, and talk about it, but it wouldn't necessarily change things." *The Times* remains the "most powerful institution in U.S. journalism," he says. "But the point is, that as activists, even with a big story, you don't get the wall-to-wall coverage that changes policy overnight."

As Walker sees it, the audience for news has changed, and fractured. It is no longer possible for any media outlet to speak to a "general" readership for an entire community, he believes. "It is just very very hard to find things that everybody cares about at the same level of engagement. The idea that I'd embraced when I first got into journalism that we were the voice of the community and we were going to try and reflect everything that was going on, I just think that's done." Instead, niche publications will be speaking to communities that share their values. Even *The New York Times*, he observes, is less a newspaper covering New York City, and more an outlet that speaks to "basically liberal, well-educated people in the U.S. no matter where they live."

But newspapers haven't abandoned their roles of serving the community, he contends. "I think the audience has abandoned that idea of a newspaper."

After nearly a dozen years at EWG, Walker was interested in new challenges. "Earthjustice, with whom I'd had a mutual admiration society, was just down the street," Walker recalls. In 2008, he became campaign director for the group, a national nonprofit law firm that represents other environmental groups trying to secure the enforcement of federal environmental laws.

But Walker soon discovered that the job wasn't a good fit. The organization would always be more about litigation than communication, he says. Realizing that you're not right for a particular role in an organization is much easier, he says, when "you have decided that the cause is of greater importance than your career."

For Walker, moving on and working in the environmental vineyards has meant becoming an entrepreneur. He now is an independent communications and campaign consultant. The work has been "fascinating, exhausting, and more lucrative" than he had expected. "I feel lucky to be able to do activism full time and to provide for my family," he emailed in August 2011.

The reporter of 1990 now is 58, but he hasn't lost his rebellious streak. In a 2008 post on the Earthjustice website, he wrote that he and his wife, Judith Barish, were living in Berkeley and parenting three children. "We're trying to figure out how to raise kids to resist authority, except when we ask them to clean their room."

Chapter 2

Leaving Mount Olympus

Chuck Lewis is slightly built, with a round face and glasses. He looks soft, almost deferential. Just don't cross him. There's a toughness lurking just beneath that jovial exterior. Without that, it's hard to see how Lewis would have had the nerve to take a leap of faith and ditch one of the best jobs in network news.

When Lewis left *60 Minutes* in November 1988, the CBS Sunday news magazine routinely drew more than 18 million viewers weekly, and ranked among the top ten network TV programs in prime time.[1] It had won 36 Emmy awards, and earned its network $3 million in ad revenues per program. The *Boston Globe* called the program a "virtual license to print money."[2] No wonder his CBS colleagues questioned his sanity. His own lawyer couldn't believe that he had given up the security of a multi-year contract with a major network. "He thought I was completely out of my mind." It was, Lewis recalls, akin to walking away from "the Mount Olympus of journalism."

But by leaving Mount Olympus, Lewis found his own unique path. As the founder of the Center for Public Integrity, he pursued a new kind of investigative reporting, one based on intensive, long-term projects involving teams of researchers and acres of documents. He also helped redefine the focus of investigative journalism, successfully convincing the media establishment that the public has a right to know not only about illegal actions by elected officials and their advisors, but also unethical ones. As a pioneer, Lewis occupied new territory, in a place that seemed to uncomfortably straddle the worlds of mainstream journalism and advocacy. Two decades later, as mainstream journalism continues to absorb the aftershocks of an economic tsunami that wiped out 30 percent of its jobs,[3] Lewis is no longer the outsider, but one of the visionaries remaking journalism's future.

No one could have predicted his career trajectory. Despite his impressive name, Charles Reed Esray Lewis III was a townie in Newark, Delaware, the home of the University of Delaware, who "snuck under the fence into the [college] football games." His father was a security guard at the local General Motors plant, and his mother a secretary at a middle school. No one on either side of his family had gone to a four-year college, and while Lewis was an over-achiever in high school, his guidance teacher told him that he "wasn't cut out for college" either. Lewis ignored that advice and attended the University of Delaware, working parttime at the sports department of the Wilmington, Delaware, *News Journal* newspapers.

Lewis's father did not have a union job at the Newark plant and identified with management, not labor. His parents were Republicans. But what Lewis terms his "radicalization" was about to begin. In 1973, Ralph Nader's study group published a scathing report on the influence of the chemical giant, the Dupont Company, on Delaware politics and public life. Dupont's influence was more pervasive there than in any other state, its authors concluded.[4] His own newspaper was owned by Dupont, he realized, and had never dug into the corporation's influence.[5]

This was the "dark side of power," corporate power unbridled in his state, Lewis said. Then in 1974, as an intern for Republican Senator William Roth, he'd seen the "dark power" of the executive branch exposed as the Watergate scandal exploded, and as many Republican senators ducked for cover, rather than display disloyalty to their party. His college work was introducing him to another facet of dark power — the federal government's power to undermine what it perceived to be unfriendly regimes. Lewis's undergraduate thesis chronicled the U.S. government's destabilization of Chile, 1970 to 1973. "Here is a democratically elected government ...[and] we brought down the government for all intents and purposes. We certainly supported the Pinochet folks at least."

In researching his 189-page thesis, Lewis met and interviewed Orlando Letelier, a Chilean diplomat who had served in the cabinet of Chilean President Salvador Allende. Letelier had been imprisoned for nearly a year after Allende was overthrown by a military coup led by Augusto Pinochet in 1973. He then moved to Washington, joining the faculty at American University as a visiting professor.[6] Letelier had suggested to Lewis that he do his graduate work at American. Lewis was in Washington studying at the Johns Hopkins School of Advanced International Studies when Letelier was murdered just a few blocks away, the victim of a car bombing linked to the Pinochet regime.[7] "He's assassinated. I could hear the sirens in the street," Lewis recalls.

The Hopkins program was a leading portal for Foreign Service jobs, and many of his peers used their degrees to go to the State Department, the CIA or multinational corporations. But Lewis, now sensitive to the abuse of corporate and government power, had a different goal. "I wanted to investigate all those places." He was 23 years old and green. The networks had a hiring freeze, the competition for reporting jobs at *The Washington Post* and *The New York Times* was fierce, and those jobs likely were not attainable to someone whose sum total of journalism experience had been on the sports desk of his local newspaper. Despite those odds, Lewis figured he might have a shot at ABC.

In the 1970s, ABC News lagged behind CBS and NBC in ratings and prestige. Roone Arledge, the hard-driving head of ABC's sports division, had recently been hired to run the news division. Scouting for new blood, he hired *Washington Post* reporter Sander Vanocur as vice president of ABC News in Washington, heading up its investigative reporting unit.[8]

Lewis wrote to him, asking for a job. He got a rejection letter. "I decided it was a mistake and I was going to ignore it. I actually wrote to his secretary and asked her to please, please if I could just have a meeting with this guy, I'm sure it would work out well for both sides. And she got me in like the next week and I was hired." Lewis keeps the ABC rejection letter framed and hanging in his home. It reminds him, he says, "to never accept 'No' for an answer if you're really determined."

There was another factor working for Lewis. He later learned that one of the professors he had listed as a reference had been a secret source for Vanocur when he was covering the Kennedy White House. "I will always be grateful to Vanocur for hiring me and taking a chance on me."

Lewis' job was off-air investigative reporter, digging into every major scandal that occurred in Washington between 1977 and 1984. Dick Wald, then the senior vice president of ABC, called him "the eyes and ears of the Washington bureau," Lewis says. "I did investigative stuff for basically every single show and met lots of interesting people, including famous celebrity broadcast types," he recalls. But his colleagues included "a lot of blow-dried–hair idiots" for whom he not only had to dig up 'scoops' but "also had to explain to them why [a scoop] was a scoop."

And over time the job was the source of other frustrations. Lewis was fond of going deep, and he'd assail his bosses with multi-page memos, which Carl Bernstein, who became Washington bureau chief in 1980,[9] used to call "the Lewis newsletter." But his memos didn't necessarily bear fruit. Lewis felt that ABC really wasn't in the business of doing investigative reporting, content with what he termed "the illusion of investigative reporting," adding a sentence or two of information to previously reported news so that the network could "breathlessly" announce, "ABC has learned." "It was bullshit, basically, and I could see that."

Lewis said that he was "miserable" at ABC. He wanted to be an on-air reporter, but he looked too young and his voice was too nasal. He wanted to be promoted to a producer, but his bosses felt he was more valuable digging up exclusive stories. He considered his position a dead-end job.

Now married and with a family to support, he had resigned himself to staying where he was. But colleagues at other networks knew of his work. What Lewis discovered later was that Lowell Bergman, then a *60 Minutes* producer, had urged that he be hired. (Bergman later left CBS after the network, over fears of a lawsuit, backed away from his story about tobacco whistleblower Dr. Jeffrey Wigand. His struggle with CBS became the subject of the film, *The Insider*.)[10]

Legendary CBS correspondent, the late Mike Wallace, called Lewis and asked if he was interested in moving to *60 Minutes*. CBS offered Lewis a one-year contract without medical benefits, and the job would require him to move to New York. "I was hired as sort of a producer in waiting. I had been at ABC for six and a half years but I had never been allowed to go into the editing room and actually edit a piece."

Lewis was days away from closing on a house in Virginia. While the job paid a bit more, that expense was offset by the cost of living in New York and the loss of medical benefits. "My wife wasn't really thrilled with it." When the offer came, Lewis was on the verge of quitting TV altogether. "But I thought, 'Oh my God, *60 Minutes*. How could I not take the job?'" The deal was that Lewis would become a full producer in about a year's time, and the network made good on its promise.

But even at *60 Minutes*, Lewis felt confined. The zeitgeist of a *60 Minutes* investigative story was the dramatic interplay between the good guys and the bad guys, Lewis explains. "No more than five characters on air. Try to make sure the bad guy goes on." His job in part was to find the "bad guys" and persuade them to agree to be interviewed on camera. "I would try to out-con the cons."

It was crucial to have the bad guys present to interrogate, Lewis says, because the audience expected the villain of the piece to "get his come-uppance" on camera. "So it meant that all the producers for Mike were pimping for Mike, trying to get the bad guy to go on, and that got really old."

Lewis says that "compared to Mike Wallace, I was like a warm puppy dog with my tail wagging." Conveying a "friendly" and "mild-mannered" persona, Lewis would take his targets out to lunch, soften them up and then put them on camera. Later, he says, he would be more direct with his prospects, warning them that if they didn't agree, "I'm going to have to stand in front of your house for a month, and we'll have you ducking into your car like a common criminal." He'd advise his subjects to "just get it over with, and take your best shot."

But Lewis also wanted to turn out investigative pieces that were more complex, based on wholly independent reporting, and found that several of his story ideas were killed. "I didn't like my stories not being done for all the wrong reasons," he says, when his bosses would find his subjects more appropriate for the Government Accountability Office or a congressional committee. Collecting a three-foot–high pile of documents and background research, he tried and failed to interest Wallace in doing a piece on then–House Speaker Jim Wright, whose net worth had quintupled in ten years. Wallace didn't think it was a story, Lewis recalls. Wallace speculated that Wright might have just made a lot of good investments. As a consequence, *60 Minutes* never followed up on Lewis' digging. Two years later the scandal broke that eventually led to the first forced resignation of a speaker of the house in history.[11] The House Ethics Committee accused Wright of evading House limits on outside income and accepting $145,000 in improper gifts over the preceding decade.[12]

Lewis' marriage to *60 Minutes* first went through a trial separation, sparked by a face-off with the late Don Hewitt, the program's legendary and famously combative creator. Hewitt had decided to hire a big-name producer for the Washington bureau, and he wanted to give his new hire a large office. The plan was to knock down some walls in Lewis' office and enlarge it, and then move Lewis to a smaller space. Lewis only found out about the plans when a colleague at NBC looked out her window and saw workmen in Lewis' Washington office, and called Lewis, who was in New York.

He might have agreed to the change if he'd been consulted before it took effect, but now Lewis was fuming over what he considered "the biggest showing of disrespect I'd ever seen anywhere." He left New York, returned to Washington and stopped working. The whole dispute came to a head when Lewis insisted that he would return to work only if he kept his old office. Lewis was threatened with termination if he did not return to work. When he refused, Hewitt fired him.

Lewis assumed he had lost his job for good, and flew back to New York to finish up his last story. "I'm sitting there in the editing room, watching the screen with the editor and I feel some wind coming in, and I turn around. It's Don Hewitt. Don says, 'You can stay in your office,' and he turns and walks out." It was a rare capitulation that must have felt like a "root canal" to Hewitt, Lewis surmises. It may have been prompted in part by the intervention of Morley Safer, at that point a 17-year *60 Minutes* veteran,[13] who, Lewis learned, had raised concerns with Hewitt about the way staff were treated at the news magazine.

The incident planted the seeds for a final break. "I spent a weekend thinking I was unemployed and I had stared, as they say, into the abyss and seen that it wasn't so bad or at least there is life after that world."

The last straw occurred about a year later. Lewis was working on a segment called "Foreign Agent." It aired in October 1988, near the end of the Dukakis-Bush campaign. It tracked ten unpaid advisors to the George H.W. Bush and Michael Dukakis campaigns who were registered foreign agents making "six-figure-plus sums" while they were advising the presidential campaigns of each candidate. Lewis tracked the campaign advisors as they balanced their dual roles, influencing U.S. trade policy and then advocating for their foreign clients with opposing trade priorities. He and Wallace argued about how much visibility one of Hewitt's friends, a politically influential trade advisor, should get in the piece. The struggle was "a nasty, tough thing," Lewis recalls. In the end, Lewis agreed to give him less visual prominence in the story.

After the segment aired, Larry Tisch, then president of CBS, gushed about it, and said it reminded him of the old *60 Minutes* (The segment was nominated for an Emmy). When Wallace called to thank him, Lewis told him he was quitting. That day, he faxed a one-sentence resignation letter to Hewitt, breaking a four-year contract.

Lewis said he had "no idea" of what he would do. "I had a lot of people tell me I was crazy" for leaving the Mount Olympus of the profession. The two people who stood by him, he says, were his parents. "They had to be thinking, 'God, the poor guy has lost his mind.' But they didn't ever say that. They just supported it — unconditional support." Lewis' marriage was foundering, and he hoped that by leaving a job where he was out of town so often he might be able to shore it up. That didn't work. The joke among the friends who helped him think through his vision was that if Lewis had not been distracted by his marital problems, he would have had more of his wits about him, and never would have done something as reckless as found the Center.

Since he had no savings, Lewis needed work, and quickly. So he initially consulted for Kroll Associates, now Kroll Inc., one of the world's most influential corporate intelligence firms.[14] Lewis called the job "a great education" because it made him realize "what amateurs journalists are." A company like Kroll, he says, had vast resources and information networks at its disposal, relying on former CIA directors and heads of foreign intelligence agencies, forensic accountants and corporate CEOs to do its work. "I saw what journalists know, which is a small percentage of what [corporations] know. I always had this false conceit that journalists know everything because they think they know everything."

Lewis did consulting for about nine months, while thinking of a concept that would eventually become the Center for Public Integrity. He got job offers from other network shows, and an offer to work on investigative documentary films. But he felt that all those opportunities were "the same old same old. I would hate it and my life span would be shortened. I just didn't go for any of it."

"I like investigative reporting, and felt I did it pretty well. I needed to find a different way to do it." Lewis grew to believe that he could use a non-profit structure to publish wholly independent investigative reports. He left *60 Minutes* in November 1988 and incorporated the Center for Public Integrity the following year. He got two friends to form a board that he chaired, an arrangement that ensured he'd be in charge. Lewis called his new venture the Center for Public Integrity in part because "all the investigative reporting names were taken." And the name fit, he says, because almost every investigative story "involves in some fashion, public integrity."

"The process by which we would function would essentially be journalism, but by being a non-profit group, right off the bat, we entered the public interest realm. We were a hybrid that helped us become what we are today," Lewis wrote ten years after the Center's founding.[15] The group, incorporated in March 1989, had a brief mission statement, essentially to "hold those in power accountable and to educate the American people about those issues."

Lewis spent about $1,500 to file the appropriate papers to get tax-exempt status. But he knew that if the Center was going to make it, he needed some gravitas. "I was just a former line producer at *60 Minutes*. I needed some heft." So using his old *60 Minutes* typewriter, he wrote to distinguished journalists and academics, asking that they become members of an advisory board for his new venture.

Over time he was able to put together an advisory board including everyone from Notre Dame president emeritus, the Rev. Theodore Hesburgh, to Bill Kovach, former Washington bureau chief of *The New York Times*, former editor of *The Atlanta Journal Constitution*, and then curator of the Nieman Foundation at Harvard, and Kathleen Hall Jamieson, dean of the of the Annenberg School for Communication at the University of Pennsylvania.[16] "One of the very first to say yes was Arthur Schlesinger, Jr.," Lewis says. After Lewis contacted Schlesinger, the historian called Wallace. He asked him, "Who is this Chuck Lewis fellow? Is he okay?"

"Mike could have responded by telling him, 'No, he's a little shit. He just quit.' He didn't say that, fortunately. He said, 'He's a very talented young man. I don't know what he's going to do, but he's just left my show.' And Arthur took a chance." And when Schlesinger came on the board, he drew many of the other academic heavyweights.

With the requisite luminaries serving as advisors, the Center's three-member board of directors then tackled fundraising. One board member thought the only ethical thing to do was to accept money from all donors so as not to show favoritism. The other board member felt that all donors had to be meticulously screened. As board chairman, Lewis came to see that the only approach was pragmatism. "I said if we don't take money from somebody, we don't exist."

ABC wanted to hire Lewis, but Lewis demurred, offering the network a chance to consult with his new Center instead. That first year, he says, he negotiated a $100,000 retainer agreement with ABC. Ultimately, ABC paid the Center close to a million dollars over the course of nine years, but the network did not get exclusivity. "They'd get to peek and see what was coming, and I would always release it at a news conference, and all they got to do was report it on *World News* after it came out at the press conference. But it gave them a way to be prepared for that. So it was a good deal for them, a good deal for us." Lewis also got support from labor unions and companies, because of his past work exploring conflicts of interest in trade policy.

Over time, the Center took hold. "You know when you're starting an enterprise, you measure success in little ways. Going from a Post Office box to having an office is a big deal. Becoming incorporated is a big deal. Getting an advisory board of luminaries is a big deal. So these are little victories. You savor them because the despair and the terrifying element of the other side of the abyss [of leaving your job in mainstream journalism] are rather profound."

And Lewis' development as the leader of a nonprofit was happening on the fly. He went from barely managing his own household expenses to building an entire organization from the bottom up. Nevertheless, in making the jump, Lewis was finding that piece of himself that went beyond reportorial cynicism and connected with his fundamental belief in democracy. "Damn it, this is our country, this is our government, and they should do what they are supposed to do."

In the late 1980s, the country had endured the savings and loan scandal, the Iran-Contra scandal, mismanagement and cronyism at the Department of Housing and Urban Development, and the resignation of a speaker of the House.[17] Journalists, including those in Washington, largely "missed those stories," he says. "So you had two problems. You had public service going to hell in a really serious, systemic way. And then, separately, you had journalists not getting it. The smugness and the arrogance of the national news media, the fact that they didn't seem to care, that they didn't get it, really pissed me off." Lewis said he'd always been aware of journalism's failings, but when "you're on the outside, looking in, you're seeing it even more clearly."

The Center would do what the media had failed to do. Lewis wanted to do "macro" journalism — looking not at the individual scandal or wrongdoer, but at systemic weaknesses and misconduct. "We would always do broadswath stuff. I didn't want micro stories because they were episodic and trivial." Lewis figured he could accomplish what mainstream journalists could not because he'd possess two luxuries that they lacked: time and people.

But the vision didn't come without qualms. Lewis confessed to "doubts" as he offered his house for collateral when he negotiated a $60,000 lease for office space. And his first employee — a college intern — sat on the windowsill for a week until Lewis rented some tables and chairs, "the kind that one usually finds in church basements."[18]

For the first three years of its existence, Lewis had his fingers in every pot at the Center, raising the money, hiring the staff, writing the checks, and serving as the lead author for the 13 reports it produced. It demanded nights working until 2 A.M., and lots of pizza, Lewis says. At times, he concedes, he missed "the stability of a fancy corporate job, a multi-year contract," and the "fancy hotels. I didn't stay in four-star hotels for a long, long time."

What Lewis did not miss was access to the powerful. "I never had it," he says with a laugh. Reporting by gaining access to newsmakers had never been his style. He'd always been the reporter more comfortable with "reading records no one read" than "cozying up" to people in power. "They're obnoxious, insincere and they're a pain in the ass."

The Center's first study, "America's Frontline Trade Officials," was released in December 1990 at a news conference covered by CNN, ABC 20/20, C-Span, and many other news outlets. It spurred a congressional hearing, a GAO report, and helped prompt newly elected President Bill Clinton to issue an Executive Order in January 1993, placing a lifetime ban on foreign lobbying by White House trade officials.[19]

Despite that initial success, the first four years, from 1990 until 1994, were "a lonely period" Lewis says, with the future of the Center still uncertain, and relatively modest support from foundations.

In the early 1990s, Lewis observes, reporters thought about money and politics differently. "If it wasn't criminal, why is there a story?"

In 1992 Lewis held a press conference releasing the Center's report, "Under the Influence: Presidential Candidates and Their Campaign Advisers." The report identified individuals in key campaign roles who also were lobbying for special interests with specific agendas before the current and future administration. But Lewis faced a number of skeptical questions. One reporter asked, "Are you suggesting ... that candidates should have nothing to do with anybody who works for a corporation?" He followed up by asking Lewis why any of this information about special-interest ties to campaign advisors was "relevant."[20]

Lewis fumed about the reaction of one *New York Times* reporter who believed that if a lobbyist was not breaking the law, a report about special interests he represented while advising the President wasn't news.

But the work continued, and the reports kept on coming. "Somewhere between 1994 and 1996 it became really obvious that we were hitting our stride," Lewis says. Big foundations—Ford, Carnegie, MacArthur—previously indifferent to the Center's inquiries, now were interested.

The Schumann Foundation started the ball rolling with a $1 million grant over three years, and then other large foundation grants followed. By then, the Center had a prosperous-looking office on I Street and a full-time staff of 24. It was publishing book-length studies. The first, published in 1996, was *The Buying of the President,* an in-depth examination of the special interest donors and their influence on the presidential candidates.

To say the book got a lot of attention is an understatement. Even the *New Yorker Magazine* took notice, commenting that the book had become "an essential reference work" for reporters covering the 1996 presidential campaign. Following the book's publication, ABC News did a two-day feature on money and presidential politics, the magazine noted, and PBS did a 90-minute "Frontline" special, based in part on the Center's reporting.[21]

The inside the Beltway media were taking notice. In April 1996, the Washington press corps, for which Lewis had so little respect, asked him to speak at its prestigious National Press Club luncheon. He was hailed as a "significant force in the nation's capital, a new government watchdog alongside the likes of Ralph Nader and Joan Claybrook. If the mainstream press is not doing enough hard-hitting investigative reporting on ethics in government," said National Press Club President Sonja Hillgren, "Lewis's Center is there to fill the void."[22]

And in 1998, just eight years after the Center was born, Lewis won a $275,000 MacArthur "genius" fellowship for his work. Even then, *The New York Times* story about the awards was a bit vague about what Lewis did, terming the Center "a nonprofit organization that produces book-length reports on issues like health-care lobbying."[23]

Lewis concedes that it was only after the Center had received numerous awards from Investigative Reporters and Editors and the Society of Professional Journalists, and after the pleading of his staff, that he relented and let them call themselves journalists. In the past, Lewis had described the Center as a "non-profit research organization" comprised of "concerned citizens" doing "investigative studies."[24]

The Center hit its "high-water mark" in 2003, Lewis says. In January of that year, the Center released a secret draft of legislation proposed by the Department of Justice then led by John Ashcroft, to greatly expand anti-terrorism law. In October, it launched its project, "The Windfalls of War," which identified the companies that won billions in government contracts for work in Iraq and Afghanistan and their political connections and contributions. That won the Center the prestigious George Polk award for online journalism.[25]

"A scrappy little group like the Center, we measure success with the awards we get," Lewis says.

Lewis says he would have preferred to have been "investigating the bastards" and "digging through documents" and "writing my own stuff," but his priority was to keep the Center in business. That meant lots of traveling to raise the Center's visibility and to meet with donors.

More resources meant being able to put 20 staffers to work on one project, and also gave the Center the opportunity to branch out, creating the first network of journalists across borders, 100 journalists in 50 countries. "If I didn't have money, I couldn't have done that."

But his 15 years of working 100-hour weeks were starting to burn him out, he says. He also found himself irritated when his staff complained about his frequent absences. They would tell him, "You're never here. You never come to see us. You never talk to us." He wanted to retort, "'If it wasn't for me you wouldn't be here, pal.' But I would keep it to myself. That just irritated the hell out of me because it was grossly unfair."

Lewis also felt some staff pushback over his media appearances. Some of the "crusty hard-bitten former Associated Press and those traditional print journalist types" at the Center felt that Lewis was veering from journalism into punditry when he was willing to comment on the issues of the day. But he felt that for the Center to expand its audience he had to be willing to use the media to publicize the Center's work. "You discuss it, describe it, and you make it simple for them. They're not going to read 200 pages. They want to hear in a sentence or two why this matters.

"Being a producer I knew what electronic media wanted in terms of sound bites. I didn't school myself for that. I didn't aspire to that. But did it help the Center? Yeah, it really helped the Center. The more [media appearances] I did, the more money people gave us because they thought we were a player."

Lewis also believes that if journalists do the hard work of researching a topic and developing expertise, their opinions are valuable. A journalist who has come to conclusions based on facts should not have to go through "this bizarre kabuki dance of trying to pretend you have been neutered and have zero opinions." The original definition of journalism, he says, is, "Someone goes into the cave and comes out and tells you what they found."

But his staff's qualms led him to ask his mentor, veteran print journalist, academic and media critic Bill Kovach, whether he was doing the right thing. Kovach assured him that he was, and that his visibility was "giving spine to the editors" throughout the country who wanted to do in-depth investigative work.

Lewis remains intensely proud of what he accomplished. With the resources he raised, the Center was able to do "cool stuff that has never been done." Its exhaustive work included investigating conflicts of interest among public officials in 50 states, an effort that resulted in the Center posting 7,400 financial disclosures online, a first, he says, in the history of journalism.

Lewis also is proud that the Center offered decent salaries with good benefits, and even paid its interns. Its last office move took it to a nice space close to the White House. He acknowledged that the Center's success came at some personal cost. "Do I feel I sacrificed a bit personally and my family to raise the money to enable us to reach that level and was a lot of it on my back? The answer is Yes. Do I regret it? No." (Lewis' second wife is Pamela Gilbert, an attorney who was executive director of Public Citizen's Congress Watch, and who also served as executive director of the Consumer Product Safety Commission.[26] He and Gilbert have a son, and Lewis has a daughter from his previous marriage.)

But Lewis had almost been too successful being the face of the Center. Lewis stepped down in 2004 in part out of concerns that the Center "was beginning to have a cult of personality about it." He did not want the Center to be "Chuck's Excellent Adventure," he says.

Lewis also was reaching his own personal milestone, his 50th birthday, and wondered if there was something more for him. "I realized if I got hit by a truck my obit was going to say I founded the Center, whether I was there 15 or 50 years. I started to realize that if I wanted to do anything else in my life," what the Center had already accomplished — "maybe 300 reports and 14 books and 30-plus awards — would be enough for me to move on."

Running the Center, he said, was both "the so-called burden and a privilege. The burden was making it all work financially in terms of management and withstanding legal threats. All that stuff. The privilege was being able to do whatever the hell I thought was important. That is the coolest thing in the world."

Lewis left the Center in 2004 the way he walked away from *60 Minutes* — without a clear plan of what he wanted to do next. "I have this habit of jumping off cliffs," he says. He took on teaching gigs at Harvard and Princeton, got a book contract, and continued to run the Fund for Independence in Journalism, which Lewis created in 2003 to ensure that the Center would have the funds it needed to defend itself against lawsuits related to its work.

As a fellow at Harvard's Joan Shorenstein Center on the Press, Politics and Public Policy, he had time to think "big thoughts" and plan the third act in his working life. He wrote a 17,000-word paper analyzing the growing importance of nonprofit journalism, and that intellectual exercise, he said, "Helped me fix in my mind my role, what I could do and why it matters and what else I should do."

Lewis sensed that if investigative journalism were to continue and thrive, the seeds would be planted in an academic setting. In late 2007 he proposed to American University that "we should do something like the Children's Television Workshop but call it the Investigative Reporting Workshop." He envisioned a program that combined investigative work with national and international media partners, and an "i" lab that would look at new economic models for producing and sustaining and increasing the impact of investigative journalism.

American went along with his vision. The Workshop began publishing in 2009, and now has a formal working relationship with PBS's *Frontline* documentary program. It has explored everything from the soundness of the nation's banks to the safety records of regional airlines. It airline reporting was featured on a *Frontline* documentary, "Flying Cheap," in February 2010. In late 2010, the Workshop collaborated with *Frontline* on a special examining the Obama Administration's enforcement of immigration laws. Its "i" lab also is keeping a running tally of the nonprofit journalism startups happening across the country, offering signs of new promise and rebirth for the still economically fragile journalism profession. Through 2011, the Investigative Reporting Workshop has received more than $5 million in foundation support, and is now the largest university-based investigative reporting center in the country. He also co-founded the Investigative News Network, which gives nonprofit news outlets a channel to disseminate their reports.

Lewis says that his role is to "push and prod and poke the profession" and those who will fund new efforts, to "encourage us to think the big thoughts about what we need. Because you can't have a democracy without information, and you can't have information without journalism."

"So I'm back in the saddle," Lewis says with a smile. "Doing 'investigating the bastards' but also doing new models."

Chapter 3

The Book of Simon

David Simon looks like he should be etched into a stained glass window. Balding and solidly built, he has the stern countenance and weary eyes of a figure from the Old Testament. The devil-may-care insouciance of newspapering portrayed in Ben Hecht's *The Front Page* may have reeled him into journalism, but he lacks the rakish élan of that era. When he talks and writes about journalism, he betrays a depth of feeling that goes way beyond the capers that Hecht celebrates in his famous stage play about reporters in the 1920s. "Head and heart I was a newspaperman from the day I signed up at my high school paper until the day, 18 years later, when I took a buyout from *The Baltimore Sun* and left for the fleshpots of Hollywood," Simon wrote in 2009.[1]

But in leaving journalism, Simon found himself at the center of journalism's conversation about itself. Simon's fictional account of life at his former newspaper, *The Baltimore Sun*, as part of the HBO series *The Wire* gave millions of viewers an inside look at what it means to be a reporter. And it gave him gravitas as a spokesman for journalism's flaws, financial problems and potential. He's testified before the U.S. Senate on the issue, addressed reporters at the National Press Club, and spoken at national meetings of investigative reporters. Quoted in countless stories about the future of journalism, Simon has become an icon to some reporters, a lightning rod to others. But nearly everyone who reports for a living knows his name and his story.

Simon fell in love with journalism as a suburban Jewish middle-schooler growing up in Montgomery County, Maryland. "To be able to sustain a credible opinion in our family was prized," he says, recalling the "very heated" debates at the family dinner table about the 1968 election, with his father declaring for Hubert Humphrey, a sister "passionate about [Robert] Kennedy" and his older brother for Eugene McCarthy. (Simon says the "real intellect" of the family was his mother, who was "genuinely wise." Marrying young, she dropped out of Hunter College, but ultimately got her bachelor's degree at the University of Maryland, attending at the same time that Simon did. She, unlike her son, graduated summa cum laude, Simon says with rueful pride.)

The dinner-table debates led Simon to become a voracious consumer of news, reading both *The Washington Post* and *The Washington Star* from the age of 11 or 12. "I loved newspapers, and I loved magazines and I loved reading, especially nonfiction. In my family books and periodicals were the currency."

His father had his own dreams of being a journalist, dreams that largely went unfulfilled, but he loved hanging out with reporters. As director of public relations for the Jewish Service Organization, B'nai B'rith, the elder Simon met a lot of reporters, some of whom he brought home. One favorite was Irving Spiegel, who covered religion for *The New York Times*. Simon remembers him as a bit of a Renaissance man, a Julliard-schooled pianist who "could recite Shakespeare in Yiddish" and who penned something he called the Metropolitan Desk Opera with lyrics that mocked his bosses and co-workers at *The Times*. "If I was his editor, he probably would have driven me crazy, but he was larger than life."

His father exposed him to the romantic, picaresque side of the journalism of the 1920s and 1930s, taking him to see a production of *The Front Page*, giving him "books of his generation about what journalism was like, among them, *Bovard of the Post-Dispatch*" (the biography of legendary *St. Louis Post-Dispatch* editor Oliver Brovard, whose 38-year editorial career, beginning in 1900, spanned World War I and the Great Depression).[2]

Not that Simon's father pushed him into journalism. "It was something he loved and I guess I got it through osmosis."

Simon worked on his high school newspaper, but he was not a natural. His early writing, he pronounced, was "awful." He was more concerned about the process of putting out a newspaper, "the pica rulers and the paste pots," than its content.

Things got more serious as Simon headed to the University of Maryland. Faced with competition from broadcast news outlets, print journalism was finding new ways to compete, surrendering its edge in breaking news to television, but touting its ability to do in-depth reporting. Simon's journalism professors predicted that newspapers would become more like magazines, and that reporters would become specialists, people who knew their beats so well they could write authoritative stories. "I thought journalism was going to become not merely the accounting of the day's events or the flash of controversy from the day's events, but something close to the most immediate, most comprehensive story of our times." Looking back, Simon concedes that vision was "absurdly ambitious," but in the mid-1970s, it seemed attainable.

But his career in journalism was almost fatally scorched by the scowl of a student editor. As a freshman new to the University of Maryland's daily, the *Diamondback*, he was assigned to write a story about a report about to be released by the Maryland Public Interest Research Group. Simon tried to get the report but was told it wasn't ready yet, and he reported that back to his editor. "She expressed her disappointment in such a way that I felt as though I had failed.... She had budgeted the story, she had created a budget line for it, and I did not have a story for her. And she made me feel so bad. Probably it was all internalized in me, but I didn't go back for a long while." Even after he returned, Simon avoided news and went over to the features side of the paper.

Ultimately, Simon switched from features to hard news, moving up the editorial ladder until he became the paper's editor-in-chief. The *Diamondback*, with its own stylebook, its traditions, and its hard-charging editors was a good paper and a very good training ground, Simon says.

So good a paper, that Simon ultimately dropped out of the journalism program. "I started to realize that studying journalism is bullshit." He grew to believe that the best way to learn journalism was to do it, and that he had all the mentors and guidance he needed at the campus daily. What he really needed, he thought, was knowledge about the world outside of journalism, everything from the plays of Shakespeare to anthropology and economics. So he became a general studies major, "so I could be an inch deep and a mile wide like every other journalist."

Writing for the paper became so consuming that Simon's academic career foundered. A pattern would develop. Simon would neglect his school work, plead for re-admission, and then ignore his classes to work on the paper. By the end of his senior year, he was about 60 credits short of graduating. He figured the best thing he could do was stay in school to earn the missing credits and string for either *The Washington Post* or *The Baltimore Sun*. Since *The Sun's* stringer was graduating, Simon felt he had a better shot there. He also felt that despite *The Sun's* being a "very good paper," he could write his way onto the full-time staff.

Simon got a break just as he was giving up his editorial duties at the *Diamondback*. One of his sources, the vice president of academic affairs, let him know that he was resigning to become president of Wayne State University. Simon got the news into the *Diamondback* for the next day's edition, and then called *The Sun*, asking the paper if it would like a brief, and if he could be a stringer. Simon dictated the brief and state editor Tim Phelps told him that if he wanted to be a stringer he'd have to come in for an interview and submit clippings of his best stories, and that he'd be in contention with other candidates.

"To me this was, 'What, are you kidding? I edited the paper!' I couldn't believe that I was going to have to have a job interview." Before the interview took place, *The Sun* took another story from Simon, about an increase in dorm fees.

During his interview, Phelps asked to see samples of his writing. Simon did not bring copies of his best stories, painstakingly pasted into a scrapbook. Instead, he submitted the last three issues of the *Diamondback* that he had edited, but whose content largely was the work of other students. Phelps was not impressed. He told him, "I've got to see your writing. I'm sorry. Put together a clip book. I don't want you writing any more for us until I see your clips."

But Phelps then went on vacation, and news broke out in Simon's backyard, once again. President Ronald Reagan visited an African-American couple in College Park who had been the target of a cross-burning. Simon called *The Sun*. He told the editor on duty: "Listen, I know I'm not supposed to write any more for you but do you want a piece on the President visiting this couple in College Park?"

The editor who answered asked, "The president of the college?"

Simon responded, "No, no. The president of the United States." *The Sun* asked for quotes from the family, and Simon contributed to the story.[3]

Then he wrote an account about commencement at the University of Maryland, and the humorous pranks students had invented in previous years to liven things up.[4] For that piece, *The Sun* gave him a byline, his first at the paper. "I went out and bought every copy at People's Drug—eight copies. I couldn't believe it. I couldn't have been more excited in my life."

By the time Phelps returned from vacation, Simon's presence at the paper was a "fait accompli," Simon said. He did submit his clip book. He learned years later that Phelps had never bothered to take it out of its envelope. As a stringer for *The Sun* in 1983, Simon wrote 100 bylined stories, so many that *The Sun*'s union complained.

But it wasn't just the quantity of the stories that would ultimately earn him a full-time slot at the paper. Simon had landed a big story—a scandal that involved Lefty Driesell, the University of Maryland's colorful basketball coach, and one of his star players, Herman Veal. A student disciplinary body had barred Veal from playing in the remaining intercollegiate games of the basketball season, and the nature of the complaint was supposed to be confidential. But Driesell was stirring things up, furious that one of his star players had been sidelined. Asked to find out what was going on, Simon used his sources and learned that a coed had accused of Veal of attempting to force himself on her sexually. "After she made the complaint, Lefty harassed her. Called her repeatedly on the phone, screaming at her, telling her he was going to turn her into a whore in the media if she persisted."

A college administrator had been in the young woman's apartment when she took a harassing call from Driesell, and had heard the abuse himself. "So now, Lefty is caught." At that point, the story was big news, Simon says.[5] In the end, Simon recalls, all the press coverage of the scandal didn't make much of an impact. The university launched an investigation of the affair, but the next year offered Driesell a raise and a new five-year contract.[6]

But it helped Simon's career. "Every day for the next couple of years I got down on my knees and definitely thanked Lefty Driesell for being such an idiot because it helped me get hired at *The Baltimore Sun*," Simon says.

New reporters don't get great working schedules, and Simon recalls that for his first two years at *The Sun*, he worked both weekend days. Nevertheless, he was "so ecstatic" about being hired by the paper that he didn't complain. He had the cops beat, and also worked on the rewrite desk, essentially being the person who assembled breaking stories from reporters' notes. In the 1980s, when newspapers in one city competed with each other and with local TV, the most challenging rewrite slot was the late-night slot, usually an assignment handed off to a seasoned veteran. It was, however, a job that fell to Simon when he was 25, "which meant I was all alone [in the newsroom] from 10 P.M. until 1 A.M.," he says. "You got beat on the 11 o'clock news, you had to reach people at home and turn it around [for the next morning's newspaper]. And reporters would call their late-breaking stories in to the desk. "I was very quick and very clean."

Simon was particularly proud of his work in January 1987, presiding over the coverage of a collision between an Amtrak passenger train and a Conrail freight train in Chase, Maryland, resulting in 16 deaths and 175 injuries.[7] Simon started to call in reporters, taking dictation from the scene, and managing coverage. When David Ettlin, the night metropolitan editor, got to the office, Ettlin stood behind Simon and watched how he was handling things. He sat down to write the sidebar, the secondary story about the crash. "It was like graduation. It was like I'd been given my diploma. David didn't take the lead story, and he could have. I would have stepped aside. But [his actions said] 'Simon's got it, don't worry.'"

Simon also was working the police beat, developing contacts, learning the ropes. He was on the beat when Jane Bolding, a Prince George's County nurse, was charged with killing three patients at Prince George's Hospital Center by giving them injections of potassium chloride. He says that he consistently beat *The Washington Post* on the story, explaining the mistakes made in the investigation, and the challenge of proving death by potassium chloride poisoning. He credits *Sun* colleague Bob Benjamin for helping him beat *The Post*. While Simon was pursuing the toxicology, Benjamin was staking out the state's attorney's front lawn, and getting crucial information about why the case wouldn't hold. "The best thing you could do if you were a reporter at *The Baltimore Sun* was beat the fuck out of *The Washington Post*. Nothing felt better." The state's attorney dropped the murder charges against the nurse in 1985, when new information surfaced she was tried, but acquitted in 1988 for lack of evidence.[8]

But this also was the time that Simon, having spent a couple of years covering the Baltimore police, was considering something bigger. He was beginning to chafe at the constraints of daily journalism, and the inverted pyramid structure of news writing, with its focus on the who, what, when, where and why. He first thought about doing a book at the end of 1985. Armed with a bottle of whiskey, he went to pay a thank-you Christmas call to the homicide unit in gratitude for their help in the previous year. It was a relatively slow night, and Simon listened to the cops until the wee hours of the morning. Sitting there, with their paper cups of whiskey, going over the events of the previous months, one detective said, "If somebody got up here and wrote the shit that happened even in a year, they would have a fucking book." Simon recalled thinking, "Of course they would."

Although Simon's background and politics were far different from the cops he covered, he thought he could capture their voices. "I'd been around them enough and they were certainly interesting to me and I remember thinking to myself, I might be ready to do this." It took the book idea some time to percolate. Simon wanted to get some magazine stories under his belt, so he could demonstrate to a publisher that he had the writing talent to do a book, and he also had to secure the permission of the Baltimore Police Department to let him follow the homicide unit.

A labor dispute kick-started the project. *The Sun*, which had been family owned, was purchased in 1986 by the Times Mirror Company, a chain known for quality journalism, a move that Simon and others greeted with optimism. But Times Mirror now wanted to charge employees for health care costs that the company had picked up in the past, despite the fact that *The Sun* was very profitable and by then had no newspaper competitors. In protest, reporters walked off the job for six days. Simon, interviewed by *The Washington Post*, said reporters would continue to withhold their bylines for a few more days. "We want to show the company they are just a bunch of cheap bastards and they should be ashamed of themselves," he said.[9]

"When we came back in I was very angry at management. I felt like this had been an abuse of the workers," Simon says. He wasn't so angry that he wanted to ditch a good journalism job, but he felt that he needed some distance from the newsroom. Shortly after the strike concluded, he wrote a proposal to the police commissioner, asking permission to follow the homicide unit. In December 1987, the commissioner agreed. Simon observes that allowing a reporter access to the homicide unit carried much less risk than letting a reporter hang out with the vice squad. "There's not much dirt to be had in death investigations," he says. "They're not about kicking over a mattress and finding $50,000."

Simon asked for a book leave, intending to return to *The Sun,* but aware that after five years of solid reporting, he had other options. He knew, for example, that *The Washington Post* had been impressed by his work on the Jane Bolding poison story, and would be receptive if he applied. "I wasn't ready to jump. I loved being at *The Sun,* I loved learning about Baltimore, and I was working for people who were teaching me."

Writing a book, he says, was a way to become a better reporter, not "pulling away" from the paper. It was a way to "service my abilities" covering his beat. In thinking this way, Simon knew he was going against the grain. The culture of journalism is largely one of moving up or on. A reporter does a good job on one beat, then gets promoted to another, more prestigious beat, or becomes an editor, or moves to a bigger paper. Simon believed that "if I stayed in one place, I would get better and better. And I would find out things about that place that nobody else knew. Or find ways of telling stories that nobody else had told."

Once Simon got the permission to be a fly on the wall of the homicide unit, the reporting was not that different. He took notes, using slim reporters' notebooks similar to the ones that the detectives carried. Reporters and cops both faced obstacles and frustration at getting the facts. "Reporters would love to have the power of subpoena to force people to tell what's true. And cops would love not to be lied to [solely because] they're cops." Over the years, too, Simon had developed relationships on his beat. "We were often simpatico, and often not," he says. "But I definitely admired the best cops. The guys who do their job. I admired them the way I admire the best reporters."

Writing the book, however, presented a far tougher challenge. To prepare, he read voraciously any "year in the life" book, finding that he greatly admired *Ball Four* by Jim Bouton, the 1969 diary of his season as a pitcher. "Such a thoughtful book about America and what its institutions were going through ... written through the prism of baseball."

Despite all the preparation, Simon found book-writing daunting. "It's terrifying. I think I spent six weeks drinking, going back and hanging out with the cops and drinking and bullshitting. And finally I complained there was so much material I didn't know quite where to start." One of the detectives disagreed, telling him in so many words, as Simon puts it, "A fucking monkey could write this book." The message was clear, Simon says: "We let you into our lives for a year. Don't act like you have problems."

It took Simon nine months to write *Homicide: A Year on the Killing Streets*. He was out of the newsroom in 1988, and for six months of 1989. He needed an additional three months to write the last version of the book, time he took in 1990. The book was published in 1991 to rave reviews and an Edgar Award, and ultimately became the basis for the television series *Homicide: Life on the Street*.

His experience writing the book expanded on his thoughts about beat journalism that had been percolating for a few years. In 1992, Simon wrote an essay on crime reporting for the *Media Studies Journal*. In his essay, Simon defended *Homicide* from journalist critics who felt he had surrendered reportorial objectivity to tell the story of the homicide unit through the eyes of the detectives. Simon disagreed, contending that the truth of the homicide unit's experience was more honestly conveyed without the intervention of the reporter as judger of facts and conduct. He also forcefully argued that by focusing on just the facts, in brief, breaking-news accounts of murders and other crimes, newspapers had desensitized their readers to the violence in their inner cities. Routine crime reporting, Simon wrote, "anesthetizes readers ... cleans and simplifies the violence and cruelty of a dirty, complex world," and "manages to reduce life-size tragedies to easily digestible pieces."[10]

This wasn't and isn't the conventional wisdom about daily newspaper journalism. Returning from book leave, "I felt a little like a square peg in a round hole," he concedes. There were struggles between Simon and even the editors he prized, like Rebecca Corbett. Simon wrote an obit for a police informant whose character would be the basis for "Bubbles" in his HBO series, *The Wire*. Simon was interviewing Bubbles for a magazine piece but the junk man, petty thief and police informant died of AIDs before Simon had completed the interviews.

To protect the man's family, Simon called the man Possum, the alias Bubbles used in New York City. The 2,000-word obit is far from conventional. This is how Simon describes his subject:

> Possum nods, the gaunt face bobbing. The Virus hangs on him, hangs on everything in the rented room. Three decades of firing heroin and thieving and turning over criminals to police at $50 to $100 a head, but it isn't a penitentiary or a bullet or a lethal dose that claims him.
> "Yeah, I been sick, you know," says Possum in a mumble, his stick-leg stretched over a table. "I been sick but I'm back now."[11]

The obit is itself a mini-drama, as the dying snitch reminisces with his law enforcement handlers about the part he played in helping them catch 500 fugitives over the years. Possum's photographic memory was matched only by his ability to remain unnoticed in his inner city neighborhood. Only in death could his accomplishments be reported, and only under an alias to protect his Baltimore family.

"I was very proud of the piece. I thought this is a part of the city that is unseen otherwise." The story got front-page play in the news section, and because of that, he says, Corbett "took grief" from some of the staff. "What the fuck is that?"

He was hearing complaints about pieces that were "trying too hard not to be a newspaper story. To which my response was always, 'What story would want to be a newspaper story if it could be any other kind of story?'

"That [story] was true and people cared about it and they read it from the beginning to the end and now they understand the interior dynamic of that world," Simon would counter. A strong piece of narrative journalism based on facts and a deep understanding of a beat served readers better than the traditional news format, he believed. Simon says, however, that the arguments were healthy and constructive. "I didn't see myself running out of room at *The Sun*. I felt like we were all growing together. It was growing pains for all of us, but we were getting somewhere."

Simon believed *Homicide* improved his crime coverage over the next four years. But then he felt that he needed to do a second book, focusing on the war on drugs, a war he believed had disrupted law enforcement. He also felt that without the "perspective of the street" his "law enforcement reporting was always going to be tilted towards the cops." He asked for a leave for 1993, giving his editors the same assurance: "I'll be back. I'll be back as a better reporter."

In 1992, shortly before he asked for the book leave, *The Sun* had offered buyouts to reporters who wanted to leave. Simon had informal discussions with *The Washington Post* about a slot in the paper's metropolitan bureau investigative enterprise unit. But managing editor Bob Kaiser warned him that if negotiations got serious and "we get down to talking money" and he turned down a formal offer with *The Post*, he would not get a second chance. "Rebecca [Corbett] and I held hands, and if she had jumped, I would have jumped. I was going to go with her and if she stayed, I was going to stay. We sort of decided that we could do good work in Baltimore."

Simon also knew that it wasn't appropriate to start a job with a new paper, and then immediately ask for a book leave. And he was put off by *The Post's* arrogance. He remembers telling Kaiser: "You know what? I sort of resent the basic presumption that we're heading towards four papers worth reading in this country, and after that we're all just farm teams for those four."[12]

Kaiser, Simon recalls, responded with a little laugh. "Let us know if you change your mind."

And so he stayed, got the leave and worked on *The Corner: A Year in the Life of an Inner-City Neighborhood*, with co-author Edward Burns, who retired as a police detective to teach in the Baltimore public schools. Doing the book was more challenging because it required gaining the trust and understanding of Baltimore's underclass. And the traditional reporters' notebook was out. "You brought a notebook in the middle of a drug deal and somebody would get upset."

The Corner tells the story of a little piece of inner-city Baltimore where the drug trade flourished. Addiction, drug-related crime, wars between drug gangs all are told as they affect real people. Its strong narrative voice compels the reader to care about what happens to the individuals who live in this broken neighborhood. The authors confess to an occasional act of kindness that may have marginally affected their journalistic narrative. "[O]ver time," they wrote, "we found ourselves caring more about our subjects than we ever expected."[13]

Simon returned to the paper in 1995. After his first book leave, his editors supported what he had done and believed it would make him a better reporter. This time, Simon experienced something quite different.

In the years Simon was away, Times Mirror's new top editors, both veterans of the *Philadelphia Inquirer*, were trying to revamp the paper. John Carroll, then *Sun* editor, and his managing editor, Bill Marimow, were and are revered in many journalism circles, and were stars in the Times Mirror constellation.

In this changing environment, Simon did not feel welcomed or understood. Feeling that the book had given him new insights into the "dysfunctional" war on drugs, something he was eager to report about, he found "an incredible resentment." Managers viewed the two years he had taken on book leave as offering nothing of value to *The Sun*. On the contrary, they felt that the leave "didn't reflect well on them in any way and that they gained nothing out of it."

Instead, his editors seemed to want to take him down a peg, sending him to Howard County in suburban Maryland, ostensibly to train younger reporters how to write a narrative story. But the buzz in the newsroom, Simon says, was that "Bill kind of wanted to take the edge off the princely return of the author" by assigning him to the boonies, "and then he was rehabilitating me by bringing me out." The editors also suggested to Simon that he work in the paper's Washington bureau. But for Simon, "the timing was off" when he was eager to use the lessons of *The Corner* to report about what was happening in Baltimore.

Simon felt that there was a poisonous environment in the newsroom, pitting new hires against veteran *Sun* reporters. The new editors at the top, Simon contended, "were about the prizes. The other thing they were about was the mythology that the paper knew nothing, nothing about journalism until they arrived. That it was completely moribund and that they were teaching us journalism from the ground up."

He had heard rumors of a "salon" at an editor's home where "a lot of bad stuff was said about the paper" and Corbett and other veteran *Sun* editors were unfairly trashed for their editorial judgment. Simon made some calls to check out what he'd heard, and then he wrote a confidential memo to Carroll, and copied in Marimow.

Simon assumed that since he was not going public with his concerns, that it was his right to voice them, strongly and urgently. "I wasn't posting it on the Wittenberg church door. It was very private. This was not good for the paper." In the confidential memo, Simon recalls advising Carroll that "you can't possibly hire enough new people to make the place over in its entirety. You need to graft what was good about the place and the talent you bring over for this place to take a leap forward. I don't understand the mythology that [before you took over] nobody knew anything."

"I speak my mind," Simon says. "One of the great joys of going into journalism used to be you could go into your newsroom and argue about anything and it was an intellectual exercise and maybe if you didn't play politics you weren't going to be an assistant managing editor, but you could be a reporter and put your feet up on the desk and talk about what was shitty, what was good and what was honest and what was not." That freedom, Simon says, was the difference between working in a newsroom and working for an insurance company or advertising firm or anywhere else where the company line mattered more. He continues: "A good journalist was an iconoclast ...you can't tell me to turn it off in my newsroom. What you can expect is loyalty to an institution and good credible work. You can't expect me to drink Kool-Aid for anybody."

When he showed the memo to Corbett, she warned, "This is going to cut it between you and John." Simon replied: "If it does, I need to know that. Because if I can't speak about the quality of the paper in my newsroom or where we're going, if I can't have that voice anymore, I can't live here anyway."

After he got the memo, Simon says, Carroll essentially cut off all contact with him. Carroll also tried to kill a feature story Simon had written, set to run on the front page. The story profiled the people who harvest metal out of Baltimore's buildings. "I had gone around with them for a few months. Drug addicts, taking the metal, selling off copper drain pipes, radiators, everything, and destroying the city bit by bit." Simon says that Carroll finally relented and agreed to let the story run in *The Sun's* magazine because "the whole newsroom had read it and couldn't figure out why it was spiked." (Marimow told *The New Yorker* that he opposed the story because he felt it "glorified" people "who were destroying homes."[14])

Simon made one last effort to confront Carroll to "clear the air." Simon said he tried to explain to Carroll that the books he had written while on leave had made him a better reporter and that since he'd returned from his second leave,

> I've done my best work in this place. And he asked, "Really, what would those be?" And I listed the articles, and it seemed that Carroll hadn't read any of them. I said, "I think we just don't want the same things out of journalism. If this is what you value, and I pointed to some prize groveling shit, and if you don't value this, and I pointed to the spiked piece, then there's probably not a place for me at the *Sun*." He said, "Probably not." So I was out.

Simon didn't equate leaving *The Sun* with leaving journalism. He still could follow up with *The Washington Post*, or pull together his work and aim for magazine writing at *The New Yorker* or *The New York Times Magazine*.

But Simon's journalism had deep roots in a particular place. "The idea of being wedded to a geographic region, to learn the ways of a single entity, being a city, to doing process books based on that city, to having books serve the journalism. There were still places to go at *The Sun* and ... until the tenor of the newsroom changed I thought *The Sun* was going to be a viable, intelligent place to work." (Simon is so quintessentially Baltimorean that Baltimore-based filmmaker John Waters, best known for the film *Hairspray* set in 1960s Baltimore, officiated when Simon wed mystery novelist Laura Lippman, who has used Baltimore as the setting for her popular and critically acclaimed books.)[15]

The buyout came with a year's salary and benefits, and in the short term, there was television. He'd written for *Homicide*, and the television series based on his book. But "to me, the TV thing was not the future. It was a lovely stepchild that was sending checks to me every now and then but it was not the future."

But television continued to pursue him. "While journalism was showing me where the door was, and offering me money to go through the door, the entertainment industry kept saying, 'What else have you got?'"

As he was finishing *The Corner*, which was published in 1997, Simon was writing for *Homicide*, learning from series producers, Tom Fontana and Jim Finnerty. They "taught me everything they could [about writing and producing for television] and I am ever grateful."

When Simon's second book came out, HBO, which had started to do grittier, edgier dramas, turned *The Corner* into a six-part mini-series. Simon took on the series because it had a limited run, and he figured "it will serve the journalism" and find new readers for the book. He still planned try to land another job in journalism. But Carolyn Strauss, who oversaw series and mini-series development at HBO, told Simon she loved *The Corner* and asked for his suggestions about future projects.

I said I was talking to Ed Burns about what we didn't do in *The Corner*. *The Corner* was the microcosm of addiction in this broken family, but the drug war in its dysfunction can be portrayed only by depicting a whole city. And then we realized what if we depict a whole city, never mind the drug war. There's a lot we can say about what's going on in urban America. So it was a journalistic impulse. This little portion of the entertainment industry at HBO was saying "What are your ideas?" And in my newsroom it was, "Please don't have any ideas, but give us the raw materials. We have the ideas as to how to win prizes."

And it was what Simon viewed as *The Sun's* obsession with winning prizes that ultimately led to his making a break not only with his former newspaper and its management but with his future in journalism. While working at the paper, Simon had been unhappy with the trend at the paper of going after Pulitzer Prizes—he calls it "Pulitzer-sniffing."

For a newspaper, there is no higher award than a Pulitzer, and even in that pantheon, the most revered Pulitzer is the one for public service, the award that recognizes that journalism can make a difference, and change things for the better. But Simon disagrees with the fundamental concept. "I did not believe in the newspaper crusade, that you write something in the hopes of getting a committee to have a panel hearing or getting a law passed." That was a lesson, Simon says, he learned from the Lefty Driesell scandal. Simon uncovered damning facts, and felt that the facts alone should have resulted in Driesell being fired. But in the end the coach emerged unscathed. "As a reporter if you want to be honest you can't put your expectations in some sort of positive societal outcome as a result of journalism," he says. "You have to be distanced." A reporter has to do good work, and expose scandals and other problems, but with the knowledge that the reaction those stories provoke may actually do more harm than good. "I'd do this five-part series on a very important issue and they will probably pass a law that will make things worse. If you start leaning into changing the world, what you end up doing is corrupting your journalism."

And that, Simon believes, is exactly what happened at *The Sun*.

"The prize thing had become its own force in the newsroom. They had stopped covering the city. They were covering their projects. There was no poverty reporter, there was no labor reporter. The courthouse was going uncovered. Institutionally they didn't give a fuck about Baltimore. Baltimore was just the terrain they were going to mine in order to get a few prizes so they could get to some better place in the world."

For Simon, there was no better symbol of the cynicism of *The Sun's* editors than their tolerance of what Simon termed a reporter "who was making it up." The reporter in question was Jim Haner, a journalist who has been defended by many in the business as bright, capable and dedicated, but who aroused wariness in Simon and others in *The Sun* newsroom.[16]

Haner's errors had led to a couple of retractions, and Simon brought it up with Carroll during his exit interview. "I said to John, 'This guy may win you a prize, but you may have to give it back.'" (Later, Simon would write a very similar line in a script for *The Wire*.) After Simon left, Haner also left *The Sun*, moving to the New York City area to join his wife, who'd found a job there. But when his wife was hired by *The Washington Post*, Haner returned to the area and was rehired by *The Sun*.

Haner was writing a series on lead paint poisoning. It was 2000, and Simon was in New York, editing *The Corner*. Simon says he got a call from a colleague still at *The Sun* who told him, "He made up another story."

Haner had written a story reporting that Maryland's Governor Parris Glendening had traveled to Baltimore to discuss the "epidemic" of lead paint poisoning in the city, and its impact on Baltimore's children. The following day, the paper corrected the story, noting that "The Sun incorrectly characterized the purpose of a visit to Baltimore" by the Governor "as a fact-finding mission" about lead poisoning, when the visit "was a previously scheduled meeting with Baltimoreans United in Leadership Development to discuss the group's legislative priorities."

The original story also had included what appeared to be a vivid exchange between a Baltimore minister and the governor about the lead poisoning problem. But the correction noted that the minister had not talked to the governor about the lead paint problem. His quote came from a separate interview with *The Sun*.[17]

Simon was incensed. "*The Sun* may have been a stodgy old lady but it was honest. He tried to contact the publisher, who referred the call to Carroll. Carroll called Simon and told him, 'This is your problem. This is in your head. You're angry about it.'

"I said, 'John, the whole newsroom's angry about it. I'm in New York. Two or three people ended up venting to me on the phone. You don't think your newsroom's angry?'

"And he said, 'This is personal to you.'

"And I said, 'Everything's personal to everybody. But what's personal to me is that I love that newspaper. It was my alma mater. And this is just shit. If I had to retract three stories as an editor by the same reporter, I'd remember it for the rest of my life.'

"And he said. 'What were the other two?'"

Simon hung up, and decided to go public with his criticism. "So I called *Brill's Content* and so the pissing war began." *Brill's Content*, now defunct, was a high-profile journal of media criticism. It ran a lengthy, balanced story, including comments from Simon and other Haner detractors as well as from Haner and his defenders. In the *Brill's* piece, Carroll, who by that time had left *The Sun* to take the reins at *The Los Angeles Times*, calls Simon "Mr. Vindictive himself," and while acknowledging there were errors in the story, calls the incident "much ado about nothing."[18]

"If John had gotten on the phone and said, 'We're going to get rid of the guy or we're taking him off the street or we realize we got a problem,' I would have never gone public," Simon says.

The Sun, Simon claims, slipped out the offending story, but submitted the Haner series to the Pulitzer awards committee. By going public, Simon then believed, he had essentially made a break with journalism. "Once you shit over another reporter and say they're making stuff up, it's going to come up at every job interview you ever have."

After he went public with his concerns about *The Sun*, Simon says he heard from many journalists who shared similar stories about their own papers.

> I realized this was sort of endemic. In the shrinking pond that was journalism, the resumes and trinkets mattered more and more and the ambitions had become stunted. *The Baltimore Sun* no longer cared about covering Baltimore for the purposes of letting people know about what was really going on in that city. It had been reduced to small chunks of personal ambition. That was intellectually unsatisfying to me. So in a way when I got shown where the door was, it was a blessing, but I didn't know it at the time.

Simon had left journalism. Few journalists have the chance to take their struggles at their newspaper as the basis for one season of an HBO mini-series.

The Wire's last season tells the story of *The Sun*, a story that clings close to the truth as it discusses cutbacks and staff morale, and yes, a reporter who makes things up. Editor characters based on Carroll and Marimow come off as less than stellar.[19]

And a series that was fiction, not journalism, rang so true to so many journalists, that Simon found himself no longer a reporter but very much engaged in the ongoing conversation about the future of reporting.

He believes that corporate greed started the death march of print journalism, long before the Internet led newspapers to offer online content for free, a decision that sharply cut profits.

As a young journalist, "I thought that talent was going to be valued because the product mattered. It's incredibly naïve." Simon believes that journalism's problems are linked to the sale of many family-owned papers to large out-of-town newspaper chains, which were concerned primarily about the value of their companies to investors.

Once Wall Street appreciated how profitable newspapers could be, Simon says, "the product didn't matter. Wall Street was coming to believe that we can make more money putting out a less consequential and less relevant newspaper than we can putting out a better newspaper. More wire copy, small news hole, less veterans, less benefits, less pay, more profit." (Since this interview, several daily newspapers, including *The Baltimore Sun*, have instituted paywalls for their content, with the jury still out on whether this will ultimately sustain profitability.)[20]

When the Internet came along, newspapers were willing to give their content away, Simon charged, because they "had contempt for their own product. They didn't believe it was worth anything." If they had, Simon says, newspapers would have trimmed their staffs through layoffs, not buyouts. The people who take buyouts, he says, are by and large the most experienced and talented reporters and editors, the people who have options. Buyouts, he contended, were a way to eliminate the people with the highest salaries and the benefits. "Let's get rid of the older reporters and fuck the content."

Simon doesn't expect print journalism to necessarily survive, but he does believe that local journalism, journalism in a city like Baltimore, could find a way to sustain itself. "The desire for high-level journalism is there. There is a readership for it." Simon concedes that online news subscriptions may never get above 80,000 or 100,000 in a city the size of Baltimore. But because an online newspaper avoids the costs of printing and distribution, that revenue could be almost "pure profit," he says. "I would pay right now to get what the old *Baltimore Sun* was online. I would pay $10, $15 a month ... somebody's going to figure that out eventually and that's where it's going to go."

As for his own career trajectory, he no longer believes that going public with his complaints about *The Sun* would present obstacles should he ever want to return to reporting. "I never really had a moment of reckoning where I said, I'll never get back. I don't think I have yet, although it seems increasingly unlikely, being in the entertainment industry for some time."

But HBO has given him the opportunity to tell stories to Americans about people and places they didn't know or care about. "I have too much respect for journalism to equate what I do now with journalism. *The Corner* is a reflection of journalism. And when we did *Generation Kill* [an HBO miniseries based on a nonfiction book by Evan Wright about the experiences of Marines at the beginning of the Iraq War][21] I was very respectful of another man's journalism. *The Wire* was written from a journalistic impulse but it was drama." *Treme*, which debuted on HBO in April 2010, tells the story of a post–Katrina New Orleans.

Both as journalist and dramatist, Simon has found a way to fulfill what he considers the core mission of his former profession. Simon's body of work, like the writing of the Old Testament prophets, exposes his audience to subjects that many of us want to avoid. His work is unflinching. For many of us, he continues to remain faithful to the reportorial mission of bearing witness.

"I don't believe *Homicide, The Corner* or *The Wire* changes anything," he says. "But I do believe that there are certain things that are true about the world [they portray] and that nobody can now say, 'We didn't know.' It makes us all a little more complicit in the status quo."

In 2010, as he turned 50, Simon received a MacArthur "genius" fellowship. The $500,000 award from the John D. and Catherine T. MacArthur Foundation honored his work as "an author, screenwriter and producer who draws from his background as a crime beat reporter to craft richly textured narratives that probe urban America's most complex and poorly understood realities."[22] In the fall of 2011, Simon began work on the third season of *Treme*.[23]

Chapter 4

Bullets and Balance

Paul Taylor did not leave *The Washington Post* at the end of 1995 because he had a beef with his editors, his newspaper or journalism. That said, Taylor's departure was influenced by a trend that has only intensified since he left journalism at the peak of his career. Taylor gave up a plum gig as a national political reporter in part because of the prospect of becoming a "wise guy pundit" who offered "smart and sassy" political coverage that veered on the cynical. "I don't think I would have been comfortable. Whatever levels of discomfort I was starting to feel 15–20 years ago, I look at the landscape now and say, the old-fashioned 'just-the-facts' political reporter ... faces a fairly unattractive set of career choices. That's not the way of advancement.... Everybody feels the pressure to be a pundit."

Taylor could have been a powerful *Washington Post* columnist, particularly with a powerful mentor like the late David Broder, considered the dean of Washington journalists, who was a Pulitzer-winning columnist and political reporter. He certainly could have played one on TV. Taylor looks like central casting's idea of an influential Washington journalist. He has high cheekbones and regular features and a bit past 60, still maintains a television-anchor-quality head of hair. His booming voice and bonhomie seem to evoke a man unbothered by the struggles faced by the rest of us.

But Taylor has had struggles, and many have had to do with his fundamental discomfort with the challenge of covering the news and commenting on it at the same time. "I remain a big believer that opinion is opinion and facts are facts and the twain should not meet," he says.

Don't shrug off that belief as the knee-jerk reaction of a reporter from the old school. It's much more visceral than that.

For Taylor, the notion of journalistic objectivity can't be reduced to merely quoting both sides of a dispute. It is a "journey" that requires reporters to be disciplined about recognizing and setting aside whatever their own biases may be, and setting out to understand "multiple points of view." It's the willingness to approach a story and have your initial premises thrown out the window by what is learned in the course of many interviews, and to reframe that story because of new information. Objectivity, in Taylor's mind, doesn't mean forgoing conclusions about the validity of various points of view, and not sharing those judgments with the reader. But it does mean that reporters don't get to come in with their minds made up, and then arrange the facts and the quotes to back up a certain position they've taken.

Taylor's very being seems committed to this way of viewing the world, no matter what the assignment, particularly his three-year stint covering South Africa for *The Washington Post*. You could perceive that vividly when Taylor and a colleague wandered into rebel-controlled territory in Angola. Before the fall of the Soviet Union, Angola for decades had been a pawn in a Cold War conflict, with the United States backing the National Union for the Total Liberation of Angola (UNITA) and the Soviets supporting the country's Marxist government. Here's how he describes a rebel soldier: "Mateus is a UNITA guerrilla, an obliging, eager-to-please true believer of 22, who is old enough to remember when the superpowers couldn't keep their arsenals out of his country's civil war, and naïve enough to wonder why Angola is a neglected orphan in a unipolar world."[1] Taylor's empathetic description is extraordinary considering that Mateus was his captor. In 1993, Taylor and a colleague accidentally wandered into rebel territory in Angola and were stopped by a hail of bullets, captured by UNITA forces, taken and held for two days in the bush.

You might say that Taylor was born to be objective. Amid his generation's "raging debates over Vietnam, the draft, the counterculture," he was a non-combatant. "I didn't really have a side." He recalls thinking that "there must be something wrong with me."

Instead, Taylor wanted to understand everyone's passion, and what stoked it. It was certainly not a habit of mind he acquired from his father, who for years headed up the U.S.-Japan Trade Council, but who also had been active in the progressive politics of the 1960s, getting more conservative as he got older. "He had very strong opinions about everything and he liked getting up on a soapbox and letting his family and people know ... I think in his heart of hearts he would have loved to have been a columnist." Taylor's mother, an employment counselor, was the one who was good with words, a "very good storyteller and also a good writer," the person who "could crystallize things in catchy epigrams" or witty lyrics, he says.

In a world of "watchers and doers," Taylor found himself pulled to watching. But he came to believe that the "act of observing" had a validity and did render a service. "Societies need good honest watchers," he says.

Taylor was barely out of his teens when he graduated from Yale. Tussling with career choices, he came to believe that journalism was the place for people like him, people with the temperament to want to explore the views of others, how people arrived at their opinions and how those positions "fit into the larger scheme of things."

Taylor concedes that not all of his views on journalism were crystallized as he began a job search. He thought of reporting as an extension of his education, a way of getting "a great front row seat" on events, something he would try and see if he were good at.

Taylor did indeed prove to be good at journalism. After graduating in 1970, he sought out a small paper where he could learn the craft, and landed at the *Winston-Salem* (North Carolina) *Journal and Sentinel*, a daily whose publisher was Wallace Carroll, a former news editor at the Washington bureau of *The New York Times*, who had been highly revered in his profession.[2] A few months after Taylor arrived, the paper received a Pulitzer prize for public service for its successful efforts to block a strip mine in northwest North Carolina.[3]

It was there, Taylor said, that he learned to put stories together. One senior editor told him that journalism "is a little like cabinet making," an art for which North Carolina has long been famous, a matter of learning how to handle the tools to produce a product, just as you would "join together a joint."

Taylor says he's always found the act of writing difficult. "The struggle to get the words on paper is really the struggle to figure out what you are trying to say to begin with." It is not difficult to understand the reason for Taylor's struggles. A reporter who already has a preconceived notion of what the story is about has only to fill in the blanks with quotes that support the scaffolding that's already been built. Taylor didn't work that way.

In a small paper, even the rookies get good beats, and soon Taylor, as the county government reporter, was covering the "sewer wars," a dispute between two counties over managing the sewage system. He learned, he says, "that players gotta play," that politicians are drawn to conflict. "It's just a little bit more alive if you're in a pitched battle, even if you're in a pitched battle over sewers."

Less than three years later, Taylor went on to the *Philadelphia Inquirer*. It was, he recalls, a terrific time to be at the paper. In 1969, the paper was sold to Knight Newspapers, which soon would merge into the Knight-Ridder newspaper chain. *Time Magazine* opined that the *Inquirer*, at the point it changed owners in 1969, was "uncreative, undistinguished." Its rival, the *Evening Bulletin*, had been far more popular, and the *Inquirer*, *Time* wrote, had been "in danger of dying an unmourned death."[4] The paper's new owners brought in Gene Roberts, a former national editor at *The New York Times*. Roberts was bent on turning the *Inquirer* from a "terrible" to a great newspaper. Taylor says, "It is fair to argue he did."

During Roberts's tenure, the *Inquirer* won 17 Pulitzers. "I never got close to one of them," Taylor recalls of his 16 years at the paper.[5] More than 80 staff members worked on the stories that won the paper a Pulitzer for the paper's coverage of a severe core meltdown at the Three Mile Island nuclear power plant near Middletown, Pennsylvania, the most dangerous kind of nuclear power accident, in 1979.[6] "Obviously a big story, not far from our backyard and Roberts was in all his glory. He marched into the newsroom one day, and said we're going to lead the world in coverage of this. Like World War II General George Patton," Roberts divided the staff into three teams, Taylor recalls. At this point, Taylor, as the paper's political reporter, had one of the paper's "top beats" and was pretty high up on the reportorial food chain. Nevertheless, for this fight, he didn't make it to the front lines. Roberts "went on to this editor, that editor. And then he came around and said, 'Now we need about three or four people to hang back and put out the rest of the paper. Paul, you take care of that.'" It was not a difficult task, Taylor says. "There wasn't much room in the paper for anything but Three Mile Island."

Pulitzers aside, Taylor rose quickly at the *Inquirer*. Taylor was in his early 20s when Roberts asked him to become assistant city editor. Taylor took on the job but only on the condition that if he didn't like it, he could come back to reporting. Eighteen months later, he was back on the beat. "Then it was the school board, and then city hall and then political reporting."

He started on the politics beat in the 1970s when Frank Rizzo, a former police commissioner, was mayor. When he headed up the police force, Rizzo had been described as a "southern sheriff in a big northern city," Taylor says. "The politics beat in a city like Philadelphia, it's pretty raw." Taylor recalls that Rizzo was perceived as a "tough cop" representing the "white backlash" against the rising minority population of the city. "The black population was reaching for a political piece of the action." He remembers, for example, Rizzo's efforts to change the city's charter so a mayor could serve more than two terms. The charter change campaign "was very racially charged."

At that point, Philadelphia had three dailies, the *Bulletin*, which died in 1982, and the *Inquirer*'s sister paper, the *Daily News*. While the *Inquirer* was broader in its scope, covering the Philadelphia suburbs, the state and national and international news, the *Daily News* "was a big-city tabloid, aggressive and hard-hitting," Taylor says. There also were a number of big-city broadcast news outlets. "It was an intensely competitive environment."

Making the beat even more challenging, Taylor was covering city hall at a time when his colleagues at the *Inquirer* were doing exposés of police brutality and rampant corruption in city government.

He took very seriously the challenge of "seeing everybody's point of view" and giving those various positions "a fair and open-minded rendering. I used to have this image that we're all in this tight little closet together. All these people are fighting each other and elbowing and then once a day I as political reporter for the dominant paper in town go out and say, 'Okay, here's what happened yesterday.'" To keep his sources, Taylor says, "everybody back in the closet" had to believe that his accounting was a "fairly accurate account of what happened."

He tried very hard to keep his sources, he says, because they could have talked to the city's two other dailies or the radio and television reporters. Losing access, he says, "would hurt me professionally and would hurt my paper." So he endeavored to "keep the lines of communication open" while getting out "the best possible story."

Taylor also did a weekly political column, but, he says, "it had almost no point of view. It was a reporter's column" that gave him a bit more freedom about the style in which he wrote. But it was not the place where he expressed his own opinion, he says. He did not and does not believe reporters can wear two hats, writing both news and opinion at the same time. (Indeed, that was the one area where he disagreed with Broder, longtime *Washington Post* columnist, who also wrote straight new stories. "Broder was my idol as a young journalist" and he cherishes the time they worked together. "But I remember thinking then that it wasn't the greatest thing in the world that he was both a reporter and a columnist." What might have made Broder the exception to this rule, he says, was that his voice as a columnist was "very judicious," the voice of a man who is "centered, who brings an open mind.")

In 1980, Taylor covered the presidential campaign for his paper. He got enough of a taste of it to believe that national political reporting for either *The Post* or *The New York Times* would be the next step.

The Post showed the most interest, particularly when the paper got wind that Taylor also was talking to *The Times*. And Taylor's father knew Donald Graham, then the publisher of *The Post*. They had met on the tennis courts of St. Alban's, an elite Episcopal boy's school near the Washington National Cathedral. Through that connection, Graham "knew of me," Taylor says.

Taylor had a day of interviews at *The Post* culminating in one with Ben Bradlee, then the paper's legendary executive editor. "He's all huff and puff and gravelly voice." Bradlee took one look at Taylor, and wisecracked, "So tell me Taylor, what's a WASP like you doing in a profession like this?" Taylor replied, "Actually I'm Jewish, evidently assimilated." The interviews culminated in a job offer, landing Taylor on the paper's national desk.

It didn't take long for Taylor to be part of *The Post* political team, headed up by Broder. His career trajectory seems smooth and absolutely successful, but the fit didn't always feel perfect. When he was a political reporter, he called himself,

> an explainer, an analyzer, and an ingratiator. Investigative reporters have a low threshold for indignation. They're quick to see high conspiracies and base motivations. I rarely see anything but nuance, and my first instinct runs toward benefit of the doubt. I find it painful to render harsh judgments about anyone in print. I find it equally difficult to praise anyone.... Sometimes I worry that my squeamishness about making sharp judgments, pro or con, makes me unfit for the slam-bang world of daily journalism. Other times I conclude that it makes me ideally suited for newspapering—certainly for the rigors and conventions of modern "objective" journalism.[7]

Not that he was unable to do the job. In 1987, it was Taylor who asked Democratic presidential frontrunner Gary Hart if he had ever committed adultery. He was likely the first mainstream journalist to have asked any presidential candidate that impertinent question. In past elections, reporters might have heard rumors about candidate misbehavior, but they did not pursue them. But Hart took umbrage at any media inquiries about his personal life, or the state of his marriage. And he essentially dared reporters to follow him around to find any evidence of less-than-stellar conduct. The *Miami Herald* did investigate Hart's activities, and, aided by an anonymous tipster, discovered Donna Rice. Rice, in the aftermath of the initial news reports, talked to the media to dispel rumors that she was having an affair with Hart, but volunteered in an interview with the Associated Press that she'd been on an overnight trip to Bimini with the candidate on a private yacht. (The day-trip became an overnight one, she said, because the Bimini customs office had closed by the time they were ready to leave.)[8]

In the ensuing media melee, Taylor asked the candidate the adultery question. "I didn't realize at the moment how much of a hornet's nest that [question] would stir up," Taylor recalls. He says that his role was minor compared to the digging by the the *Herald*. Nevertheless, he did realize the question's significance. "I thought about it a lot afterwards, and never wavered from my feelings that all in all I was pretty pleased with the way I handled my role."

But Taylor is not a man without qualms. "On the one hand I felt I made the right decision, but on the other hand the whole story was so tawdry. Being a part of probing and prying into private lives is not a comfortable situation." The scandal forced Hart out of the race.

The Hart experience, he says, had a role in his rethinking his career as a political reporter. "Hart for me crystallized something I understood in myself — that I wanted the people I covered to be better than they turned out to be." He realized, he says, that it might not be fair to have that expectation, and disappointment in the politicians you are covering can soon lead to cynicism, something he did not want to creep into his coverage.

His immediate response to these qualms was to take a six-month leave from the paper to write a book about the campaign, *See How They Run: Electing a President in an Age of Mediaocracy*, rooted in his own disappointment about the way the 1988 campaign had turned out. Writing in 1986, Taylor looked at the field of candidates and predicted debates that would evoke a "new mood" in the country "about things like a national sense of community, moral revival, civic virtue and imperative of doing good."[9] Instead, this was the campaign in which Massachusetts Governor Michael Dukakis duked it out with George H.W. Bush, dominated by the image of Willie Horton, a black murderer convicted in Massachusetts. Horton escaped after an unsupervised weekend prison furlough, and ten months later terrorized a couple in Maryland, raping the woman and stabbing the man. The Massachusetts law that permitted the unsupervised furloughs was passed when a Republican governor was in office. Nevertheless, Horton became a major theme in the campaign, and fodder for ads supporting the Bush candidacy.[10] It helped create the impression that Dukakis was soft on crime.

"The way the campaign played out, record low [voter] turnouts, a feeling that this campaign was driven by these images of Willie Horton," Taylor says. "It just seemed to me that the whole system wasn't working very well, and that really became the framing of the book."

"The premise of this book is that the political dialogue is failing because the leading actors in the pageant of democracy — the politicians, the press, and the voters, are bringing out the least in one another," Taylor wrote.[11] Taylor observed that voters shied away from politicians who tried to discuss substantive issues. Successful candidates stayed on script and did not discuss the real problems confronting the country. But he didn't let his colleagues off the hook, either. He called the "disagreeable" presidential campaign "the subject of a disagreeable sneer campaign — in the press."[12] He also noted that "critics said our mocking tone fed the cynicism of the voters and the surliness of the candidates."[13]

The fact that the campaign inspired the lowest voter turnout in 64 years was a "consumer boycott," he concluded.[14] But Taylor did more than report, he also offered a solution.

"I gave myself a pass in the book to do something I would never have been comfortable doing as a working reporter," Taylor says. What Taylor proposed was that all radio and TV over-the-air broadcast stations in the country give presidential candidates five minutes of free time to talk directly to the American public during the last five weeks of the campaign. Each candidate, or his or her vice presidential nominee, would appear on alternate days, and would have to agree to appear in person. No political ads or stand-ins. In essence, Taylor was asking the media not to mediate and interpret and let the candidates speak directly to the voters, at least for a few minutes every other night.[15] "I thought, 'Boy this is a great idea.' I'm going to put it out there and ... the light bulb will go on in all the right places, and people will say, 'Aha, Taylor's come up with a solution. Onward we go.'" Instead, Taylor says, his family and friends read and liked the book. "That was the end of it."

Disappointed by the response, Taylor felt it was time to "go do something else." He first did some reporting on family and children's issues. But although he found the issues compelling, he didn't think he was very good at covering them. He didn't feel that he could tell the "human side" of stories that well, that his brain was too analytical.

In 1992, Taylor gave up the comfortable gig of political reporter to become *The Post's* South Africa bureau chief. At this point, he had two sons and a daughter, all teens, so that a posting to a foreign bureau was doable. His time there coincided with the death of apartheid and the birth of a multiracial democracy. When he took the assignment, he knew he was going to an exotic land exposing him and his family to "different people, different worlds. That's part of being in the front-row seat at the circus." He knew that South Africa was "going to pop one way or the other and that it was just a huge story." But there was also danger in that reporting, something he hadn't fully anticipated. A reporter had to be able to predict how a story assignment was likely to end. "Is somebody going to get killed and is it going to be me? I wasn't very good at making those calculations because I was brand new at it."

During his sixth day on assignment in the country, he was shot while in a black township a few miles outside Johannesburg, covering a massive strike of black workers. Taylor and a white South African reporter were attacked by a band of car thieves. (Taylor, always willing to see the other point of view, found that the first band of thieves "seemed reasonable enough," but that a second, tougher band was not.) The tougher thieves, eschewing conversation, shot them both. Taylor got away relatively lightly, with wounds to the left arm and shoulder. But still it was a harrowing experience, as Taylor described for *The Post*. "Here we were a couple of white guys, lying bleeding in the suddenly deserted intersection in the middle of a black township in the middle of a region seething with suspicion and hatred." Taylor wrote that salvation came in the form of Felix Gabanakgosi, a young black computer technician who was on strike and who'd heard the shots as he sat in a nearby bar. He went outside and heard some in the crowd murmur, "Let's finish them off."

Risking his own life, Gabanakgosi told the crowd, "Look they're human beings." The crowd's mood changed, and some helped hail a car to take Taylor and his colleague to a hospital. Anti-apartheid leader Nelson Mandela visited Taylor in the hospital, as did a police lieutenant. The lieutenant, "with four centuries of Afrikaner defiance surging through his ample frame," asked Taylor what he thought about the black townships now. Taylor wrote that he had answered that they were dangerous places. But Taylor concluded: "[T]hey are also places where the Felix Gabanakgosis of this world live. That's the lesson I learned the first week on the job ... the one that provides hope that this haunted nation might yet find its way to a better tomorrow."[16]

A few months later came the Angola kidnapping. "They filled our car with bullets, riddled our car with bullets, blah, blah, blah but it ended fine," Taylor says with a smile and a shrug. What he discovered, he says with a laugh, is "that even rebel movements have bureaucracies. The unit commandant found himself with two Western journalists and no one spoke the other's language," and he didn't know what to do with them. When the unit leader radioed his unit commander, he was told to let the two journalists go. The reporters were released after two days.[17]

Back in South Africa, Taylor also said he had the "crap beaten out of me" by an angry mob of white racists, and found himself in the middle of political violence so intense "literally 30 people were killed all around me."

It was, he recalls, the best period of his reporting life of 25 years. You have to remember, Taylor says, that the South African experience, while sometimes dangerous, also had many other dimensions. Taylor and his family were living the "over-privileged" life of white South Africans, living in an exquisitely beautiful country, in one of the most exclusive suburbs of Johannesburg, with a tennis court and a gardener and pool. At their weekly barbecues, he and his reporter colleagues would gather, and tell their "war stories about who ducked what bullet" and compare notes on the transition negotiations to form a new South Africa. "I remember thinking. This is the best story you will ever cover."

Reading Taylor's news stories from that three-year period, one is impressed by his ability to go beyond covering South Africa as a struggle between blacks and whites, or those who support apartheid and those who would continue it. Taylor draws fine distinctions among multiple political players and South African citizens, refusing to summarize the country's status into a two-sentence sound bite. Writing in 1993, he observed: "To understand the dynamics of the transition that has ensued, begin by tossing out your old moral compass on this country. It will only confuse you. The fundamental divide in present-day South Africa is not between black and white. It is between the multiracial center and the multiracial extremes."[18]

The South Africa experience made the prospect of returning to national political reporting even less palatable. It wasn't just the desire to avoid being one of those reporters who spend the next 20 years of their careers recalling the exciting exploits of their past. It also was linked to Taylor's growing unease with the dominant trends in political reporting. The reporting Taylor did — straight-up, fact-based, nuanced — was fast losing favor in newsrooms all over the country.

Taylor did not feel comfortable with the cynicism creeping into political reporting. Commenting on his decision to leave journalism, Taylor told the PBS news program *Frontline*: "From my perspective, it became increasingly dreary. And then in terms of what editors expect, the way it works in newsrooms, you've got a whole culture of newscraft that mixes analysis with commentary, this sort of sneering tone. That is increasingly what is prized and valued." Taylor believed that he had been captured by that tone at times. "I found myself hoping that I was never a cheap shot artist."[19]

In considering this giant career leap, Taylor was also rethinking the second act for his life. His career arc had been spectacular. Despite that stunning career success, Taylor faulted himself for what he had not achieved. "For most of my years in journalism, I was pretty frustrated with my performance. I just felt I was never quite as good as I wanted to be, and that used to gnaw at me." Taylor concedes that by any outside standard, he'd done "pretty well" as a journalist. But he also recalls reading his stories and cringing. He'd fault the stories for unanswered questions or awkward sentences, or regret not making another point or observation. "It was just a death," he says.

There was something else tugging at him, the vision of the possibilities of democracy. "My God, given its 400 years of tortured history around race and the way that plays out ... if they [the South Africans] can get it right, if the human spirit can summon forth at a critical juncture the better angels of our nature, maybe that little system reformer that came out in the last chapter of that book I had written ... maybe I want to take a shot at that."

In 1995, when he returned to *The Post*, he was writing half time and teaching at Princeton half time. He was teaching the book he had written in 1990. He asked Federal Communications Commission Chairman Reed Hundt to speak to his class, the class that was going to discuss the book's idea for reform. He discovered in Hundt a "kindred spirit, a guy in the administration in an important position with the FCC who agrees with me." And Hundt encouraged him to act on his reform ideas. He told him, "Do it. We need somebody to help make it happen."

So for all these reasons, six months after his return from South Africa in 1995, Taylor told his editors at *The Washington Post* that he was leaving. The astounding part was what he intended to do, start a nonprofit to implement his ideas about free broadcast time for national candidates. "I was quitting to be a do-gooder. And they all thought I had completely lost my mind."

In retrospect, Taylor calls his career move taking "a leap blind." He was in his mid-40s with three children, two in college and one about to enter college. But the good fortune that had shone on his journalism career seemed to be with him as he waded into the new waters of the nonprofit world.

He wanted a clean break with no conflicts of interest. So Taylor left *The Post* before he made any efforts to secure funds for his fledgling nonprofit. As it turned out, he didn't have to worry. Broder had put in a good word with Rebecca Rimel, president of The Pew Charitable Trusts. When Taylor made what he thought was a cold call to the foundation in early January, he found that Rimel was ready. Pew gave his startup nonprofit its first grant, and over the nearly eight years that Taylor ran it, he estimated he raised more than $7 million in support from Pew and other foundations.

Taylor also didn't have to worry about credibility. When he made his farewell visit to Bradlee, Bradlee asked if he could help. Taylor said he'd really hoped to get in touch with former CBS news anchor Walter Cronkite, someone the industry pointed to as an example of its commitment to public service. "I said, 'I'd love to get Cronkite on board. It would be fabulous. Just beat them [the broadcasters] with their own halos.'" Bradlee tapped on his knee. "Hear that? Titanium. I just got it put in six months ago, and Walter got his new knee put in six months ago. We talk all the time about our titanium knees."

By the time Taylor reached his home office that afternoon, Cronkite called. "I understand from Ben that you've got a crusade. I'm very interested in helping you," Cronkite told Taylor.

"I was out of the box in a big hurry," Taylor recalls. In relatively short order, he recruited, along with Cronkite, former presidents Jimmy Carter and Gerald Ford. In the early days of his Free TV for Straight Talk Coalition, later called the Alliance for Better Campaigns, it was "me and a fax machine and great letterhead. " Early on, too, the media were quite interested in his new nonprofit. He thinks the coverage was prompted in part by curiosity about why anyone in Taylor's shoes would leave "our profession."

For whatever reason, his first media event was a big success. "Three months before, I was a reporter and suddenly you know you had a lot of important people paying attention to what I felt was this good idea." These beginning months, Taylor says, were "very exciting, very heady."

But Taylor soon discovered that turning that a good reform idea into reality was not an easy lift. Good-government groups such as Common Cause liked the idea of free time for candidates, but they were after bigger game — pushing, for example, for stricter campaign contribution limits that would eliminate huge unlimited gifts to national political parties. Taylor could use his foundation support to contribute to such organizations to enlist their grassroots efforts for free TV for candidates, but it was never going to be the issue on which any good-government group focused all its energy.

On the other hand, the people who were against the free TV idea were strongly opposed to it because it threatened their self-interest. Incumbents weren't that keen on handing over TV time to challengers who likely weren't as well known or as well funded as they were. For broadcasters, time was money and they didn't want to lose any by providing candidates with a public forum free of charge.

"It was always a long shot. I started the change theory with the hope, well with Cronkite for it and Carter, we'll beat them over the head with their halos and shame them into doing better. There was an inch of progress here and an inch of progress there," Taylor concedes. Broadcasters gave just enough to avoid being criticized for being bad corporate citizens, but not enough to actually deliver on the free TV goal.

When it didn't seem that Taylor could shame broadcasters into doing the right thing, he tried to get change through federal regulation or legislation. He stuck with it for nearly eight years. He left in part because he didn't see a way to move forward, but more importantly because the media landscape had changed. The networks and their affiliates had been the "keepers of the public square," Taylor says. But then cable channels exploded, and with them many more sites to get political news. "I used to spend months going around the country talking to station managers," asking them to air city council and other political debates, Taylor says. But cable discovered that "politics can actually be interesting."

Just at the point when Taylor was looking around for a third act in his career, his ties to the Pew Charitable Trusts proved very beneficial. He got an email from a Pew executive he knew, saying that Pew was going to consolidate a number of its information projects and was looking for someone to manage them. Taylor proposed that he would be the right person.

Taylor has no regrets about his do-gooder phase. He tried his best to move forward on an idea he cared passionately about. But even so, the role of an advocate was one that wasn't entirely a good fit. Taylor said he was effective "as a framer of a message, but there's something in me that wasn't totally comfortable" in arguing for one position, and not "seeing a situation for all its complexity.

"I would occasionally check in with myself and say, 'Am I really telling the whole story here? Maybe the broadcasters do have a point.'" He'd "give himself a pass" by reminding himself that he'd taken on a new role, as an advocate.

"Now that I'm back in the fold of seeing all points of view, I think temperamentally that's a more comfortable role for me," he says.

As executive vice president for the Pew Research Center, Taylor characterizes his position as "half-way into journalism." Pew does extensive surveys of the American public on a variety of issues. Taylor offers as an example, a Pew survey on race that he worked on. He helped to formulate the questions and refine them after they were tested on focus groups in the field. The survey asked 2,000 Americans 60 questions on race and looked for differences in views across many demographic groups. When the results came back, "you have the Ph.Ds. with their skills" and "people like me who have story telling skills. It feels more and more like I'm in the information generating business."

The role of the Pew Research Center, he says, "is very closely aligned with the civic mission of journalism. We believe that self-governing societies, in order to function, need a certain basis of facts." Indeed, Pew Research Center calls itself not a think tank but a "fact tank. We say we generate the facts, numbers and trends that help you understand your world."

Taylor has always found it difficult to criticize his former colleagues in journalism. But he is dismayed by the trends that were part of the reason he left in 1996 and that have morphed and become more problematic over time.

The "sneering" Taylor worried about in the 1990s now has become "red sneering" and "blue sneering." Not only is political commentary increasingly rancorous but now it's also partisan, he observes. "This is a world that I just would have been extremely uncomfortable in as a journalist. I couldn't find a place for myself." Taylor stresses that he maintains deep friendships with journalists and avoids criticizing his former profession. But he does worry that the values he embraced as a young reporter, the striving to be objective and fair, are fast losing ground. "News marbled with opinion is vivid, entertaining and easy to get. You can build an audience around it and certainly that's the world of cable and talk radio." The sad part, he says, is that some of those behaviors have "migrated up into the world of high-end journalism, rather than the highest values of high-end journalism creeping down."

Taylor remains at Pew, where he oversees Pew's Social and Demographic Trends project and the Pew Hispanic Center. In 2011, the studies he co-authored included groundbreaking reports on the increasing wealth gap between blacks, whites and Hispanics; differences in economic well-being among various age groups, and current attitudes of adults under 30 about marriage and parenthood.

Chapter 5

Divine Intervention

In the worst of worlds, journalists are cold and detached observers, who violate the privacy, impair the dignity and exploit the suffering of people caught up in tragic events in the interest of bringing back a good story. In the best of worlds, journalists bear witness to suffering and loss because they are empathetic members of a compassionate community. They are players–bit players, to be sure, but players nonetheless, in the great human drama of good and evil, order and chaos that has been unfolding since the beginning of the written word.[1]

These were Joan Connell's comments in an email interview in 2010 for a college publication. Her answer illuminates her approach to journalism. For Connell, reporting always has been about the big questions and the core values. She's never let anyone off the hook, including her colleagues, on what those questions and values demand. When corporate mainstream journalism failed to meet those standards, and uphold those values, she left the profession, only to return to what she terms "public service" journalism as online editor of the progressive weekly *The Nation*.

In an interview with Connell, it quickly becomes apparent that she is used to the writing life. She speaks in clear sentences, using exact descriptors. She is precise about dates and places. She stops to spell out unfamiliar names, and includes middle initials. Slightly built, with a throaty laugh, she is unfailingly considerate and polite during a multi-hour interview. She insists on serving tea and cookies in the spectacular Manhattan high-rise with awe-inducing views of the New York skyline that she shares with her journalist husband. Sensing a chill in the air, she insists on offering a pashmina shawl.

But if that description makes one think "kindly grandmother," the impression is all wrong. Joan Connell has a mind sharp enough to slice through concrete. Without the support of any friends and family in the profession, and over the objections of her father, Connell became an award-winning journalist — a finalist for the Pulitzer Prize. Connell did benefit from

70

one bit of good timing. She entered the profession shortly after a pioneering group of women editors, who hired and mentored her. While she's done her share of breaking news stories as both a writer and an editor, her real métier has been covering religion and ethics—subjects that for a brief time merited the attention of regional dailies across America. That focus on deeper issues led her to think long and hard about the nature of war and its coverage, and the ways journalists can best serve communities and respond to their audience.

But nothing so lofty first propelled her into her chosen field. The middle child in a family of five, the daughter of a lawyer and a mom who was an avid reader, she was beguiled by journalism as a youngster. "Very, very early, I read the [Buffalo] *Courier-Express,* from the police reports to [gossip columnist] Walter Winchell," she recalls. Connell was a fan of comic-book news hound Brenda Starr and aspired to the reporter's life. Her father strongly disapproved. "My father said, 'No daughter of mine is going into that profession. You'll meet terrible people. You'll stay up all night. You won't be happy.'" So she majored in English literature, and with the family budget stretched with a grandmother in a nursing home and two older siblings away at school, Connell commuted to the State University of New York at Buffalo. "I was a townie," she says. It wasn't the ideal college experience, she says, but it got her a "great education." She married young, accompanying her husband to Iowa City, Iowa, to further his life plans. The marriage soon foundered, and at 28, Connell found herself the single mother of a toddler.

Her prospects were slim. She couldn't afford journalism school, but it was the 1970s, and the Writers' Workshop at the University of Iowa was flourishing. The workshop, founded in 1936, had become a haven for students pursuing creative writing, and its visiting instructors had included poets Robert Frost and Robert Lowell.[2] There was, Connell recalls, "a great spirit of intellectual generosity" on campus. She was not a student, but the editor of the campus paper, *The Daily Iowan,* told her she could "hang around" and learn how to be a reporter.

She got her first break on a wintry Iowa City garbage day. Pushing her daughter in a stroller, she noticed a mysterious bit of garbage. She found "an animal form wrapped in yellow tape" marked," 'caution radioactive materials,' sticking out of a garbage can." The animal turned out to be "a dog, a radioactive dead dog," she says. Her story, written with the help of a more experienced student reporter, broke the news that the university was disposing of radioactive materials "in some fairly unorthodox ways via the city trash system," Connell says. "Oh my goodness, this was a real story," she says. The story was picked up by the public radio station in Cedar Rapids, and eventually earned her an award from the Iowa Press Association. It was not "the most perfect story," Connell says, but to a "single mother in Iowa City without a job and a very empty resume, it was a big deal."

It turned out to be her ticket out of the Midwest to a region that had long attracted her, the Pacific Northwest. She found work at a twice-weekly suburban paper in Seattle, the *Highline Times*. After a year, she went from being a reporter to serving as an editor. It was community journalism and it allowed her to write and to learn on the job.

It was the kind of publication where the staff did almost everything, she says. "We practically delivered them too." But there were other realities that were not so pleasant. "It was very hard in Seattle to be a working mother, having a child in day care and to earn pretty much less than my neighbors in our apartment building who were on welfare," she says. "And to keep it all together was really, really difficult."

Her "unachievable" goal had been to land a reporting job at *The Seattle Times*. Knowing the odds were against her, she networked, putting feelers out for openings in other parts of the state. That was how she landed a job in a more supportive and family-friendly environment in Bellingham, Washington. She was hired by a rarity in those days, a female managing editor — Diane Borden. Connell, ever precise, pauses to give Bellingham's estimated population — 25,000, and location — in the northwest corner of the state about 40 miles from the Canadian border. The *Bellingham Herald* was her first daily reporting job, and now she could afford to buy a house. "I had good clips and I had won awards," and knew how to report in a "very passionate" way, she says.

It was an afternoon paper, which meant that Connell's reporting day started early but concluded by 3 P.M. She could be at home when her daughter returned from school. The job, she says, "worked beautifully for me both personally and professionally." She was, she says, "majorly ambitious." Looking back, she is grateful for her editors' receptivity to some of her projects. She was interested in Buddhism, and when the Dalai Lama visited Seattle, she would explain concepts such as Tantric Buddhism to her readers. She laughs at the memory. "I'd write these things and they'd publish them."

Connell knew that she was going to outgrow Bellingham, so she became adept at applying for journalism fellowships, and study opportunities in the summers she could pursue while her daughter spent some time with her father. The secret of her success in landing them was the ability to write "passionate applications," she says.

Courtesy of the National Endowment for the Humanities, she studied journalism ethics at Yale. Teaching the course was Professor John Edwin Smith, one of the great lights among philosophers in the U.S., whose tenure at Yale lasted for nearly 40 years. After his death, Smith was hailed as "one of the great philosophy teachers of his time."[3] He "made philosophy and ethics really come alive and apply it to the work that journalists do every day," she says. For a "self-educated journalist" like herself, she says, that month at Yale was "a signature moment." She came away feeling that what she was doing "*was* worthwhile," and that journalism "*is* a noble profession. You have to do it right and there *are* rules."

Another NEH fellowship allowed her to study at Duke University during the American Dance Festival. The fellowships were for dance critics, but Connell had grown interested in Tai Chi and was fascinated by the "whole idea of movement and expression and body-mind connection." Since Bellingham had an arts community vibrant enough to attract traveling dance troupes, it was possible to make a case for training in dance criticism. Connell also figures that she often was the "token" small-towner in the group.

"How do you write about dance and movement in an analytical way, and how do you report a dance?" She learned how to answer those questions, sitting at the feet of America's best dance critics— Anna Kisselgoff of *The New York Times* and Arlene Croce of *The New Yorker*. She even danced with a member of the renowned Martha Graham Dance Company, since each fellow had to take a dance class. "You'd see all of us schlumpy out-of-shape journalists at the bar doing pliés, it was just hilarious," she says.

But Connell really won the fellowship lottery the year she was named a Gannett Foundation fellow in the Department of Asian and Pacific Studies at the University of Hawaii at Manoa. At the time —1983 — Gannett had recently launched *USA Today*, but the chain was better known for owning dozens of small and medium-sized daily newspapers across the country. The *Herald* was then a part of the chain, and Connell suspects that helped her prospects. The one-year fellowship gave her the chance to study Asian religion, philosophy, aesthetics and history. She and her daughter lived in Honolulu for the year, and her daughter attended public school there.

After her stint in Hawaii, she remained at the *Herald* for another year. With her daughter about to start high school, they both were ready for a move, and Connell landed a job at the *San Jose Mercury News*. She had been at the *Herald* for eight years, from 1978 until 1986, covering the school board and the university, doing arts criticism, serving as features editor, and serving as a member of the paper's editorial board.

Her growing interest in religion and philosophy coincided with a flourishing of reporting that went beyond breaking news and explored religion and ethics in a deeper and more intellectually stimulating way. One of the first papers to take that approach was the *Mercury News*. Editor Judith Neuman had moved the paper's religion section away from " the 'church lady' mode of bake sales and new pastors" to coverage that was "issue-driven," Connell says.

Connell was well equipped for this beat. She had grown up in the 1950s in a very Irish Catholic household. "We were on our knees a lot. Said the rosary a lot. We loved the Pope." She had relatives who were nuns and priests. "I was saturated in our little religious world." That devotion all went by the board's in the 1960s, she says. But while no longer a practicing Catholic, Catholicism "was still culturally a part of my life." She also retained deep respect for the "great, unselfish, inspired work" of some religious orders.

There was, she says, "a level of rigor" at the *Mercury News* that enhanced her reporting skills. "I had a lot to learn." One of those eager to teach her was copy chief Dean P. Wright. She filed a story. "He kind of flung it back to me with copious questions," she recalls.

"Copious questions" from an editor usually incite reporter hostility. Reporters can often deeply resent editors, and the number of editor jokes among reporters is legion — like the reporter who, upon discovering that his young daughter had head lice said: "Oh, you've got *editors*." But Connell found them instructive, and probing, and a signal that she had to up her game. "I have always loved editors," she says. Writing a story, she says, is "a communal act," that demands "great levels of trust and caring between editors and writers. You can't do this work without trust and caring for one another. The editor's job is to make the writer look good and to tell the story in the appropriate way and to leave as few fingerprints as possible on a piece."

Wright had a lot to teach. He'd arrived at the paper at about the same time Connell had, coming from the national desk of the *Louisville Courier-Journal*. Experienced in hard news, he also had a longstanding interest in culture and entertainment. "Our interests and emotions aligned very nicely," Connell says primly. The two became romantically involved, but kept it secret. "We kept company for about a year," she says, going public only shortly before they married in 1987.

As Connell's personal life was flourishing, so was her professional. One of the first stories she did for the *Mercury News* described a surrogacy clinic in San Francisco. The whole science of infertility was taking off, and women with fertility problems were finding doctors who used surrogate mothers. The surrogates either were artificially inseminated with the father's or a donor's sperm, or carried the couple's embryo. In each case, the surrogates went through the pregnancy and the delivery and then agreed to surrender the infant to its adoptive parents.

Connell wrote about the Hagar Institute, a for-profit clinic that was helping women "rent their wombs out," she says. She termed it "the birth equivalent of an adoption mill or a puppy mill. It just didn't seem right." The science had outpaced the law, and there were no laws in place to regulate surrogacy. A quarter century ago, readers looking at the front page of the religion section of the *Mercury News* would have seen this headline: "The Big Business of Babies—Kids by Surrogate: A High-Tech Harvest." She didn't mince words. "The product is babies. The means of production: surrogate mothers. The market: childless couples willing to try their luck with the emerging technology of fertility. The cost: About $22,000, from conception to birth." Connell went on to describe how the Institute operated, and she quoted California officials who conceded that no laws on the books anticipated surrogacy, and that the possibility of abuse was real.[4]

Connell took on other hot-button issues, writing about "the abortion wars, the culture wars." She maintained sources on both sides of the controversies, including the father of a co-worker who was a pro-life protestor, keeping vigil outside abortion clinics. "He was a lovely person, very passionate." Connell says that a lot of reporters would have dismissed this source and other pro-life activists as crazy, but "as a reporter, I couldn't do that. You have to report fairly and not depict people as crazy except when in fact they are and they kill people." She says her effort "to cover that issue with equanimity" was something she believed her community largely respected. She also covered the growing Muslim community. Her tolerance for unfamiliar religious rites like self-flagellation earned her the trust of Muslims, and in turn she'd write stories that emphasized their humanity, like the challenge for Muslim teens in keeping the month-long fast for the feast of Ramadan. The headlines sometimes were "a little sassy," Connell recalls. "Young, Muslim and Misunderstood: Devout Teens Must Rely on Their Faith and Each Other to Endure Culture Shock," introduced South Bay's Muslim teens this way: "They do not go to dances. Proms hold no appeal. Dating is out of the question. Their formula for a good time is boys and girls and a chaperone. They actually like to spend time with their parents." Connell interviewed teens who were fasting between sunup and sundown during the holy month of Ramadan, who discussed the difficulties they encountered. One teenage boy noted that the first day of Ramadan was especially difficult. "You're surrounded by food, you're always thinking about food, you really want to eat, and you can't." Another teen said that her non–Muslim friends thought she was on some exotic diet that promised terrific weight loss. She explained, "[W]hen you fast you just feel better.... It's not dieting, it's discipline. You feel like you're doing it for a reason, a good reason."[5]

Connell received an award from the South Bay Islamic Association, recognizing the contribution her stories made to promoting understanding.

Connell says she was covering religion during the "golden era" for such reporting. Faith, she says, should be covered with the same rigor as science. "I've always taken an anthropological approach to it. What is it about this belief system that motivates these people to make the choices they make and to pursue the path they pursue?" During the 1980s and 1990s, she says, there was a cadre of reporters who were "irreverent and hard-bitten and tough as nails," but very good at covering religion. People like George Cornell of the Associated Press, Don Lattin of the *San Francisco Chronicle*, Bruce Buursma of the *Chicago Tribune*, and Bill Bell of the *New York Daily News*. "We'd go around in a pack, follow the Pope, cover the big stories," she recalls. "It's so easy to sentimentalize religion, or to sensationalize it or to reduce it to its most elemental and often erroneous dimensions," she says. She and her colleagues avoided that, and kept their own beliefs to themselves and out of their coverage.

Connell spent five years working at the *Mercury News*, from 1986 until 1991. Then, she says, "the wonderful Deborah Howell," the new Washington bureau chief of Newhouse News Service, hired her to cover religion, ethics and morality. Howell, she says, "was my mentor and my friend and believed in me." Under Howell's leadership, the Washington, D.C.-based news service transformed itself. Its 12 correspondents had "atypical beats and our mission was to write the counter story. You know how Washington is, 5,000 people chasing the same story every day," Connell says. "We were going to be doing things differently." Connell focused on the moral dimensions of public policy and popular culture. She remembers going to a clinic in Paris, France, sitting with women taking a new drug, RU 486. "The question was, is this a more ethical alternative to the surgical abortions ... is this a more compassionate way to deal with problem pregnancies?" In the early days of the drug, she recalls, ending a pregnancy took more than one pill and more than one trip to the clinic. "It could take hours or days." She heard the stories of the women who took the pill, and the doctors who administered it.

Then she boarded a train for what she termed a "sublime" experience in Taize, an ecumenical monastery near Dijon in eastern France. Taize music had become a trend in the U.S., she says. The monastery was known for its hospitality to young people and its liturgical music. "Young people were coming to Taize from all over Europe to have religious experiences and fellowship and music." Connell remembers simple food, "heavy on carrots," and "beautiful candlelight liturgies with singularly beautiful meditative song" composed by the monks.[6]

She looked at the intersection of sports and religion, observing that "the growing influence of a muscular Christianity has made the post-game prayer circle, the end-zone genuflection, and the touchdown-for-Jesus as much a part of the pageantry of pro football as the cleavage of the cheerleaders and the roaring of the crowds."[7]

She critiqued the way mainstream media largely dismissed religion and people of faith. Writing in 1993, she observed: "Americans who practice religion and Americans who practice journalism eye each other across a chasm of mutual misunderstanding and mistrust." At a time when religion was a factor in so many violent conflicts throughout the world, journalists must understand the power of religion to shape world views and to help believers make sense of an otherwise chaotic world, she contended. And she urged journalists to understand that the language of faith — emotionally fraught and dependent on "moral absolutes" — was very different from the more neutral language of democracy.[8]

She covered the movement to protect the environment as a moral issue. She traveled to the slums of Rio de Janeiro, wrote about the lives of the people who lived and died there. "Millions of people living in these favelas."

Even menopause touched her beat, as New Age practitioners started to hold "croning ceremonies" to celebrate the end of a woman's fertile years and her entry into "'cronedom.' I would kill myself before I would have a croning ceremony," she says with a laugh.

That wide-ranging work led to her being named a Pulitzer finalist for beat reporting, but the prize was awarded to reporters exposing spending abuses at a Michigan state agency.[9] "What's new about that?" Connell says.

But that was the problem. The people who ran the newspapers in middle America weren't hankering for innovative in-depth stories that challenged their readers, particularly if they ran more than 800 words. Connell's work was offered to the papers that subscribed to Newhouse News Service, but her stories could be cut sharply, or not published at all. Indeed, the stories Connell so vividly remembers on RU 486 and the monks of Taize no longer exist in the most commonly used news databases. Howell left Newhouse News Service in 2005 to become ombudsman at *The Washington Post*, and died in a traffic accident in 2010.[10] Newhouse News Service closed its doors in 2008.

In the early 1990s, Howell and Connell had persuaded Steve Newhouse to buy Religion News Service. The service was more than 60 years old by then, founded by the National Conference of Christians and Jews to ensure that religion was covered in an unbiased way by reporters who knew something about it.[11] Connell became its editor. Connell took the helm of the wire service with relish. "Even though I loved writing, I was getting kind of tired of it." And, she says, this position gave her the chance "to drive the boat. I love that." She added that although writing "is wonderful, the writer is often the lowest person on the totem pole." She adds that wasn't the case at Newhouse or Religion News Service, but happens "as you get into larger media organizations. ... I found that if I wanted to set the agenda, I was going to have to be in charge."

She had to give up doing "the deep, delicious Newhouse News Service stories," but continued to pursue compelling issues. "Bird-dogging the religious right, tracking the effect of conservative Christianity on American politics and popular culture, following the Catholic Church pedophilia scandals." She was, she says, "creating a culture of news, working with writers, editors, contributors," meeting morning and afternoon daily deadlines, "staying on top of" stories that were moving and fluid.

The solid reporting from around the world was complemented by an array of columnists "reflecting a vast array of denominational and faith perspectives—Christian, Jewish, Muslim, New Age, you name it."

She vividly recalls the work of a "very brave" correspondent, writing from Rwanda, during the massacres in 1994. He was explaining the origins of the animosities between the Hutu and Tutsi ethnic groups that resulted in the slaughter of hundreds of thousands of Tutsis. The animosity was fostered by Rwanda's Belgian colonial rulers, who favored one tribe and demonized the other, breeding years of resentment, injustice and intolerance.[12]

It was, Connell says, "fascinating, brave work, but could you get a paper in Peoria to run it? Of course not. They weren't even covering the massacres."

Connell found it frustrating that even her major clients—such as major broadcast news outlets and NPR—often weren't interested in the stories her news service was exploring. They relied on the service for the basics. "But some of these stories, though important, just couldn't get a home."

Meanwhile, the world was changing. In Silicon Valley, when Connell had been at the *Mercury News*, there was interest in a precursor search engine called Mosaic. Microsoft, too, was intrigued by the potential of search engines and online content. Among those *Mercury News* vets interested in going to Redmond, Washington, and Microsoft and the fledgling MSNBC.com in the late 1990s was Connell's spouse. At that point, he was working at the Associated Press. Connell suggested that he go to Redmond, and check it out. Six months later, Connell was ready to leave for Redmond, too.

Connell was familiar with interactivity between journalists and their audience. As far back as 1989, Connell, then at the *Mercury News*, asked readers to respond to the kinds of ethical questions that are common in newsrooms, questions that concerned the appropriateness of a gruesome picture of an injured earthquake victim, the newsworthiness of a scandal involving a public servant after the official in question resigned, the fairness of a story about a student athlete and leader in an affluent community who was arrested for possessing and distributing drugs, without identifying him by name, but after the news of his run-in with the law has circulated widely in the local high school. Readers were asked to cut out a ballot printed in the paper, fill it in, and mail it back. Connell wrote that the response from more than 800 readers had been "impressive," particularly the "comments ranging from salty, well-chosen epithets scribbled in the margins to eloquent, sensitive essays."[13]

What she found in Redmond, she says, was a new alliance of software developers working with "very grounded" journalists. "Software engineers who thought like journalists and journalists who thought like geeks." All of them were engaged in exploring new ways to tell a story. They were, in the parlance of the 21st century, developing apps, she says. In 1999, she remembers doing a year-long series about the new millennium and how things were changing. "I had a different theme every month," she recalls. There was a feature on the city of the future, complete with a clickable map. Another story predicted computers that will be wearable. The series featured all kinds of digital "bells and whistles."

MSNBC.com was a joint venture of Microsoft and NBC. "Microsoft provided the engineers," she says, but initially NBC was pretty removed from the operation, providing the money for the startup, with the journalists recruited primarily from California and Washington State. Connell began her tenure by writing a weekly column called "NetEthics," exploring moral and ethical issues in cyberspace, because "that's what I knew how to do." Indeed while still at Newhouse, Connell had written a probing story about the coming Internet revolution and the "ethical road maps necessary to negotiate this electronic terra incognita."[14]

She was particularly drawn to the new technology's capacity for public engagement. As an editor and executive producer, she oversaw a multi-partisan opinion section for the website. Her contributors ran the gamut from former Marine Lieutenant Colonel Oliver North, a hero of the far right because of his role in the Iran-Contra scandal,[15] to former counselor to the Clinton Administration and Democratic strategist Paul Begala. In the beginning, the audience was small, largely consisting of the subscribers to dial-up connections to the Internet through AOL or MSN. "It skewed very male, very young, very conservative, just because the geeks' world was that way," she says. They couldn't really do video because the available bandwidth was too low. But they did embrace the 24-hour news cycle. Connell's philosophy was that if something happened in the morning, she'd put out commentary by that afternoon. "We just did everything. Covered the Lewinsky scandal. The impeachment trial. The 2000 election where the newspapers had that Dewey/Truman moment on election night. It's Gore. No, it's Bush. No, it's Gore." She said that her designers had come up with alternative designs for the next morning's web page, one featuring Gore as president, and one featuring Bush. "The results were so crazy and I thought I had all the options covered." She discovered she had to ask her artists to design a picture of America waking up to both Bush and Gore.

As an MSNBC editor, she found herself handling multiple tasks, not only editing copy, but also writing text, assembling slide shows, and deciding whether a story needed an illustration or some type of special presentation. "It was very intense, very demanding, but a lot of fun. And you move so much faster than in traditional media because you don't have to wait for the presses to roll."

It was, she says, not that great a jump. Even though she had delighted in doing long-form, in-depth journalism, she'd also done her share of breaking news stories throughout her news career. Newhouse and Religion News Service both had been wire services, working on a 24-hour news cycle. "Something happens, you do it." And she says, as an editor at both wire services and then at MSNBC, she found herself working intensely with correspondents across time zones, often people she'd never met, with whom she developed close bonds. "We never saw each other but we had a deep instinctual understanding of one another."

Connell's job was changing as MSNBC.com changed. *Slate*, the online magazine, was a strategic partner and eventually became the website's portal for opinion. In late 2001, Connell had temporarily relocated from Redmond to work at the MSNBC operation in Secaucus, New Jersey, just outside Manhattan. She was trying to integrate the on-air portion of MSNBC into the online portion, getting correspondents to file for the web. "It was very hard, very painful, not a lot of fun, but it had to be done." It was, she says, "a slow educational effort."

It was the aftermath of 9/11 that offered her "a moment of truth about corporate media." What Connell found troubling, and ultimately unbearable, was corporate media's coverage of the decision to invade Iraq. "In the wake of 9/11 you'd see anchors wearing little [American] flags and there'd be triumphal music," she recalls. In that environment, she perceived a "lack of discernment on the part of media about whether this war was a good idea or not." In April 2003, U.S. and other coalition forces received a specially designed deck of playing cards identifying the 55 most wanted members of Saddam Hussein's regime. Each card displayed the name, face and titles of the sought-after Iraqi officials.[16] One of her colleagues, she says, suggested that MSNBC develop an online app based on the deck of cards, and make a game out of it. The concept, she says, sickened her. (Other entrepreneurs had the same thought and the Iraqi deck of cards app continues to be offered for sale at iTunes.)[17]

When a reporter writes about religion and ethics, she will inevitably write about war, its morality, and its toll on the human spirit. Many of Connell's most poignant stories touched on these themes. At the *Mercury News*, she wrote about a cathedral overflowing with worshippers coming to grips with the 1991 Gulf War. "They came in tears, they came in silence, with lighted candles in their hands and faces transfigured with pain. The house of God became an arena for anguish, as people came to terms with a world suddenly at war."[18] The service, she later wrote, "made me understand what faith is for."[19]

The question of what constitutes a "just war" and the moral implications of violence always had been on her plate as a journalist, both at the *Mercury News*, and at Newhouse News Service. Her correspondents at Religion News Service brought home the ravages of civil war and genocide in Rwanda and elsewhere.

So it is not surprising that Connell had grown weary of the "jingoism of the moment" and "all the pressure from NBC to jazz things up." Some members of her staff were saying, "I can't support this war. I can't do this work ... I can't sit and listen to this ... beat the drum."

"My personal feelings about war and peace and my good sense as a good journalist told me that something wasn't right here," she says. "I don't want to say that I was making any kind of grand gesture," she adds. "I just thought it would be good to get out of the news at this point because I was struggling with this lack of objectivity about the war.... For the first time in her career, she says, "the news felt like a garment that didn't fit."

She made a decision that she does not regret. She went to the business side of Microsoft, returning to Redmond. Web publishing was about selling products and delivering eyeballs. She tried mightily to lay down some standards, winning some battles, but losing some too. It was, she says, "very lucrative and just the hardest job I ever had."

But if Connell had escaped corporate media, she hadn't finished with journalism. She missed the news business. When her spouse moved from Redmond to New York for Reuters, Connell found herself back in the media capital of the country wondering, "I'm 58, who's going to hire me in New York?"

She needn't have worried. *The Nation* was thrilled to have her as an online editor, and her career in "public service journalism" began. She coined the term "public service" journalism, she wisecracks, because *The Nation* can't afford to pay decent salaries. Nevertheless, she terms her tenure there "a labor of love." Founded in 1865 by abolitionists, the weekly publication has been one of the major voices of progressive politics in the country.[20]

Going to *The Nation* in 2005 meant a transition from objective journalism to journalism with a very distinctive point of view. Connell concedes that *The Nation* is "very, very, very, very, very 'lefty.'" She recalls with a laugh how her son-in-law took the news that she was joining the staff. His response was, "Oh my God! *The Nation*! Really?" But Connell says that while *The Nation* is "passionate" and "has a point of view-damn it, we check the facts. We're not just bloviating.... The reporting is scrupulous."

Among her fondest memories is covering the 2008 presidential campaign.

"Evolving that year-long story was just so exciting." She also is very proud of the way *The Nation* covered the financial crisis. Bill Greider and Nicholas von Hoffman, she says, were two

> consummate professionals who have a social conscience who had the deep knowl-
> edge of our economic system and our business system and the compassion and
> the social vision to know that we were getting screwed by [Bush Administration
> Secretary of the Treasury] Henry Paulson and the Bush bailout and the whole
> thing. They saw it, they shed a light on it, they called it out. Covered it, day in
> and day out, beautifully. Those kinds of experiences have been the highlight of
> my life as an editor.

She also speaks fondly of the young writers willing to accept $50 or $100 for their work, or to do it for free "because they have a story to tell."

Connell was happy at *The Nation*. But she was growing weary of its demands. "It's a wonderful thing to be able to sit at that desk and have these relationships with faraway people and do these stories," she says. "But I have to say that 24/7 when you're the only one doing it, gets old. I did have some helpers, but I was always on."

Ready for something new, she left reporting and editing in 2009, jumping to the Dart Center for Journalism and Trauma, a project of the Columbia University Graduate School of Journalism, becoming its associate director. She jokes that she calls herself a "journo-bureaucrat." She is managing editor of a website, and involved in strategic planning, keeping track of budgets and payrolls. The Center's mission is to provide resources, training and support to journalists who cover disasters and wars. It brings together mental health clinicians, researchers, working journalists and educators in an attempt to be a "center for ethical reporting around traumatic events," she says.

Connell recalls a conference the Center co-sponsored with the Carter Center in Atlanta, Georgia, for reporters to address the coverage of soldiers fighting in Iraq and Afghanistan, and their families. Connell says that the conference, which enabled reporters to learn from trauma scientists, returning vets, and military experts, was "enormously gratifying" because it gave real-world guidance about how reporters should approach military families, and how they can interview a soldier via Skype who's been deployed to Afghanistan. This type of reporting, she says, "requires some skill. You just can't wing it.... It's just fascinating to teach these people and then see the difference in their work."

She remembers one of the conference attendees was a reporter from a Fox affiliate in Georgia. She asked him how he could use this information in his current job. He told her, "I don't know, but sometimes they give me four minutes to do a story."

Another attendee was a young Hispanic journalist from a public radio station in the Midwest. After the conference, she interviewed a local family with a father and two sons deployed, two in Iraq and one in Afghanistan. The story profiled the entire family, and included a Skype interview with the father from his tent in Afghanistan. The reporter sent Connell a link to the final story, and Connell beams. "It's beautiful, it's sensitive, it's ethical, it's respectful. Complicated. It's everything you want journalism to be." The reporter, she says, was "already good to start with." But the Center's training made her better, and "she is on her way to being a marvelous witness to this huge story of returning soldiers."

Dart also brings together journalists who have covered earthquakes, wars or other violent events, so they can discuss what they saw and experienced, and get some expert help about how to handle their own traumatic stress.

Dart often deals with this "burning cohort of independent journalists who are going to dangerous places and doing difficult things without the support of an employer, without a health plan, without employee assistance plans.... These people are still wanting to practice journalism and we want to support them, but how are they going to do it?"

But Connell notes that all journalists, by the very nature of the profession's own precariousness, are suffering a sense of dislocation. "The whole profession is in trauma as people try to reconcile their passion to report the news and tell the stories that need to be told" with the "abysmal financial outlook for news publications."

The very existence of the Dart Center, she says, "is making a leap of faith.... There's a trust there will be a journalism and then training the people you can find."

There was, she acknowledges, a lot that failed to work in current mainstream journalism, which, she observes, is neither "public spirited," nor "intuitive" and "doesn't speak to much.... Maybe this moment of crisis is an opportunity as we search for new business models, as we figure out what kind of work these idealistic young are people going to do." It may be, she says, a chance to "somehow reset our expectations. And regain our integrity."

In 2010, after a collective 75 years in daily journalism, Connell and her spouse moved back to the Pacific Northwest to pursue a new path. They now are independent media consultants (Connell Wright Media) in Bellingham, Washington, working with a variety of news organizations as they evolve strategies and ethics for the integration of social media into the news process. Connell also joined the journalism faculty at Western Washington University in Bellingham, teaching online news writing with special emphasis on ethics, social media and emerging platforms for storytelling.

Chapter 6

Globetrotter

Ted Iliff's novel, published in 2009, weaves together many of the skeins of his life and career. Set in Germany in the years right after World War II, *The Golden Times* vividly describes the German countryside, whose beauty was barely marred by combat. His hero is a young, eager wire service reporter from Kansas City, as Iliff once had been.

The tale is told with the clarity and structure that one sees in all good reporting. When the reader first encounters Mike Falwell, he's struggling with his luggage and his typewriter in its "battered aluminum case." Falwell, we learn, has been a war correspondent for the Military News Service, now assigned to report from Karlsruhe, Germany, near the French border.

He doubts that the posting will be interesting, but his bureau chief assures him he's wrong.

> What were you reading in Frankfurt? The funnies? We've got ex–Nazis hiding from the French. We've got denazification that makes the Spanish Inquisition sound like a radio quiz show. We have a town full of displaced refugees, released POWs, widows, orphans, disabled German veterans, bored GIs, sanctimonious socialists who think they should run the place and spotty basic services for us or the Germans.... There's a 400-word piece on every corner.[1]

That bit of dialogue, like a good wire service lede, sets us up for the entire novel. The way Iliff handles his love story may not tally with the popular notion of a hard-bitten cynical journalist. But in real life, Iliff does not come across as either hard-bitten or world weary.

He continues to have the passion of the wire-service reporter he was more than 40 years ago. His love of writing has been matched by his passion for travel. His German heritage always has been important to him. And there is something romantic about the way he took an unexpected job loss and re-created himself. Goodbye Ted Iliff, executive editor, CNN. Hello, "Ted Iliff

Global Consulting, Media and Business Consulting with a World of Experience," as his website defines him.

Iliff's career led him to Radio Free Europe just before the fall of communism, to *USA Today* when the national newspaper was a startup, and to CNN as it became a full-fledged player on the media stage. But he hasn't been content to think about past media triumphs. Painstakingly developing his brand, Iliff has taken on assignments across the globe, and for a time, zestfully segued out of journalism altogether. In 2011, he was working as editor-in-chief of a radio station at Kandahar Airfield, Afghanistan, one of his many international media development consulting jobs.

In his early 60s, Iliff is a big man with a mustache reminiscent of a prospector in the Wild West. But there is nothing rough or uncouth about his demeanor. During a three-hour interview, he uses no profanity. He laughs easily, and yet it's very clear that he is serious about journalism. Consult his blog, and you realize how much he cares about words and how they're used.

Iliff first was drawn to reporting because he wanted to live in Germany. "My mother's German and I had a great affinity for that side of the family," he says. But his career goals remained unformed until his sophomore year at the University of Kansas. By then he had taken a basic journalism course, and then took a course in writing taught by the city editor of the *Topeka Journal*. "He threw out the textbook literally in front of us, and taught with real-world examples. And the fire got lit, as inelegant as the phrase is," Iliff recalls. "That's what set everything off."

The attractions of journalism? "Drama," he says. "The jolt of being the first to know anything and tell everybody else." The relating of the news is really about story-telling, he adds. He also liked the glamour that went along with the job. "You told people what you did, and they said, 'Oh wow.'"

He soon got himself a job freelancing for the *Journal* as its University of Kansas correspondent. He spent his summers interning at dailies in Kansas City and Rochester, New York. He spent his academic years concentrating only on his journalism courses, which led him to drop out of school just one semester short of finishing. (Iliff ultimately earned his degree in 1988 through an external degree program offered by the State University of New York.)

He ended up in his hometown, Kansas City, taking a job at a semi-weekly suburban newspaper. He covered school boards, city councils, police departments, sports, politics, and zoning commissions, "one of the most important governmental agencies in anybody's life."

The work he had done for the student paper at the University of Kansas occasionally had been picked up by United Press International, and Iliff used his contacts to land a job with the wire service. He spent two years covering the statehouse in Topeka, and then returned to Kansas City. Then, Iliff, now married, was transferred to Detroit, and promoted to assistant bureau manager.

Iliff recalls his wire service days with great relish, vividly describing it over the course of one interview as "wham bam journalism," "mile-a-minute journalism," "reporting on steroids," and "rock-and-roll journalism." He had the right skills to flourish there, he says. "I was fast and I was good fast.... I had the knack for being able to take material and put it into usable wire service copy, either print or broadcast." He called it "the hardest work I've ever done."

Iliff was one of those reporters who actually relished the call at 3 A.M. to cover a fire or a murder or another disaster. He remembers the surge of triumph he felt when he got the news of the death of former President Harry Truman on the UPI wire first, beating the rival Associated Press by a few minutes. What he learned at UPI, he says, "set me up for everything else that I ever did."

It was only as a he matured as a journalist that he realized that speed wasn't always an advantage and could lead to errors. UPI's moniker for "being first and worst" was often undeserved, he says. But he concedes, "I think I have every story that was ever printed that I wrote for UPI. I don't think I want to read them. I certainly don't want to have somebody go back and check every single fact."

The "International" part of UPI's name also had drawn Iliff because he hoped it would get him to an overseas bureau. But in the late 1970s, after seven years stateside, and with UPI's financial prospects looking dim, Iliff answered a blind ad in the trade publication *Editor and Publisher* for a newsroom opening in Germany. The opening was at Radio Free Europe/Radio Liberty. Funded by the U.S. government, RFE/RL operated as an alternative news source about their respective countries to millions of listeners behind the Iron Curtain.

Iliff had some qualms about answering it. Initially funded by the CIA after World War II, RFE/RL had been harshly criticized for broadcasting reports that misled Hungarians into thinking that if they rose up against the Soviet Union, U.S. troops and tanks would rush to their rescue. The Hungarian revolt killed several thousand Hungarians, and displaced an estimated 200,000 more. It is not clear how complicit RFE was in inciting the rebellion, since U.S. politicians also made promises of support that they did not keep.[2] Investigations into RFE reports did not uncover any specific incitements to riot. But its broadcasts did little to challenge the belief in American assistance.[3]

Just approaching 30, Iliff figured working for RFE was a gamble well worth taking. He arrived in Munich in 1979, after CIA funding of the operation had ended,[4] and put in nearly 10 years in Germany, as he explains it, "winning the Cold War." It was, he says, "the most rigorous newsroom I've ever managed, much less worked in." Efforts were made to ensure balance, and to eliminate any hidden biases, he says. "It was very careful, very heavily edited."

"Hungary weighed heavily on everybody's conscience" during his tenure in the newsroom. And in 1980, when Polish workers in Gdansk started agitating for change,[5] RFE did straight reporting of what was going on. "One night very soon after that strike started, we were watching German television and they had gotten some film out from the Lenin shipyard in Gdansk, and here were guys walking around with short-wave boom boxes on their shoulders acting as town criers relaying the news that Radio Free Europe was reporting." That wouldn't have happened, he says, if the workers didn't trust RFE to tell them the truth.

Early on, the Reagan Administration tried to use RFE/RL as a "weapon for the Cold War and control it in a certain way," he says. But that attempt, he says, "backfired." Once word got out about "ideologues ... in charge in certain spots," he says, the threat to RFE/RL's credibility caused the administration to pull back. "RFE/FL's credibility was the most important thing to preserve and they backed off and let us do our job."

More evidence of RFE/RL's influence came in 1981, when then–Romanian President Nicolae Ceausescu paid the notorious terrorist known as Carlos the Jackal to bomb its Munich headquarters, causing $2 million in damage and several injuries. "I was in the building when it went off," Iliff recalls. "It was a Saturday night, so there weren't that many people. But when that happens, you figure you're doing something meaningful." (The perpetrator of the bombing wasn't known until 1989.)[6]

As much as he loved writing stories and promoting understanding, Iliff found himself increasingly drawn to editing. He had always liked puzzles, and editing was trying to find the "nuggets" in a reporter's story that need to be changed, while retaining the other nuggets that work. He found, too, that the opportunity to teach, mentor and train was rewarding in and of itself. "Some people need to be the one whose name is attached to that story. I prefer being the person who makes the story attached to the name just a little bit better, or in some cases, saving it from all kinds of trouble."

About three years into his posting with RFE, he became restless and a bit homesick. He returned to the states in 1982, ostensibly to attend the Detroit Grand Prix auto races, but also to look around for opportunities. He wasn't sure how long RFE was going to stay open in Europe, since there had been talk about the operation relocating to the U.S. He got nibbles from the fledgling CNN and National Public Radio, and also interest from "this thing called *USA Today.*"

Gannett Corporation, which owned dailies throughout the country, including one in Rochester, New York, where Iliff had interned, was starting a national newspaper. Gannett offered him a job at a "pretty decent salary." What Iliff liked, he says, is that the new paper was a startup. So he took a chance, figuring that since the paper's offices were near Washington, D.C., if things didn't work out, there would be other opportunities. The startup paper was not met with open arms by many journalists. It was accused of being frivolous, and derided as "McPaper," the butt of jokes by *Doonesbury* cartoon creator Gary Trudeau. "If USA Today is a good newspaper, then I'm in the wrong business," Ben Bradlee, then executive editor of *The Washington Post*, was reported to have said.[7]

Iliff has heard all the criticisms, but remained committed to the concept. "I was there when it started. I believed in it. It forced newspapers to look at two things—one, the length of their writing, and two, color." He was indifferent to the color issue, he says. But he had grown to believe that "newspaper writing was way too ponderous." He was asked to teach the staff to write shorter. He says that the news briefs that to this day run on the left margin of *USA Today's* front page were something he developed to "show people that it [writing very concisely] could be done."

Iliff says he is proud of the work he did at *USA Today*, and the product Gannett produced. "Is it the definitive form of journalism? Of course not. It's one form," he says. "*USA Today* found a niche in the market.... It was the right thing at the right time to introduce new concepts to the business." But for many reasons, including his wife's strong desire to move back to Germany, his stay at the paper lasted less than a year. He returned to Munich and RFE. "You sometimes don't realize that you miss something until you don't have it anymore," he recalls.

Back at RFE, Iliff resumed his editing duties, and grew to appreciate all the perks of the job — the free housing, "down to the towels and forks and knives," and generous vacations, with both German and American holidays off. By 1987, he'd been named a senior supervising editor. But it was clear to him that as the Cold War was thawing, the need for RFE/RL as he knew it was ebbing away. Iliff remembers a short trip he and his wife took to Budapest in 1988, their first behind the Iron Curtain, when Hungary's Communist Party had started liberalizing its policies. The hotel desk clerk knew about RFE, but considered it passé. She replied, "We used to listen to RFE. Our radio stations are much more interesting now."

Taking that comment as a sign, Iliff kicked up his job search and found that his former UPI Detroit bureau chief was now at CNN and eager to welcome him back to the states. He came on as a copy editor. By then, the all-news cable network was nine years old. It was, in Iliff's parlance of news events, "after Challenger [the space shuttle explosion that killed 7 astronauts][8] and Jessica and the well"[the saga of 18-month Jessica McClure who fell into a well and was rescued 58 hours later, riveting millions of TV viewers].[9] But it was before Hurricane Hugo and the Gulf War," so CNN was "just on the cusp, just about to make it big."

The Berlin Wall fell in November 1989,[10] after Iliff had been on the job for three months, giving him the informal "fall of communism editor" title at CNN, where it was up to him to write entire news blocks on eastern Europe. "CNN was like an adolescent boy learning his strength," Iliff says, meaning that the network was just beginning to understand its influence on the media and the world stage. It had a young staff, but it was serious about the news. It didn't have any competition from cable, but it was fighting the broadcast networks, he recalls. CNN was experimenting, doing breaking news. What "sealed the deal" for the network was the Gulf War, Iliff says. That was when "it became an adult. I was there for it."

In 1990, Iraq invaded U.S. ally Kuwait, launching the Persian Gulf War. The following year, the United States and its allies attacked Iraq. The night that U.S. forces made their move "will mark the moment that CNN came of age," predicted TV critic Robert Goldberg in *The Wall Street Journal*. CNN was equipped to give viewers a minute-by-minute real-time experience of the war. The country was riveted as three CNN correspondents, holed up in a Baghdad hotel, described the sounds and sights of the battle.[11]

Iliff felt that as CNN matured, it was crucial that he convince broadcast news writers on the staff to recognize that cute and clever wasn't enough. News copy had to be authoritative and accurate. It also meant that CNN began to hire more experienced and capable producers and anchors. "There was a higher level of professionalism in the newsroom," he says.

Three years into the job, Iliff was one of nine staffers tasked with ramping up CNN International. CNNI had started off as a news source for business travelers looking for news from home on their hotel TVs. Now, the network had much larger ambitions. "We started doing international news for an international audience," he says. CNN International literally had been housed in a little closet under the stairs at CNN's original offices in Atlanta, Iliff recalls. "It was known as the network under the stairs." But now CNN International got its own newsroom, its own anchors, and its own perspective. "The challenge is to try to rise above your time zone, your hemisphere and even your culture," Iliff told the *Los Angeles Times* in 1993. Writers, he said, were cautioned not to use baseball metaphors, which would be unfamiliar to many international viewers. And governments, even the U.S. government, got equal treatment. "If Iraq says they shot down U.S. warplanes, and the Pentagon says they didn't, we give both statements equal credence. We don't say, 'Iraq claims,' implying we don't believe them, while 'the Pentagon says,' implying we're sure the Pentagon is telling the truth."[12]

Along the way, Iliff took on more and more responsibilities, and the title of executive producer. "I was scheduling and hiring and deciding all the editorial rules," he recalls. One "amazing" part of the job was determining which world cities were listed on the network's weather list. "I got offers for trips and bribes and everything else from mayors who wanted their cities on that damn weather list." And world newsmakers were beginning to take notice, stopping at the studio in Atlanta, everyone from then–President Bill Clinton to the Dalai Lama.

Iliff had his own encounter with a "star," but not as part of CNN. He sings barbershop, and his group performed at the opening ceremonies for an Olympic sailing event in Savannah, Georgia, in 1996. The master of ceremonies was former CBS news anchor and ardent sailor the late Walter Cronkite. A thunderstorm occurred right before the event, and in the scramble for shelter, Iliff found himself standing next to Cronkite. It turned out that they had been trained by the same editor at UPI. "I'm in the business for moments like that," he says. "Everybody is an old wire service reporter, it just seems to me."

In 1998, Iliff's scope became much broader, when he was named CNN's executive editor, with "editorial responsibility for all the CNN networks." He had the chance to focus on improving writing and reporting and insist on accuracy. The most rewarding part of the job, he says, "was having the authority to influence the editorial product of CNN in a way that I thought was important, and to have CNN staff generally accept my recommendations in that spirit."

Television, he observes, is a medium that depends on visuals and popular news personalities, and not a lot of folks at the network worried about the words. Iliff says he was happy to be doing that. Looking back, he says, reaching the lofty heights of CNN was the "pinnacle" of his career. "No two ways about it, it was pretty heady stuff." Recalling Marlon Brando's words from the film *On the Waterfront*, "I could-a been a contender," Iliff says that he *was* a contender at CNN.

But CNN now was in a battle for ratings against its major cable rival, News Corporation's Fox News, trying to grab a larger share of younger viewers. In 2001, CNN *Headline News* brought in Teya Ryan to shake things up. She had been a longtime producer, and was well regarded, Iliff says.

Ryan quickened the pace of *Headline News*, adding jazzier music and more visuals.[13] She also hired Andrea Thompson to anchor *Headline News*. Thompson was a stunning and shapely actress with very limited journalism experience, best known for her role on the series *NYPD Blue*. (Thompson raised eyebrows when she began her tenure as CNN anchor by saying, "Hi, I'm Andrea Thompson — and unless you've been living in a cave, you probably already know that.")[14]

Iliff offers not one critical word about Ryan. But media reviews of her changes were mixed. Some media critics questioned the professionalism of Thompson, who left the network after less than a year.[15] Others found the snappier *Headline News,* with its screen loaded with fast-moving bites of information on a news ticker, dizzying and devoid of real content.[16] Ryan's innovations, however, were credited with making *Headline News* more attractive to younger viewers.

Iliff didn't see new career challenges for him on the horizon, and figured it was doubtful CNN would make him a vice president. He had started looking for another job and was scheduled to have a job interview on Sept. 14, 2001. He declines to say what the job was. But after September 11, he took himself out of consideration for the position. "After 9/11, there's no way I can leave CNN.... And then we had the Afghan war, so things were really hopping."

By February 2002, Ryan had been promoted to executive vice president and general manager of CNN's domestic network. "When she came in I knew there was going to be a change," Iliff says. When he heard about the promotion, he says, "I told a friend of mine at CNN, 'I'm outta here.'" "Ryan did the rounds and talked to everybody, asking 'what do you do,' and I probably didn't do a very good job explaining what I did," Iliff says. "I don't think she ever understood what I did.

"All of a sudden in early May I get a call one night from a friend of mine who's in the management structure of CNN," Iliff recalls. His friend warned him that some changes were happening the next day and that Iliff might "be a part of them or not. So I said, 'Well, that's great.' So we met at a pub in Atlanta and talked about the possibilities. The next morning I get called in and I'm told they're eliminating my job."

Managers asked him to stay for a month, which caused Iliff to ask why, since "you don't want me around anymore." Their answer was "for transition." Determined not to burn any bridges, Iliff stayed. At one point during that last month, Ryan told him that he was "a very elegant man," a compliment he cherished. "No one had ever called me that before. That was pretty cool," he recalls. Nonetheless, in those intervening weeks before he finally walked out the door, "you go into panic mode."

Ryan soon found that her tenure at CNN was not secure, either. News accounts in February 2002 hailed her as a "rising star."[17] Eighteen months later, she was described as "beleaguered."[18] Ryan resigned in September 2003 "to pursue opportunities outside the CNN organization."[19]

"I had never been let go before so this was an entirely new experience for me," Iliff says. Now single — he and his wife divorced in 1999 — he says he had put his financial house in order, and had a "contract with a very generous severance clause in it. I was in great shape to get pushed out the door."

"And then," Iliff beams, "that's when the adventure started. If I ever see Teya Ryan again, I will kiss her on the cheek, if she'll let me. She pushed me into the next adventures of my life."

He'd networked all his working life, and Iliff now drew on those contacts to build his brand. At 51, he judged himself "too old" to take a job as a writer at another network. But for other positions — editor, news executive, manager, writing coach — his age posed no obstacles, he figured. And at CNN he had developed a storehouse of TV knowledge that he didn't realize he had. "That was a revelation," he says, when he started to do consulting.

"I knew CNN was a great brand name," Iliff says. "I had to figure out how to cash in on the CNN in my resume," and to exploit his tenure in the "Oh, wow" position of executive editor for the network. His severance, he says, gave him some time to map out a strategy that would capitalize on his experience and skills and build his brand. It didn't take long for him to settle on international media development consulting as a new direction.

A colleague from his RFE days now was president of IREX, created in 1968 as the International Research & Exchanges Board, a nonprofit founded by major U.S. universities to manage student exchanges between the United States and the Soviet Union and Eastern Europe. Over the years, IREX grew and evolved to support programs and partners in more than 100 countries, helping their citizens to use technology to build strong communities improve educational options and foster independent media.[20] Iliff had been an advisor to the group. Shortly after he left CNN, Iliff was invited to moderate IREX panel discussions in Istanbul for all its media managers for programs in Eastern Europe and Central Asia. He met them, and soon they were asking him to advise them on a number of media projects. "From that extended weekend I got two years of consulting work," he says. "That was the giving back, the teaching without being in academia, that was international travel, and truly an adventure.

"I was learning how to blend the standards of journalism that we have with the cultural realities of the countries I was working in — Montenegro, Albania, Kosovo, Armenia." Being "exposed to different cultures," he says, "was all mind candy to me." International consulting in this arena has to be targeted, he says. Since he did not speak the language of his various clients, he did not advise on content. If it was a startup television station, for example, Iliff would concentrate on production values and administration. "What are you doing in the control room? How are you structuring your [story] rundown? All those non-cultural technical things that would apply any-where." There were broader discussions about journalism and ethics, he says, but they would be "over a cup of coffee or over dinner and it would be very carefully couched not to be a lesson or a lecture."

In Kosovo, he says, he helped set up an Internet-based radio news service that was just like creating a "little UPI." There was a staffer to write the news, but "I worried about the structure, the schedule of the news, how it was designed for small radio stations to use easily, to rip and read."

In Armenia, he conducted the equivalent of a six-week seminar. In a classroom setting, he taught the fundamentals of doing a news rundown, set-ting up an interview, and, since Armenia's a very religious country, how to cover news about the church.

Again, Iliff stayed away from content, feeling that teaching through an interpreter was too likely to cause confusion and distortion. Rather, he'd ask questions about specific stories they told him they were covering. "I would say, 'Are you talking about this, and talking about that?' That's about as far as it would go."

He found the work very rewarding, particularly when he could see progress, and continues to keep in touch with the some of the media contacts he made there. "It was fun. It was hard sometimes. They were not always luxurious loca-tions; in fact, none of them was." But the experience made him realize how much he had picked up about the nuts and bolts of broadcast news: production techniques, control room management. These were things he absorbed when he was working at CNN, sitting in the control room watching "some of the best in the business" do their jobs. The teaching was a two-way street, he says. He dis-covered what he had learned when he taught them what they needed to know.

In 2003, Iliff took on a consulting job in Baghdad, working for the Iraqi Media Network. The contract was supposed to last a year, but things changed suddenly as the American government decided to disband the Coalition Pro-visional Authority. Iliff had turned down a job offer from the Voice of Amer-ica, and now he called VOA back, saying he'd like to take the job. He joined VOA as associate director in 2004. "It seemed to be the ideal next step." But it turned out to be far less than ideal. "In terms of just atmosphere, that was the worst job I ever had."

Like RFE/RL, the Voice of America was funded by the U.S. government, and its mission was information. But Iliff walked into a far different envi-ronment. The government-funded Voice of America aims to broadcast news about the United States to an international audience in a way that promotes the values of democracy while giving an accurate portrayal of U.S. policies and policy disagreements. During the Bush years, many faulted the admin-istration for attacking VOA's editorial independence.[21]

Longtime VOA staffers chafed under the leadership of Kenneth Tomlinson, named in 2002 by George W. Bush to head the Broadcasting Board of Governors, with authority over VOA. Tomlinson was criticized for political interference with the journalism at VOA, pushing a pro–Bush agenda. Tomlinson and the BBG board hired former *Time* correspondent David Jackson as VOA news director. Jackson also drew the ire of many VOA staffers, who leaked memos from Jackson that implied that he wanted VOA to pump up positive news stories about Iraq.[22]

In February 2004, Iliff says, "I walk into what was already an untenable management situation. The agency had been terribly polarized with Tomlinson and Jackson on one side and some VOA staffers on the other side. They felt that David was a neocon trying to warp the VOA message to fit the Bush Administration's goals. He felt that elements of VOA news division primarily were rogue journalists with their own agendas, who didn't think they had to answer to anybody."

An entire book could be written about that conflict, and who was right, he says. "They both had points. But the main thing is, I walked into the middle of this. And all I was supposed to do was integrate television news into the VOA," which was primarily radio at the time. "David always treated me very cordially," he says. "Some in the news division did not." Things got even worse when the news director was reassigned, and Iliff took on the duties of acting news director, as well as associate director. "I should never have done that," he recalls, "because I was trying to put one foot in each of two camps" that were at war with each other.

He found himself in the crosshairs, viewed by many in the news division as "David's lackey" while feeling "tension" from Jackson when he refused to take action against several news staffers that Jackson wanted him to deal with. "I was ineffective," Iliff says. "I couldn't do what I thought I should do."

Iliff also felt burned by media coverage that he felt was inaccurate and unfair. One story concerned Iliff's decision to move VOA's Asia news desk out of Washington to Hong Kong. Iliff had lined up two Americans and an Australian in Hong Kong to take the jobs. "It was going to place our news desk in Asia during the Asia business day." To Iliff, the decision was not controversial, had already been approved by the BBG board, would save money — $330,000 annually — and would not cost jobs. However, it would result in a pay cut for staffers who had been earning a bonus for working an overnight shift.

Many VOA staffers who already were suspicious of the VOA management saw the move as one more sign of bad faith and ill intent. The staff, according to media accounts, was angry about adjusting to new working hours and lower pay. "The irony of transferring our operation to a communist country is not lost on anyone," one staffer told the publication *Government Executive*.[23] Some VOA staffers went to Capitol Hill and complained that he "wants to hire Chinese communists to write the VOA news, which was absolutely absurd," Iliff says. "I got hauled up to Capitol Hill to a room full of very pleasant congressional aides who had no idea about journalism, media or business, and couldn't understand why proximity [to the news] was an advantage. It was just hopeless."

What made it worse, he says, was VOA's insistence that he not aggressively rebut the allegations when they got media attention. VOA assumed that "nobody's going to pay attention anyway. Well, I did and Google did," he says.

In June 2005, NPR did a story raising concerns about political interference at VOA. It referred to an Iliff email to news correspondents that reminded them: "Whatever the case, be sure that for any story you produce, it includes a reference to U.S. policy or reaction as necessary for the story."[24] Iliff doesn't recall the NPR story very well, but doesn't think it gave him "any heartburn." The story gave both Jackson and Tomlinson the opportunity to rebut the politicization charges. Iliff adds: "VOA's job is to cover the American government and American policy. That's the charter, that's the mission." He was not asking reporters to be pro–American or report "only the American view," he says. "Let's just make sure all aspects of the story are covered."

At CNN, he says, if there were some consternation about his message, people would have walked into his office and talked to him about it. "I love to be debated because that's how I learn stuff." But at VOA, Iliff's office was across the hall from Jackson's. The news staffers would not go near what they considered "the den of iniquity," Iliff says.

The last straw for Iliff was a story in the summer of 2005 in *The American Prospect*, a magazine with a progressive slant. The story paints a picture of a news operation that, under political pressure from Tomlinson, had turned into a propaganda machine. One of the anecdotes supporting the author's premise is Iliff's decision not to assign a VOA reporter to Kenya to cover a trial of a malaria vaccine conducted by physicians from Walter Reed Army Medical Center. Instead, the reporter was asked to cover a joint anti-terrorism exercise in Senegal for television, even though a VOA radio reporter was covering the same event. According to the piece, Iliff felt that the malaria story would be too costly to cover and was "not compelling" enough, but the reader doesn't know where the "not compelling" quote comes from, since Iliff is not quoted in the story.[25]

Before the story was published, Iliff said he spent 45 minutes on the phone talking to the writer of the piece. He told him that the malaria trial had been covered. "The story was on the web. It was there. I told him that, and I told him what the URL was." It was a fact that he "totally ignored," Iliff charges, "because it would have ruined his story."

After his experience with *American Prospect*, "I realized not all journalists work by the same standards that I work by. That rules that I had lived by for decades apparently were no longer in vogue. That people could get paid to write stuff without telling both sides of the story. That was a very bitter shock for me."

Iliff concedes that journalists often will emphasize one point of view over another — paraphrase one side and quote the other side. "There are ways to build in a little point of view in your story." But that's far different than "to wholesale ignore one side of the story even when it's provided in its entirety for your use. To me that was shocking, and very demoralizing.

"There were a lot of things that I stopped liking at VOA, but that was the final straw," Iliff says. "I figured if that kind of crap is being written about me, and I can't rebut it, I don't need this."

This is when Iliff's career path took a very different direction. A longtime friend was president of the National Board for Certified Counselors (NBCC), a not-for-profit whose mission is to promote high standards for mental health counselors through a certification system.[26] Iliff had been invited to join the board as a "public" member because the organization wanted to expand into international work. As a board member, he was helping the nonprofit develop an international strategy, and create an international division.

In December 2004, Iliff said he'd had a conversation with his friend, laying the groundwork for him to run the international division at some point in time. By the summer of 2005, Iliff had told VOA that he would be leaving. At about the same time, the NBCC held a conference in Istanbul, Turkey, which Iliff attended. Iliff met a Turkish university president, who was impressed with his CNN credentials. The man offered him a job on the spot, teaching media for a semester at Bahcesehir University in Istanbul. The plan was for him to teach a semester, then move from Washington to NBCC headquarters in Greensboro, North Carolina, and take on his new management duties.

"That's exactly what happened," he says. He spent that semester teaching, and finishing his novel. "Came back, sold my place [in Washington] and moved out to Greensboro.

"I had totally jumped out of media. Totally right-turned out of it. It felt great because I was so relieved to be out of VOA." And the added draw, he says, was that "my job was to travel. I was making a good living, living in a nice place, and traveling all the time, internationally." He also felt good about what he was doing. "Counseling is a noble profession. So you can feel good about advocating for counseling. And that's what I did."

Iliff was surprised at how little he missed the news business. When a big story broke, he found himself "looking at it like a producer," and "editing it. But I didn't feel, 'Oh, boy, I wish I was there.' I had been at CNN for the Gulf War, for the 2000 election, for 9/11, for incredible stories, and I didn't feel like I needed to do that anymore."

Iliff once again was working on a startup. "I was creating all the rules. It was brand new." He had a good rapport with the NBCC president, and "we were making progress. Then the economy got nasty," Iliff says. The president prudently cut back on international travel, and Iliff took on the duties of communications director, focusing on internal communications—"getting the website up and modernized, editing the newsletters, editing the news releases."

Three years into the job, Iliff was getting bored and pitched the idea of his moving back to Washington and doing the communications work from there, figuring he could advance NBCC's goals by working with foreign embassies and international NGOs. Instead, he was asked to resume a part-time consulting arrangement with NBCC, and consider other options. That news didn't come as a blow. "I missed Washington a lot. Almost all my friends are here." And he was starting to get feelers for media consulting work.

In 2009, Iliff found himself in Kabul, Afghanistan, consulting for Internews Network, a California-based nonprofit working on international media development. Iliff helped Nai, an Afghan NGO, which provides training to the fledgling Afghan media. "They're trying to develop professional standards and help Afghan journalists learn the basics. Most of them don't know the basics." The work is rewarding, but challenging, he says. Afghanistan, even more than Iraq, has a media landscape fragmented by ethnic divisions. Audiences for news divide along ethnic lines.

Afghanistan also is a place where tragedy is never far off, an environment he deftly evoked in a 2010 blog post. He recounts a late-afternoon visit to a local physician in Kabul. He needed a few stitches removed from his nose before he left for another consulting assignment. The doctor took Iliff into a room that would have been well-lit, had the electricity not gone out, and she didn't have to rely on her generator. She warned him that the procedure might hurt, and asked if he preferred to lie down. "I don't want you to faint," she told him. Iliff, perched on the hospital bed, looking at the linoleum below, joked that he didn't want to faint, either. "If I do, you'll need five guys to pick me up."

"We wouldn't pick you up," she said.

The deadpan exchange tickled Iliff's sense of humor. "Coming from a doctor in a Kabul clinic, it almost put me on the floor," he writes. He was still smiling after the procedure, which turned out to be painless, when he

walked into the reception area. He started a conversation with a young recep-
tionist, who also laughed when he recounted the doctor's "great line." He
then noticed a vase of flowers and a framed photo on the file cabinet behind
the reception desk.

> Before I could ask, the receptionist turned instantly somber and said, "She
> worked here," then left for the day without another word. "She" was Dr. Karen
> Woo, a member of the charitable medical team massacred in northeast Afghan-
> istan two days earlier. The entire clinic staff was in mourning, but you'd never
> know it by the way they went about their business. That's the thing about Afghan-
> istan. No matter how hard or how long the laugh, there's always something to
> stop it.[27]

Iliff went on to serve as editor-in-chief of 88.5 FM in Kandahar, and is
based at the sprawling Kandahar Airfield, which employs 30,000 people. The
station, sponsored by the military, broadcasts to Pashtun southern Afghanistan. "I oversee the whole operation," Iliff emailed me from Kandahar in
August 2011. "I have a news editor, and a studio manager, both Americans,
and a staff of 11 Afghan journalists, including four field reporters." Iliff says
the station is a startup, and that the military has been very respectful of the
"firewall between news and military messaging."

Iliff made light of the dangers of working in Kandahar. "A rocket or two
is fired in the general direction of the base every once in a while, but I feel
safe here," he emailed in August 2011. He concedes that he never goes "outside
the wire" but that the airfield is so big that there are enough diversions
within—stores and restaurants—to keep him occupied.

His hope, he wrote, is that when the Americans pull out of Afghanistan,
the station will be able to make it on its own as an independent media outlet,
and "does not turn into a mouthpiece for the government or some faction."
His one-year contract ended in late January 2012.

His exotic posting certainly hasn't dimmed his reverence for words, as
evidenced in a few blog posts from 2011. You can visualize him wincing when
he catches a *Washington Post* reporter confusing an acronym with an abbre-
viation, or when an Associated Press writer, recounting an incident that damaged a Southwest Airlines plane, forcing an emergency landing, wrote that
the "hole" in the plane's ceiling had "ruptured." "Holes don't rupture, things
that rupture develop holes," Iliff wrote with spare precision. He lamented:
"The noble Associated Press did this. Another sign of the Apocalypse, at least
for journalism."

Is his career path a template for the journalists of the 21st century? Interviewed in Washington in early 2010, Iliff thinks that, to a certain extent, it
is. Not that he expects journalists to be as footloose as he's become. But
he does believe that the reporters of today and the future will be more

entrepreneurial, more versatile. "They have to view themselves as independent agents, even if they're on salary, even if they get a contract. They have to constantly assess their marketability," Iliff advises. As in many industries, journalism no longer can guarantee permanence, he says. The job that a young journalist takes in 2010 may no longer exist in 2030, he says. So the challenge is to constantly update your skills, continually learn new things.

Like Mike, the optimistic and resourceful hero of his novel, he remains confident about the future. "There will be an enduring market for my services," he says with a smile.

Chapter 7

The Quiet "Race Man"

Richard "Dick" Blood, a *Daily News* editor, came to brief us about covering cops and crime. There was a stretch during Blood's lecture in which he described members of the NYPD as if every member of the 30,000-member force were infallible. Maritza Arrastia [a classmate] ... could not stand it anymore. She stood up and glared at me like an annoyed big sister who wants her little brother to stand up to a bully. "Wayne," she said, "tell him what you witnessed."

I dutifully stood and spoke.... My eyewitness reporting of a riot provoked by police was included in a Village Voice investigative report. A crowd peacefully assembled in Bedford-Stuyvesant and marched to protest the fatal shooting of a mentally disturbed youth. The mother called the cops for help, then was horrified to watch her 19-year-old son get riddled with bullets from a crowd of police. Residents were horrified, too, so they demonstrated. A cop in a police cruiser ordered demonstrators to disperse. When they did not, he plowed his cruiser through the crowd, hitting pedestrians.

Blood listened to my account without comment. I did not give an opinion; I just reported what I saw.

Wayne Dawkins recounted this anecdote in a blog post about the year he spent as a student at the Graduate School of Journalism at Columbia University.[1] It tells a lot about the person and his character. Over the next 30 years, Dawkins would be more concerned about getting the facts than confrontation. He would nurture the relationships he made at Columbia, particularly those he formed with other African-American students. And yet, for all his calmness, he wouldn't shy away from controversy. Asked what drew him to journalism, he responds: "Well, I'm not afraid to say it. I think I'm somewhat of a race man, although I may not come off as combative or militant to a lot of people." He says that he wanted to cover the lives and issues of people of color in ways that went beyond the stereotypes.

Dawkins's career has played out during times of great change, both for the media industry, and for the role of African-Americans in journalism.

When Dawkins studied at Columbia, it had been only a dozen years since the National Advisory Commission on Civil Disorders was convened by President Lyndon Johnson in 1967 to study the riots in black neighborhoods that had occurred in cities across the country.

Chaired by Illinois governor Otto Kerner, the commission excoriated the U.S. media for doing very little to reflect the country's diversity:

> The media report and write from the standpoint of a white man's world. The ills of the ghetto, the difficulties of life there, the Negro's burning sense of grievance, are seldom conveyed. Slights and indignities are part of the Negro's daily life, and many of them come from what he now calls "the white press"—a press, that repeatedly, if unconsciously, reflects the biases, the paternalism, the indifference of white America. This may be understandable, but it is not excusable in an institution that has the mission to inform and educate the whole of society.

The report faulted journalists for excluding African-Americans from their ranks: "The journalistic profession has been shockingly backward in seeking out, hiring, training and promoting Negroes. Fewer than 5 percent of the people employed by the news business in editorial jobs in the United States today are Negroes. Fewer than 1 percent of editors and supervisors are Negroes, and most of them work for Negro-owned organizations."[2]

Media outlets were beginning to recognize that their newsrooms needed to better reflect the country's diversity. But that in no way made the path smooth for Dawkins and his colleagues. About 20 percent of his class consisted of students of color, Dawkins estimates, including about 25 African-American students, evenly divided between men and women. "The push was on to really integrate the media because the numbers were still abysmal," he says. If African-American reporters were sparse in the media of the day, things were even worse at the managerial level. "You could count them on your hand," he says. "You knew who they were," there were so few.

He said the media "gatekeepers" kept saying, "We can't find qualified minorities."

"We had to face up to the reality that we were green. We were trying to get in the door, quickly learn the craft, and advance," mindful that they needed to ensure that succeeding generations of black reporters would find a place, too.

While he knew the challenges would be daunting, Dawkins counted himself in the "optimist" camp. He knew there were going to be struggles, and setbacks, but also triumphs. "I wanted it all," he says. "I was in it for the long haul."

What Dawkins could not imagine was that as his generation of black reporters advanced in their careers, a tsunami would hit the entire profession, sweeping both them and their white counterparts up in a wave of unemployment. Writing in 2009, Dawkins noted that the ranks of black reporters had started to decline in the wake of all the layoffs. "Of course, all journalists today are anxious. But journalists of color feel more pressure than their mainstream or Caucasian peers...." Citing statistics about job losses between 2008 and 2009, Dawkins continued, "It looks as though, especially in broadcast news, journalists of color—having just achieved certain positions—may be the first to go."[3]

Dawkins was one of those journalists who felt that he was being squeezed out when newspapers began getting more anxious about profits. He left before the ax fell. But he ultimately found a second calling teaching journalism at a historic black college, inspiring the next generation of African-American reporters.

Dawkins grew up in the Bedford-Stuyvesant neighborhood of Brooklyn in a family of readers. His mother grew up in the U.S.-controlled Panama Canal Zone. His father, a Jamaican, met his mother when he went to Panama to work at the canal. They made their way to the states in the 1950s.

His favorite subject in school was history—making him "kind of an oddball to my neighborhood friends." Dawkins knew that one of his uncles had been a journalist at an English-language newspaper in Panama. "Midway in high school, I decided I'm going to become a journalist."

In eleventh grade, he was a sports writer for his high school paper, and then rose to the paper's editor in his senior year. The teacher advising the newspaper arranged for delivery of *The New York Times* to the school each day. Dawkins took great pleasure in getting *The Times*. The other students "used to be rib me about that. 'Who do you think you are? You read *The New York Times*. What's your problem?'"

He went on to Long Island University, where he majored in journalism and minored in history. But when it came time to choose a graduate school, he thought he should be "sensible" and get an advanced degree in public planning or public administration. But the schools he investigated sent him materials that were written so ponderously, they turned him off. The way the materials were written "was counter to everything that I was learning in journalism — how you take the complex and make it simple and digestible."

As he was becoming disenchanted with graduate school plans, he got work at a startup, Trans-Urban News Service (TUNS), founded by Andrew Cooper, an African-American civic and business leader.[4] The news service gave aspiring African-American reporters the training they would need to get a job in mainstream news outlets in New York City. Its clients included *The New York Times*, CBS News Radio, and the *New York Daily News.* While at TUNS, Dawkins did some of the reporting for a pioneering series on the tensions between Jewish and black residents in the Crown Heights section of

Brooklyn, more than a decade before that neighborhood exploded into racial violence.[5]

While at the news service, Dawkins met legendary *Village Voice* investigative reporter Wayne Barrett. "He and Andy collaborated on some exposes, and Barrett was adjunct teaching at Columbia," Dawkins recalls. Barrett "just kind of bore into me," pushing Dawkins to get his advanced degree in journalism at Columbia. The advice got through, Dawkins applied and was accepted.

But he was floored by the $5,600 tuition for the ten-month program. Columbia initially offered him student aid totaling $2,000, but that still left thousands more to pay. "I was thinking, 'How am I going to pay for the rest of this?'" A few weeks later, another letter arrived, informing Dawkins that he would be receiving $5,000 in aid as a recipient of a scholarship from the Philip L. Graham Fund, named for the late publisher of *The Washington Post*.[6] "I may not have worked at *The Washington Post,* but *The Washington Post* paid my way through graduate school and I'm indebted to them," he says.

When he began graduate school, he says, he was very shy. "The Columbia experience gave me permission to be much more assertive," he says. Perhaps the greatest coup of Dawkins's Columbia year was his interview with noted black photographer and filmmaker Gordon Parks. The assignment was to view Parks's new photo exhibit at a Manhattan gallery and to write about it. But Dawkins had bigger ambitions. "I knew that the photographer was a trailblazer at *Life Magazine,* and had broken new ground when he directed the movie *Shaft,*" Dawkins wrote in his blog on his Columbia year. "Wouldn't it be cool, I thought, if I could interview the legend?"

Dawkins' naiveté came to his rescue. Having found Parks's address in the reference book *Who's Who,* he made his way to the swanky apartment house where Parks was living. He explained to the concierge that he was a Columbia journalism student on assignment. "I just walked in and asked for an interview with a cultural superstar," Dawkins wrote. Parks gave him the interview then and there.

The verdict of his teachers was that it was good reporting, but they found flaws in the writing. His copy, he wrote, "was bloodied with red ink." Nevertheless, he found the criticism "nurturing." His teachers included Anna Quindlen, "youthful and perky," a city hall reporter at *The Times,* soon to become a *Times* columnist, and then a successful novelist. Another professor, Phyllis Garland, who had strong ties to African-American journalism, assaulted students' copy with red ink, yet "the slaughter was so appreciated and the comments were constructive, even funny," he recalled.[7]

He also could look to role models outside Columbia, such as journalist Nancy Hicks Maynard, one of the first black women to work on the reporting staff of *The New York Times*.[8] Maynard once said that she had gotten into journalism because she was upset about a story that had misrepresented her neighborhood, Dawkins says. "She did something about it. She became the best journalist she could be. It's kind of that foot soldier mentality. You go out and change things. What sold me on journalism was that people who go out into the field often are change agents. They crusade. They feel they're on the side of the angels. I bought that hook, line and sinker."

The new graduates didn't know what the future would bring. Over drinks in May 1980, Dawkins and a dozen colleagues founded the Black Alumni Network (BAN). "We knew 1980 graduates were storm troopers on a mission to integrate the media," Dawkins wrote in 2010. "We could not complain or sulk about that longtime established old-boy network." The answer, they concluded, was to build "a comparable pool of talent."

Armed with an Olivetti typewriter, Dawkins became the editor of a monthly newsletter for the 25 African-American Columbia graduates, a group that over the years has grown to more than 600 black alumni.[9] It exemplified the kind of networking at which Dawkins excelled, and he soon found ways to link BAN members to members of the National Association of Black Journalists (NABJ). Time and again, those linkages supported Dawkins during professional crises.

Dawkins' first job out of Columbia was with a Gannett Westchester-Rockland newspaper, the *Daily Argus* in Mount Vernon, New York. (In 1998, the *Daily Argus* was merged with all the other Gannet newspapers in the region to form one daily, *The Journal News*.)[10] "The first year was pretty bumpy because I'm learning how to be a reporter at a daily newspaper," he says. Mount Vernon is a small city but with a population density similar to New York's, with its share of homicides and other crimes. Dawkins was covering crimes and cops. "It has old housing stock, so often fires break out, and I'm learning how to do this at an afternoon paper." Dawkins was the only reporter working on deadline, which for afternoon papers, generally was late morning. This was before the advent of the 24/7 newsroom, where newspaper websites update news constantly. In contrast, reporters working for morning newspapers had deadlines of about 9 P.M.

"Sometimes stories about events that had happened at six or seven that morning would get printed in the paper so quickly that the public could read them by eleven," Dawkins wrote in 1995. "When you're writing with not that much time, you have to work hard to get it right, and when you get it wrong, you hear about it — that day."[11] He was expected to work 10-hour-days, he says, but calls it a good place "to cut my teeth" and "learn how to be a reporter and ask the right questions."

Dawkins also met fellow reporter Joyce Ingram. They started dating and ultimately married. Dawkins left in 1984 because Ingram got a job offer from the *Philadelphia Daily News* that was too good to turn down, he says. She was named assignment editor. He told her, "You have to take that job, and I will figure out what to do." Dawkins landed at another Gannett paper, the *Courier-Post* in Cherry Hill, New Jersey, minutes away from Philadelphia. (Ingram and Dawkins divorced in 1987. Dawkins remarried in 1988. He and his wife, Allie Crump have one daughter, Carmen, who graduated from Virginia Wesleyan College in 2010. Ingram died in 1998.)

By the time he'd left the *Daily Argus*, Dawkins had graduated from crime and cops to covering housing and urban affairs. That turned out to be a good background for the Cherry Hill job, since the paper's circulation area covered nearly 100 municipalities in three counties.

His first beat involved a lot of reporting on municipal government and development in the growing towns of Burlington County. Since reporters did a rotating weekend shift, he didn't escape the crime, occasional disaster or special event story. He remembers a nor'easter that hit the Jersey shore, and in 1987, being at Philadelphia's Constitution Hall for the 200th anniversary of the Constitution. "It was really cool," he says, adding that Gannett papers throughout the country picked up his story. "That was back in the day when we lived for those moments," he says.

Dawkins also didn't forget the larger goals he had in mind when he began his reporting career. Camden, New Jersey, part of the paper's circulation area, was an old industrial city with a largely black population. "It was still depressed, but I could write [about it] with a little more context." Lawnside was an incorporated black town a few miles from Camden Township, portions of which were founded by abolitionists as a home for freed slaves.[12] "New Jersey is an old colonial state and there are all kinds of stories that could be done, and I would go and find them," he says. "I didn't get resistance from the editors if I could bring back a good story."

The chance to tell a larger story increased when Dawkins was named a member of the paper's editorial board. Then, in the early 1990s, he says, a new editor came on board, who "wanted to shake things up." Dawkins got his own weekly column. "I didn't need permission to have an opinion now," he says, and "could tell other kinds of stories." Dawkins joked in a blog in 2007 that he owed his promotion to Clarence Thomas. "I was so infuriated with the Supreme Court nominee's behavior I spit out 750 words of rage in an op-ed."[13]

Sometimes, he says, his desire to write about issues in a multi-faceted way irked black readers, who felt that he was casting a negative light on the black community. But he would tell them, he intended to write about it all, "the good, the bad and the ugly. Let's get as whole a picture as we can. That's been my mantra."

After serving as a columnist for three years, in December 1994 Dawkins got a note from his executive editor informing him that he was being shifted back to reporting. "I didn't like the way I was reassigned," he says. "It was done in a very abrupt way. And my column was taken away."

"The other reporters and editors saw me go to a new desk among the reporters," he told *The NABJ Journal* in 1995. "It was a week of people left in the dark and a very humiliating experience for me."[14] While Dawkins made clear that he did not like the reassignment, "I did understand this management prerogative to have people where they're needed. A column is not a Supreme Court appointment. It can be given and it can be taken away."

But Dawkins became a bit of a cause célèbre among black journalists. Other black columnists who had fought their own battles with mainstream media came to his defense. Those speaking out included columnist Earl Caldwell, fired by the *New York Daily News* in 1994. Caldwell claimed he was sacked because he had publicly charged his editor and *Daily News* owner Mort Zuckerman with censorship motivated by racism after they refused to run his column about a white New York police officer accused of raping five black men.[15] Also springing to Dawkins' defense was Lisa Baird, who had been a columnist at *The Record* in Hackensack, N.J. Baird, now deceased, quit the paper after several of her columns were killed.[16]

"People complained on my behalf, although I did not wage a campaign," he says, noting that the Garden State Association of Black Journalists protested the reassignment. The NAACP also registered its opposition to the move. Paul Harris, president of the Eastern Camden County NAACP, told executive editor Everett Landers that Dawkins "was the only local reporter that really understood the African-American community, and he was the only one I could talk to." In the end, the executive editor kept Dawkins on as a reporter but let him have his column.[17] Landers also insisted that the reassignment was temporary.

Dawkins could understand why his editors made this decision. The paper was in close proximity to the *Philadelphia Inquirer* at a time when the paper was flush with resources and noted for its Pulitzer Prize–winning journalism. The *Inquirer* had begun to wage a war for some of the "high-growth towns" in the *Courier-Post's* circulation area. Feeling besieged, the editors were beefing up their reporting staff to beat back the incursion. "It was what the paper needed," Dawkins says. "It may not have been what we wanted for ourselves," noting that the reassignment also pushed a white female editorial writer back on the reporting staff. "We worked a horrible shift," — 2:30 P.M. to 10:30 P.M. Sunday to Thursday." But their work, he says, made a difference in Burlington County. "The *Inquirer* failed in its effort to come over and bully us and take our readers, basically take our lunch money. A handful of us beat them back."

Despite his pride at having helped his paper, Dawkins saw the reassignment as a sign that he should move on. It was 1996, and he'd worked a dozen years at the *Courier-Post*. This was a time when big newspaper chains were still healthy, and Dawkins had friends in the business who urged him to go to the Knight-Ridder newspaper chain, at that point the second largest newspaper chain in the country, with a reputation for quality journalism. Dawkins took the chain's "famous editing test." The six-hour battery of tests challenged not only your knowledge of grammar and punctuation, but your stamina, he recalls. Four hours in, he recalls, "I just wanted to get up and walk out." Instead, he counted to ten, and stayed, showing he could handle the stress. He was offered an editing job at the chain's Gary, Indiana, daily, the *Post-Tribune*.

The position didn't turn out to be a good fit. "This was my first experience with a [newspaper] guild shop. I was assistant metro editor, where I'm not a manager, I'm a supervisor, so I'm in the ranks with the reporters. I put in a lot of overtime hours." While he was "at the paper all the time, working long hours," Dawkins' wife and daughter were pining away for the Northeast. It was their first time in the Midwest, he says, and "the culture shock was too great."

In the meantime, the *Post-Tribune* found itself a pawn in a media chess game. "I got caught up in something interesting," he says. This was the era of big media mergers, and in 1995, the media behemoth Disney agreed to purchase Capital Cities/ABC for $19 billion. After the merger, Disney started to sell some of the merged companies' papers, and Knight-Ridder scooped up four of its dailies, including the *Kansas City Star*, and the *Fort Worth Star-Telegram*, for $1.65 billion.[18] "They get two high-quality papers. They also get a billion dollars in debt," Dawkins says. And the chain's answer to its fiscal challenge was to "shed a few of its less profitable papers. They tend to be the smaller ones. I worked at one."

In 1997, shortly after he arrived, Knight-Ridder sold the paper to another chain, Hollinger International Inc., then the parent of the *Chicago Sun-Times*, and 106 papers in the U.S., 58 in Canada, and major dailies in both Jerusalem and London.[19]

"I had to reapply for my job. And they said, 'Yeah, we'll keep you.'" During all this turmoil, Dawkins got a call from the *Daily Press* in Newport News, Virginia, owned by the Tribune Company, asking about his interest in a potential editorial writer opening. The paper was based in a diverse community in Southeast Virginia near the Atlantic coast. He said to himself, "I have to nail this opportunity." And he did, moving to the paper in February 1998.

When he went to the *Daily Press*, he entered a different newsroom culture, with less emphasis on breaking news, and more on long-form pieces.

"In the Northeast, people live at a frantic pace. Here, there's a lot more attention paid to writing."

"When I got there, they exposed some weaknesses in my writing," he says. "I was always well read, a critical thinker. I was a good writer," he adds, but he had grown up in an era with "strong editing desks. If you were a competent writer, your stories would go through okay. If your grammar and spelling were not the best, there was a safety net there to catch you. In this more modern age, this is not the case. At the *Daily Press* ... they really challenged me." And Dawkins did learn from the critiques. "I quickly worked on what I needed to do and recovered."

During his tenure at the *Daily Press*, he wrote a number of provocative columns. One concerned the death of Dr. Charles Drew, an African-American physician who played a leading role in the creation of blood banks. According to widely accepted accounts, the irony was that when Drew was severely injured in an auto crash, he was denied a life-saving blood transfusion because of racism. Dawkins was concerned when he heard an African-American teen retell that story at a community event. Dawkins wrote that the story wasn't true.

Drew did encounter racism during his career, Dawkins wrote, but for far different reasons. Drew strongly objected to the government's policy that donor blood given to the armed forces would be segregated according to race, a practice that had no foundation in science. But there was no evidence, Dawkins continued, that Drew died because of bigotry. There were efforts to give him a blood transfusion. Dawkins wrote that Drew's family believes the story took hold because it resonated with "many people's recollections of black achievement devalued by an ungrateful nation." But he concludes: "Drew excelled under considerable odds and fought racist practices. There is scant evidence that he died because of those practices. That story needs to be told — unembellished — over and over to future generations of American children."[20] "When I wrote the piece debunking [the story] there were folks who said, 'You shouldn't do that. You can't do that.' But Dawkins said it was crucial "to tell as honest a version of history as possible.... There are times you have to tell uncomfortable truth," he says.

Dawkins' columns often prompted letters, usually a good sign of reader interest. One that generated some heat concerned his column on the "blending" of America as inter-racial and ethnically diverse marriages increased. "Three years ago, the face of Betty Crocker changed on cake boxes. General Mills took photographs of dozens of American women and digitally blended the images into this future American. The former blonde, blue-eyed Midwesterner evolved into a dark-haired, brown-eyed woman with hints of Italian or Hispanic heritage."[21] It was the verb "evolved" that rankled some readers.

But these thoughtful, provocative columns didn't mean that Dawkins had the approval of his bosses. "I was told I needed to be more assertive," even though as associate editor he did not directly supervise anyone. "I was part of management, so I was told to be assertive. At one point, I was told I wasn't assertive enough in editorial board meetings."

Later, however, when he would argue with a colleague during editorial meetings, he was considered "too aggressive." In the minds of his bosses, he says, he just wasn't making the grade. "What I was doing wasn't good enough or wasn't working.

"I just faced up to the fact that sometimes you hit a wall in a career and you have to change or do something different. There had been a lot of staff turnover," he says. "I was being pushed out."

Does Dawkins believe that racism was a factor in how he was treated? "That crossed my mind, but I couldn't prove it," he says. "I also recognized that the *Daily Press* is not a big paper, but it is a very demanding place. I still tell people pound for pound it is one of the best papers in the country, one of the most innovative." Reporters, he says, got good experience, but the work was very draining. Reporters who did well at the paper either burned out or moved on. "There weren't too many people who were going to be lifers."

"I loved journalism but at the time journalism wasn't loving me back," Dawkins says. At this point, Dawkins felt that he was "just holding on by my fingernails." He told himself, "I need to find a way to leave with my dignity intact." He cashed in his company stock options. He got his financial house in order, paying some bills. His wife couldn't understand why he was giving up a good-paying job and called him "a deeply disturbed man."[22] Undeterred, he submitted his letter of resignation to the paper in the spring of 2003. And as he began a new chapter, he relied on the huge network of black journalists built through his work with Columbia's Black Alumni Network, and his long-standing leadership in the National Association of Black Journalists (NABJ).

His exposure to NABJ began in 1981, and intensified over the years as he painstakingly took on the role of volunteer historian for the group, seeking out the founding members, nailing down facts about the group's origins, and ultimately writing the organization's history. He also served as a regional director of the association.

As he prepared to leave the paper, he contacted his network to seek free-lance assignments, and they responded immediately. Things brightened even more when he attended the NABJ convention in the summer of 2003 and met radio personality Tom Joyner. Joyner wanted to upgrade a site he owned, blackamericawebb.com. Dawkins accepted a job as managing editor for the news site. Web work kept him going until early 2005, but by that time, his relationship with the site had lapsed. In the meantime, Hampton University had contacted him, asking if he might be available to do some adjunct teaching for them.

Hampton, a historically black college, has deep roots. The site of the college was a place of refuge for escaping slaves during the Civil War. A school grew up there, and ultimately, by the late 1800s, it was the site of the Hampton Normal and Agricultural Institute, which Booker T. Washington attended. It formally attained college status in 1930 as Hampton Institute.[23]

Hampton was the first historically black college to start a journalism program, when it founded its Department of Mass Media Arts in 1967. The school's program got a boost when the Scripps Howard Foundation, the corporate foundation of the E.W. Scripps Company, committed $10 million to revamp its communications and journalism program, and to build a facility that could accommodate state-of-the-art journalism labs and broadcast facilities.[24] The new building opened in 2002 as Hampton inaugurated the Scripps Howard School of Journalism and Communications.[25]

But the journalism program was in turmoil, losing two directors in two years because of disagreements with the administration over press freedom for the student newspaper.[26] The department lost numbers of its faculty as well. Things started to turn around in 2004, Dawkins says, when the "iconic" Tony Brown became dean of the program. At that point author and commentator Brown had been the host of PBS's news and commentary series *Tony Brown's Journal*, for 25 seasons, focusing on issues of interest to African-American viewers.[27] Brown was looking for veteran journalists to join the faculty. Dawkins took a teaching position at the school along with seven other media professionals, he says. "We averaged at least 23 years of journalism experience each, but we had minimal teaching experience. So there were some snickers from some quarters saying, 'Oh, yeah, they're topnotch journalists, but do they know how to teach?'"

Dawkins believes he and his colleagues have been up to the challenge. He is particularly proud of their efforts to upgrade the school's introductory reporting and writing classes. "We emphasize to students that writing is at the foundation of whatever we do in whatever medium." He says that students who decide on a media major because it is housed in the Hampton building with the "coolest toys" soon are "disabused of that notion." The professors' message: "You better come with the hunger to learn. Then we'll let you play with the toys."

Dawkins says that he and his colleagues endeavored not to let their own life experience — spending years in journalism and then finding themselves dispensable — affect their teaching. "What Tony Brown made very clear was that he did not want to hear about victimization. He really did not want to hear about affirmative action.... His mantra was, if you can write well, you can write your ticket for whatever you want to do. We were all on board with that."

Brown left as dean in 2009, but Brown's vision remains. Hampton's state-of-the-art facility, Dawkins says, has helped him teach his students to work "across spectrums, knocking down silos." He exposes his students to newspapers and radio, particularly NPR News. He will make the point that NPR resurrected a medium that was considered dead after the coming of TV, and made it work. Most of his students, he says, don't read a daily newspaper or listen to NPR when they begin his course. He changes their behavior, emphasizing that while the "tools may change," the ability to research and write are the "core values that will set you apart." He stresses that students must consume media, including books, television news, and newspapers.

"Most of my colleagues who came in with me are still here," he says. He adds that students soon find out that in the journalism and communications program, it doesn't pay to "professor shop." All the professors are tough. The program has produced good results, he says. In a challenging media market, "our graduates are getting good jobs." He acknowledges that the jobs are cropping up in out-of-the-way places, and not big cities. "The reporting opportunity is in Binghamton, New York, or Montgomery, Alabama," something that students might have "turned up their noses at" 15 or 20 years ago. "But now it's a real job in a field you want to be in, so you need to go get this."

One of his students, a recent graduate, hoped to land an internship at the *Philadelphia Daily News*. Instead, he's learning the ropes at an E.W. Scripps paper in Evansville, Indiana. Dawkins told him he didn't get the Philadelphia slot for lack of talent, but because other students had already done internships there. If he does well in Evansville, he probably will get what he wants eventually, Dawkins says. The student sent him a video he shot along with his print news story. Dawkins beams. "He's living that dream of being across the platforms. He's there with a very good editor.... He's in a good place at a good time."

And, he says, some exceptional students are getting exceptional offers. One of his students had accepted a post-graduate editing internship at *The Washington Post*, but then got five other offers for jobs and fellowships. "She got kind of flustered," Dawkins says. "Why are all these people after me?" Her teachers told her to realize "You are so good, these organizations want to associate themselves with you."

He does lament that news operations, by firing older staff, lost institutional memory. But the implosion created "opportunities for these young people. What we need to do is just prepare them as best we can, get them into these positions."

Not that Dawkins is content with the current level of newsroom diversity. "If you look at minority representation in media," he says, "it was getting better, and then the industry imploded, and the publishers aren't counting [minority staff] anymore, or not keeping to any goals." Digital media in particular has been reluctant to disclose its numbers, saying that disclosing that information would harm their competitive advantage. "Many of us are contending, 'You don't want to tell us, because your numbers are abysmal.'"

When CNN's *Reliable Sources* program took viewers inside an editorial meeting at *Politico* in 2010, they saw "just a sea of white guys," Dawkins says. *Politico*, a print and web operation is an influential niche media outlet covering politics in Washington. (*Politico* said the shots were misleading and that it is committed to diversity, but did not release any data about the number of women and minorities it employs).[28]

The Sunday public affairs shows also have been "the most segregated hour in America" because the norm for both hosts and guest experts is to be almost exclusively white, Dawkins adds. Roland Martin's *Washington Watch* program is the exception, he says. (Martin's program runs on TV One, a cable channel primarily serving a black audience.)[29]

When news operations lack diversity, he says, "blind spots" concerning people of color harm their coverage. All media, digital and otherwise, have "a social responsibility to create a newsroom that is neither so monolithic nor tone deaf, so that you cover America and the world well."

Whether it's diversity in the newsroom, or finding a publisher for his books, Dawkins doesn't give up. In 1990, Dawkins received a distinguished alumnus award from Columbia for his service to journalism. His acceptance speech about expanding media diversity piqued the interest of an agent who had heard him speak. She suggested he write a book. He started writing about the history of the NABJ. He worked painstakingly to assemble facts and figures about an organization that had been pretty careless with its history, something Dawkins found frustrating. "At that point NABJ didn't even know how many people founded the organization," he says.

Dawkins spent years assembling the facts, talking to all but one of the 43 founders still alive. (The 44th founder, ABC news correspondent and anchor Max Robinson had died by then.) Unable to land a contract with a publisher, Dawkins opted to start his own publishing house, August Press. "I felt it was important to do it because no one had really decided to tell this history," Dawkins says. *Black Journalists: The NABJ Story* was first released in 1993, and re-released and updated in 1997. Some historians "sneered" at the book, thinking it was "too general or popular." But Dawkins's retort was, "You're still talking about it. You haven't written anything."

August Press became the vehicle for publishing other works of African-American authors, everything from *Good Night Sweetheart, Good Night: The Story of the Spaniels*, an examination of a largely unknown rhythm and blues group and its impact on rock and roll, to *Black Voices in Commentary*, collecting the essays of 23 black newspaper columnists throughout the country, and even a novel. Dawkins' second book about NABJ, *Rugged Waters: Black Journalists Swim the Mainstream*, came out in 2003.

Dawkins now is working on a biography of Andrew W. Cooper, the founder of Trans-Urban News Service, who went on to found the African-American weekly *The City Sun*. Cooper also played a pivotal role in securing better representation for New Yorkers. He was the lead plaintiff in a federal lawsuit challenging the redistricting of Congressional districts in Brooklyn, which diluted the power of black voters.[30]

In 1967, a federal court ruled that the way districts had been drawn in Brooklyn violated the Voting Rights Act.[31] Court-ordered reapportionment created the 12th Congressional District of New York, laying the foundation for the 1968 election of Rep. Shirley Chisholm, the first black woman elected to Congress.[32]

Dawkins was executive producer for the Hampton University faculty and student documentary *Voting Rights, Northern Style,* which was on Cooper and the seminal case. Hampton was one of seven historic black colleges to receive the first round of funding to make its film. The *Eyes on the Prize* Black College New Media project, which aims to inspire a new generation to make documentaries on civil rights issues, was a collaboration that included the Corporation for Public Broadcasting, the Ford Foundation, and Blackside Media, the original producer of the iconic documentary, *Eyes on the Prize.*

Dawkins carries no rancor about the abrupt way his own career in journalism came to an end. "Look, I tell my students, people of my generation, we had a bull's eye on our chest because these companies wanted to move us and our higher salaries. We did get all this experience but now we're costing them. They were able to move a bunch of us, but that created room for the younger people now."

"I'm even on cordial terms with the bosses at my former newspaper," Dawkins wrote in 2009. "My students are their interns."[33]

In September 2011, Dawkins received the Edward L. Hamm, Sr. teaching award from Hampton. His book on Andrew Cooper will be published by the University Press of Mississippi in 2012.

Chapter 8

Collateral Damage

Sometimes getting too close to history can singe a reporter. For nearly 20 years, Viveca Novak was the consummate "inside the beltway" Washington journalist, adept at working sources, the lawyers and lobbyists who make the wheels turn in the nation's capital. Novak's beat at *Time Magazine* was the Department of Justice, not the Pentagon. She never was sent to Iraq to cover the war. Yet she became collateral damage in the controversy that erupted over the legitimacy of the claims then–President George W. Bush made to justify invading that country.

To understand what happened, it's crucial to recall the backlash against the Bush Administration for pursuing the Iraq War. Those who pushed for the war claimed it would last a few months and topple an unpopular regime, bringing democracy to a downtrodden people. But the war soon became a costly multi-year occupation costing billions of dollars and thousands of American lives.

The war's proponents argued that Iraqi leader Saddam Hussein must be stopped from using his weapons of mass destruction to support terrorism. But thorough post-invasion searches of the country uncovered no large caches of chemical or nuclear weapons. Key to making the case that Saddam possessed weapons of mass destruction was the administration contention that Iraq had purchased "yellowcake" uranium ore, crucial for making nuclear bombs, from the African country of Niger. But Joseph C. Wilson IV, the former U.S. ambassador dispatched to Niger to investigate that claim, had told the administration that it was groundless. When the administration continued to use the Niger story to advance its case, he wrote an op-ed in *The New York Times* charging "that some of the intelligence related to Iraq's nuclear weapons program was twisted to exaggerate the Iraqi threat."[1] To discredit Wilson, one or more administration officials implied that he got his Niger assignment because of nepotism, leaking the identity of Wilson's wife, Valerie Plame, to the media.[2] Plame was a CIA officer whose cover was blown and career destroyed by the exposure.[3] Bush named a special prosecutor to investigate.[4]

In 2003, Novak found herself having a glass of wine with a longtime source, when the Plame investigation came up. That particular reporter-source relationship would have terrible repercussions for Novak, and make her the target of media criticism questioning both her sense of ethics and the propriety of her relationships with Washington insiders.

It is ironic that Novak should have found herself in that situation. She is precise and measured, someone who hates hype and sticks to the facts. She also has thought seriously about the proper way to deal with sources. "You need to develop source relationships and you need to know the way the city works to get stories," she says. "But there are boundaries, I think, that are crossed way too often."

If anyone knows how to navigate relationships, it is Novak. While she spent a good part of her career reporting on campaign finance abuses, her husband, Robert Lenhard, has been an election lawyer, offering advice to labor unions on how to navigate campaign finance laws. Novak was the author of ground-breaking campaign finance stories while employed by Common Cause, the good-government group most responsible for the enactment of the Bipartisan Campaign Reform Act of 2002. Lenhard was part of the legal team that challenged the constitutionality of that law.[5]

Novak was not prepared for the media backlash against what she considers her minor role in the controversy. Seeing the media from the other side, and its potential for error and unfairness, helped prompt her move to FactCheck.org, whose mission is to monitor the veracity of political speech.

She is contained, careful and acutely aware of the implication of words. Don't characterize me as a former journalist," she says. "What I'm doing here [as deputy director of FactCheck.org] is journalism, it's just not mainstream media journalism anymore. Thank goodness!"

Blonde and elegant, her voice is soft, just a little north of sultry, velvety. It comes as no surprise to learn that in her early 20s, she was a disk jockey for a radio jazz program. Journalism wasn't the career path she originally explored. A foreign affairs major at the University of Virginia, she worked for Senator Richard Lugar (R-IN) on the Senate subcommittee on housing and urban affairs. Some college grads come to Capitol Hill and find it addictive. That didn't happen to Novak. "There seemed to be a lot of artifice about the whole thing. It didn't feel to me like I was doing anything useful." Trying to find her way, she took the LSAT (Law School Admission Test) at the last minute without any preparation. When she scored in the 98th percentile, she figured it was a sign. "Oh well, that must mean I'm supposed to go to law school, but I don't know, some part of me resisted."

In her spare time, Novak, who was living in Washington's eclectic Adams Morgan neighborhood, was freelancing for a neighborhood publication, the *Rock Creek Monitor*. She also was volunteering at a politically progressive Pacifica Radio station. After Ronald Reagan assumed the presidency in 1981, she'd branched out beyond jazz to do public affairs programs. She focused on the environment and worker health and safety, areas vulnerable to cuts from the new administration.

"I realized that what I really liked were the journalism parts of my life," she says. At the last minute, she applied to the Graduate School of Journalism at Columbia University in New York. "I got into journalism really not because I loved to write ... it was still difficult for me when I started, but more to save the world." Her motive, she says, was "more afflict the comfortable and comfort the afflicted."

After graduation, she drove around the country, interviewing at small and large newspapers, finding her first job in 1983 at *The Anniston Star* in Anniston, Alabama. *The Star*, whose history dated back to 1911 and which was once known as the *Daily Hot Blast*, was a family owned newspaper with progressive views on civil rights. Its publisher, H. Brandt Ayers, was well-respected in media circles, and the 30,000- circulation daily was considered one of the best small newspapers in the country.[6] "It was a good enough newspaper that it had been attracting Yankee reporters for a while, but the community didn't necessarily like Yankee reporters," she says. Sometimes it was a "challenge" to get acceptance, she says, but adds that it was a fun place to work with a lot of camaraderie. "I still have some good friends from that time."

As a cub reporter, she found herself covering a county commission at the edge of the paper's circulation area. "I remember stopping when I saw my first cotton field and running out and touching the cotton and thinking about its meaning in American history," she says. She was a good enough reporter to sense that an investigative reporter would uncover some good stories on her beat, but she was green enough not to be able to pull it off. "Sitting in those county commission meetings with those five good old boys who thought it was so funny that this Yankee girl was trying to write about them. I was getting little glimmer of things that I just never could break open."

Ultimately, she was assigned to work on more project-oriented stories, a development that meant she no longer had to dread driving home alone at night in rural Alabama. She and another reporter won state journalism awards for a series on the state's county coroner system. In Alabama at the time, coroners did not have to have any special training, and often were funeral home directors "who could direct the corpses right to their own funeral homes," she says. They would be the ones who filled out the cause-of-death certificates.

Digging into those records, she says with a laugh, she found causes of death that included "hit over the head with a slop jar" and "cerebral hemorrhoid."

By then she'd been at the paper for about two years, hitting the point at which young reporters "begin to panic" about their future prospects. She left *The Star* in 1985, successfully applying for a one-year Yale University Law School fellowship offering training on legal issues to reporters. "There was some concern that people covering these things for newspapers didn't always have the background to understand and put in perspective some of these issues," she says. Five journalists took the same courses and exams as the law students. She found the experience quite "civilized" and intellectually stimulating, and she did well academically. "Please don't mislead people into thinking I had a J.D. [a law degree]," Novak says. The one-year fellowship earned her an M.S.L., Master of Studies in Law.

It was the mid–1980s, and her boyfriend at the time was doing a summer clerkship for the attorney general of the Federated States of Micronesia, an exotic island-nation east of the Philippines. Micronesia gained its independence from the U.S. in 1986.[7] "We both thought it would be fun if I could come," she says, and she was able to land a clerkship with the Legal Services Corporation there. That Pacific adventure over, Novak decided that her best shot at getting reporting work was in Washington.

In 1980, Fred Wertheimer, who became the president of Common Cause, helped create *Common Cause Magazine*, a glossy publication that aspired to the standards of mainstream reporting. Novak started freelancing for the publication, and ultimately joined its staff, working there from 1987 to 1992.

While Novak had some qualms about joining the staff, she knew that serious journalists worked there, and that the organization gave the magazine "a degree of autonomy." The staff kept its physical distance, too. They worked in a room apart from the rest of the organization, with a window facing the rest of the office. "We called it the fishbowl," she recalls. "And we always resisted any appeals to come and stuff envelopes or anything."

The journalism community respected the magazine's work. Over its 16-year history, the magazine won five awards from Investigative Reporters and Editors (IRE) and a National Magazine Award for general excellence.[8]

The monthly publication gave its staff lots of time to dig deep. In the 1980s, journalists tended to avoid stories on political contributions unless they were illegal or bribes. But Novak and her colleagues at *Common Cause Magazine* reshaped the media landscape on money and politics. The magazine pioneered scrutiny of "soft money"—unlimited donations from corporations, unions and individuals to national political parties—and how soft money donors influenced public policy. Novak remembers their "groundbreaking" reporting on donors to the campaign of George H.W. Bush, and how contributors were rewarded by the administration. The story, "George Bush's Ruling Class," was unique because it linked Bush donors of $100,000 or more specific to public policy outcomes, everything from water rights to ethanol subsidies and a White House push to weaken clean air rules. The story got extensive media play and was featured in a PBS *Frontline* documentary.[9]

It was not uncommon for magazine staffers to go on to plum reporting jobs at NPR, *The New York Times*, the *Los Angeles Times*, and *The Washington Post*. Novak was no exception. In 1992, she moved to *National Journal*, a publication not well known throughout the country, but one of the must-reads for the movers and shakers in the nation's capital. "I was covering budget and tax, fiscal policy, which was totally new to me," Novak says. She worked hard, consulted many experts, and tackled the new beat as one would tackle a college course. But, she says, during her entire tenure, "I never liked the beat." Partly because she still felt "unfamiliar with the material," but also because "I felt like I wasn't really doing what I'd gotten into journalism to do.

"I didn't think budget policy was going to change the world," she says, adding, "I don't like to write about the same things everybody else is writing about. If you're writing about budget policy for *National Journal*, you're probably not breaking any new ground. You may be putting things in perspective, you may be helping people understand things, but it wasn't lighting a fire under people."

But the beat Novak didn't like turned out to be her ticket to the big time, and a source helped her get there. The Whitewater scandal began to break during President Bill Clinton's first term. "Let's just say that I learned through a source some interesting information about the original real estate transaction that was Whitewater," she says. The Whitewater reporting she did at *National Journal* led to a job offer from *The Wall Street Journal*.

"I had always wanted to work there," she says. And when she joined the paper, she found herself in the middle of the scandal, navigating its twists and turns. As convoluted as a Russian novel, with nearly as many characters and side plots, Whitewater revolved around the Clintons' investment in 1978 in an Arkansas real estate development deal that went sour. Their partners in the development were James and Susan McDougal, the owners of an Arkansas thrift that made fraudulent loans and for which Hillary Clinton did some legal work. The thrift failed in 1989, costing the federal government $73 million. Susan McDougal was accused of fraudulently applying for a $300,000 loan backed by the Small Business Administration, $50,000 of which went to the Whitewater development. The loan was never repaid.[10] David Hale, a former Little Rock municipal judge and then a businessman whose firm issued the loan, charged that Bill Clinton had pressured him into making it.[11] In 2002, after years of investigation, the Clintons were not charged with perjury or obstructing justice. However, the independent counsel overseeing the conclusion of the investigation did find that both had made "factually inaccurate" statements.[12]

"There was a lot of pressure. It was a very competitive story," she says. But she began to feel that while the scandal was "badly handled by the Clintons," there may not have been any conduct that rose to the level of criminal.

"I don't know that I went to anyone at *The Journal* and said, 'Look, this is much ado about nothing,'" she says. "It's very hard to prove a negative. So the best I could do was to do the stories but not be hyperbolic, not write them in a sort of inflammatory way, try to be as calm and as cool-headed about the whole thing as I could. I do think that I served a purpose that way. Some perspective was what was needed and I did my best to help provide that."

As early as February 1995, Novak and co-author Ellen Joan Pollock wrote a 2,300-word front-page story about then-independent counsel Ken Starr's investigations into the affair that began this way:

> Here's a word of advice to anyone in Hollywood hoping to make *Whitewater, the Movie.* Don't expect high drama. Anyone counting on riveting scenes of Hillary Clinton meeting with shadowy figures in the Arkansas woods, or on a solution to the mystery of a top White House official's death — was it really suicide or was it murder? — is destined to be disappointed.

The authors concluded that few journalists and "Beltway cognoscenti" believed that the Whitewater investigation "would ensnare the Clintons in criminal charges."[13] Nevertheless, Whitewater continued to be a story that had to be covered. The Republican-controlled Senate investigated vigorously, and in August 1995, a pregnant Novak found herself lugging binders of briefing books to hearings, "just lugging them all over Capitol Hill, this huge belly, sweating, it was just awful."

Whitewater wasn't the only story vulnerable to media distortion. Janet Reno was attorney general during the Clinton Administration. *The Journal* asked Novak, who covered the Justice Department, to do a profile of Reno, based on the premise that she was the most political attorney general in decades. Their views, she hastens to add, weren't driven by the politics of *The Journal's* conservative editorial pages. *The Journal's* Washington bureau, she says, "was not a political place. We were quite insulated from the editorial page." Her editors simply felt that such a story would be widely read and get a lot of attention.

Nevertheless, Novak resisted. "Janet Reno may have had many other flaws but she was not political. In fact, she did not have a political bone in her body. So I basically refused to do this story. I tried to refuse nicely, and

I tried to come up with other thoughts, but they weren't happy with me at all.

"I think in general with the corporate media outlets I've worked for there was a tendency to hype things to a degree I was uncomfortable with," Novak says. Novak was facing other challenges at *The Journal*. Covering the Justice Department meant writing a lot of stories about some of the drier and more arcane aspects of the department. For example, Novak spent a lot of time writing about the Department's antitrust efforts, enforcing laws to ensure business competition. "For the *Journal's* readers, it was very important," she says. "I did a pretty good job of it and they wanted me to keep doing it and I didn't see any way out," she says. *Journal* White House correspondent Jeffrey Birnbaum had moved on to *Time Magazine* and let her know about a job opening there. Birnbaum recommended her, and she got the job. "It was better money and it sounded like I wouldn't have to do any more antitrust, but I could cover the Justice Department, which I still liked quite a lot."

In the aftermath of the 1996 presidential campaign, she returned to the issue that first made her career as a journalist: campaign finance abuses. Writing several stories about the excesses of the 1996 campaign, Novak and *Time* colleague Michael Weisskopf pulled no punches. "The Busy Back-Door Men" was typical of their coverage. It opened with this sentence: "Virtually no one with a checkbook was turned away from Bill Clinton's fund-raising party — not convicted felons, not Buddhist monks bearing someone else's money, not even a Russian mobster." The story went on to explain how Carl Lindner, head of Chiquita Brands and known for his generosity to conservative Republican causes, had found a way to secretly support Clinton's campaign. Lindner needed a favor from the administration — help getting Chiquita bananas into European markets. The administration offered its assistance and Lindner funneled nearly $500,000 to Democratic state parties. Lindner also got a night in the Lincoln bedroom.[14] In 1998, the stories earned Novak, Weisskopf and bureau chief Michael Duffy the Goldsmith Award for investigative reporting sponsored by Harvard University's Joan Shorenstein Center on the Press, Politics and Public Policy.[15]

Novak also was becoming a pretty well-known pundit on the television talk show circuit. Novak says that it took her a while to get comfortable in the role. "I was still very nervous, and I'd be very precise with my answers." It was her nature to say, "I don't know" when asked about a subject on which she wasn't informed, rather than to deflect the question and speak about what she did know. "I didn't like the TV thing for a long time because I'm a print reporter, I'm not a TV personality. I don't care about television. I think this is hype, it's stupid. The people who are asking me questions don't know anything about my story. I kind of looked down on the whole thing." However, *Time* encouraged on-air appearances. The magazine gave its writers television training, and paid them $200 for each television appearance they made. Because of that "monetary incentive," she says, "we all tried to do as much TV as we could."

The 1990s were still flush days for *Time,* and the magazine had a history of generous staff perks, everything from generous expense accounts to the notorious drink cart carrying alcoholic beverages to staffers putting the magazine to bed.[16] Novak remembers that after each of the births of her two children, *Time* sent her a sterling silver porringer from Tiffany with the child's initials engraved on it. A porringer, she explains, is a "kind of bowl with a handle, but it's kind of fancy. It would come in a lovely box with a note from your managing editor.

"*Time* was in some ways a very benevolent workplace," Novak recalls, noting how her editors responded to a health crisis. In the fall of 2001, she'd discovered a lump in her stomach. "I had all kinds of tests and finally I went to a very good surgeon who said, 'I think it's malignant and I think we should operate Saturday.'" Hospitalized for two weeks, she learned that her doctors puzzled over exactly what type of tumor they had excised and what its implications were for her future. One type of tumor would respond to a very expensive drug, but if the tumor were the other type, the medication—costing about $20,000 annually—would have no impact. Novak started placing calls to oncologists all over the country to get their views. "It was pretty hard," she says. She recalls one evening, after-rounds visit by her surgeon, who was convinced that her cancer required the expensive drug and who pulled out a chart putting her chances of living more than five years at 40 percent. She didn't feel that she could share that news even with her husband, who was trying to hold the family together, caring for their three-year-old son and five-year-old daughter.

As it turned out, her surgeon was wrong about the nature of the tumor and her prognosis. But shortly after returning to work in 2002, "I could barely get up in the morning. I felt like a huge weight was sitting on my chest. I couldn't eat dinner with my family. But I had a wonderful bureau chief who said to me, 'Why don't you take the summer off? We have disability here.'" Novak spent the summer gardening, going to films with friends, de-stressing. She needed the time, she now realizes, to complete the recovery.

Novak's experience with serious illness and its psychological aftermath may have helped prepare her for a major writing project in 2005. *Time* again was understanding, granting her a leave to co-write *Inside the Wire,* a book which evolved from her reporting on the post-9/11 creation of the Department of Homeland Security. Her coverage of some of the terrorist cases led her to scrutinize the U.S. Detainee Camp for accused terrorists based in Guantanamo Cuba. She traveled to the base, and although under tight supervision, she was able to "soak up the atmosphere of the place, describe the place, give a sense of color to the place. I just sent back reams and reams of material."

A *Time* story in December 2003 contained some of the material Novak had sent back. The story describes Gitmo as "a prison and a jewelry box," a place where there is no chance for escape, whose jailors are keenly aware of the valuable intelligence prisoners might give up. She describes the security unit for the least cooperative inmates, including its exact dimensions: 6 ft. 8 in. by 8 ft. its toilet — "squat-style," and the orange clothing each inmate received. Inmates who cooperate live in a much more comfortable unit. "Real, colored prayer rugs, thicker mattresses, pillows even, and soccer shoes. Pure-white clothes instead of glaring catch-me-you-if-you-can orange. A librarian comes around with books, and lunch is on picnic tables, family style." Authorities increased the emotional pressure to give up intelligence by prominently displaying posters depicting the faces of children who in Arabic ask a question that, loosely translated, pleads, "Dad, how can I grow up without you?"[17]

Uncertainty and its toll was something Novak knew about from her health crisis, and that theme was something she discussed on Public radio's *Fresh Air*. Novak said that beyond the examples of the individual prisoners facing abusive interrogation, "We're losing sight of perhaps the most extreme form of abuse — the psychological torture of not knowing your fate. We're keeping these people for years. They never know if they're going to see a lawyer. They didn't know if they were going to be charged with anything. Many of them didn't know why they were there. Just that open-endedness is very, very tough on the psyche."[18]

Novak's *Fresh Air* appearance was to promote the book she co-authored with someone who'd experienced the prison firsthand. Shortly after her trip to Guantanamo for *Time*, Novak was approached by an agent who asked her to work with Erik Saar, a former Army sergeant at the base who wanted to write a book about his experience there. Saar, a linguist fluent in Arabic, had been eager to use his skills to extract useful intelligence from the detainees, but soon grew disillusioned over the unjust and sometimes cruel treatment he witnessed. She had a good initial meeting with Saar, and then the abuses and pictures at Abu Ghraib prison in Iraq broke into the headlines, and Saar's book, which explored the maltreatment and mishandling of Guantanamo detainees, suddenly became very topical. So the decision was made to rush the book into print. Originally the book was going to include more of Novak's original reporting, but now it focused almost exclusively on Saar's story. Adding to the pressure was the fact that in January 2005, the Associated Press got its hands on book materials that Saar had submitted to the Defense Department for clearance.

Saar had gotten a call from an AP reporter and called Novak to get some advice on how to handle it. "Unfortunately, he'd gotten too curious," Novak recalls. By the time she reached him, Saar had already called the AP back. Somebody from the Pentagon had leaked a portion of the book, Novak says. The wire service had "our most incendiary anecdote."[19] After the AP wrote about the incident, Novak described it for *Time*. Her vivid account is an exception to her usual dispassionate reporting.

The incident Novak described concerned the attempt to prompt an inmate, a very devout Muslim, to feel guilt, and thus to weaken his connection to his god, a tactic that would weaken his resolve and lead him to divulge more information. The female interrogator's strategy was to sexually arouse the inmate by accentuating her breasts and rubbing them against his back. She also convinced him that she was menstruating and was touching him with her menstrual blood.

> When she and the first translator re-entered the interrogation booth, she told the detainee she was having her period. She stuck her hands in her pants, then withdrew a hand and showed the detainee what appeared to be blood on it. She asked again who had sent him to Arizona, and he glared at her silently. When she wiped the red ink on his face, he let out a shout, spit at her and lunged forward so forcefully that an ankle came loose from its shackle. The Saudi began sobbing uncontrollably, and the interrogator left, telling him the water in his cell had been shut off. He would not be able to wash, as Muslims are supposed to do before they pray.[20]

The decision was made to rush the book into print. "We figured I could finish it by March, we could have it out by May," making it the "fastest book ever published in the history of Penguin Books." Novak arrived each day at her *Time* office in Washington, shut her door, turned on all the lights, and "just typed, typed, typed, typed. Called Erik 30 times a day to get details of various stories. I just worked. I got it done." The book was titled *Inside the Wire: A Military Intelligence Soldier's Eyewitness Account of Life at Guantanamo*. "It wasn't a great work of literature, but it was what the publisher wanted at the time. And we got it out. We did it."

If *Time* editors could be accommodating about health and book leaves, the calculus of fitting *Time* stories into a limited number of magazine pages was not. Each week, stories, some fully edited, were dropped from the magazine. "I felt there was so much wasted effort at the magazine," she says. Her colleagues at *Time*'s Washington bureau were "really, really excellent people, which made it the more painful to have all these stories being killed left and right."

Journalists usually recall the heartbreak of one story in particular that never made it into print or on the air. For Novak it was a long project on the pharmaceutical industry that she and colleague Weisskopf worked on. "This was before everybody was writing about it." It scrutinized drug companies' lobbying, campaign contributions, marketing and pricing policies. "We produced three long stories and sent it up to New York," she recalls. "We thought it was pretty good work. It got lost and never appeared. It sat there for a while, and we kept trying to revive it, and then 9/11 happened and there was no hope of ever bringing it back."

Like any good Washington-based reporter, Novak kept in touch with a number of influential lawyers and lobbyists, among them attorney Robert Luskin. Luskin was a longtime Democrat and larger-than-life character, adept at getting positive media attention for his clients.[21] "He was a source and I knew him to be a very smart lawyer, and I also knew that he has tried to spin me on various occasions about other clients," Novak recalls. They would meet occasionally for a drink at the Café Deluxe near Washington's National Cathedral. In October 2003, as they were sipping wine, Luskin asked Novak what she was working on. She mentioned the Valerie Plame leak investigation case, and he told her that he was representing Karl Rove in the Plame investigation. She was surprised because of Luskin's liberal sympathies.[22] Rove, after all, was not just a high-ranking official in the Bush Administration. To those who opposed Bush policies, Rove was a political mastermind, someone whose political skullduggery won Bush the presidency, and who stayed on to call the shots at the White House. A Google search of "Karl Rove" and "evil genius" yields more than 35,000 hits.

The investigation continued into 2004, and Luskin and Novak continued to meet for an occasional drink. During one of those meetings, Luskin told Novak that Rove "did not have a Cooper problem," Novak says. (*Time* correspondent Matt Cooper was one of the journalists approached by administration officials with information about Plame's CIA employment.)[23] Luskin was indicating that Rove was not one of Cooper's sources. But Novak's instinct was to think that Luskin was trying to mislead her. "I thought how can he be saying that to somebody who actually works at *Time Magazine*? I pushed back." She doesn't remember her exact words, but her reaction, she says, apparently raised a question in Luskin's mind that there may have been contact between Cooper and Rove. Luskin's surprise, she says, seemed genuine. Novak stresses that she wasn't trying to trade information with Luskin about the Plame affair. "If I had known I was giving him a piece of information [about Rove's dealings with Cooper] ... that he didn't know, I wouldn't have given him that particular piece of information."

In October 2005, Luskin informed Novak that he had told Special Counsel Patrick Fitzgerald about their conversation from the year before. Fitzgerald asked to talk to her informally. Novak did not inform her editors, believing that the conversation was insignificant, and wary of not being able to contain the information, once it got out. In November, when Fitzgerald told her he would need to talk to her again, this time under oath, she let her editors know.[24]

As Fitzgerald's inquiry into her conversation played out, Novak had a hand in two *Time* stories touching on the Plame investigation. Novak's byline was on a profile of Fitzgerald published on Oct. 30, 2005, "Mr. Fitzgerald Goes To Washington." had been commissioned by *Time* "months and months before," she says, and she had done most of the research before Fitzgerald contacted her. It was a joint effort with another reporter and there was confusion about whose byline would go on the piece. All of her reporting "indicated that Fitzgerald was a fabulous prosecutor and a very upright guy widely admired." That view certainly comes out in the profile, which notes: "He works harder than God; he can be creative (sometimes controversially so) in his application of the law; he does not tolerate being lied to."[25]

"Woodward Unveiled" was published on November 20, 2005. The story discussed the admission by Bob Woodward, the investigative reporter known for breaking open the Watergate scandal, and a *Washington Post* editor, of his connection to the Plame investigation. Woodward had just disclosed that an administration official had told him about Plame's CIA ties in mid–June of 2003, a crucial piece of information he had kept from his editors for more than a year. Woodward, as Novak wrote in her *Time* piece, "said nothing then or in the months that followed ... and all Washington was consumed by a debate over spies and secrets and sources. Woodward kept what he knew secret even from Post executive editor Leonard Downie, Jr."

Woodward had learned about Plame from an administration source as he was writing his book *Plan of Attack.* He only came forward when it became clear that he may have been the first journalist to have heard about Plame from a White House official. Novak concluded that Woodward's reticence to reveal any of this information earlier stemmed from being "trapped between his loyalty to the *Post* and its readers and his parallel franchise, writing best-selling books drawn from sources deep inside the Administration." She wrote that Woodward had publicly criticized the Fitzgerald leak inquiry as "disgraceful," and pointed out that when asked point blank by CNN talk show host Larry King if he knew who the leaker was, Woodward categorically denied any knowledge of the Plame disclosure.[26]

Novak believes the Woodward story was fair, and was not influenced by her own Plame predicament. "I was writing about his situation, not mine. While I found it personally fascinating, I did not feel like I had reason to pull punches, and I didn't." She maintained that neither the Fitzgerald nor the Woodward story was compromised by her connection to the Plame investigation. But she concedes, "In a perfect world I should not probably have written either of them."

On November 20, the same day that her Woodward piece came out, Novak drove to the home of Washington bureau chief Jay Carney, (who went on to become White House press secretary for the Obama Administration), and told him about Fitzgerald's inquiries into her discussions with Luskin. Jim Kelly, *Time*'s managing editor, was informed. "Nobody was happy about it, least of all me," Novak wrote.

She adds that the fact that she didn't confide to her editors about the original Luskin conversation wasn't that surprising or beyond the pale of typical reporter-source relationships. "Like a lot of reporters, my tendency is to do my work without checking in frequently with editors, and my exchange with Luskin was all supposed to be off the record anyway. Yes, the conversation was a bit odd, and maybe I should have said something to my bureau chief. But the fact that I didn't do so wasn't unusual." Novak wrote the equivalent of an apology, published in the magazine in December 2005, that explained the Luskin encounter and what followed and expressed her regret for how things had played out.

But she believes that she had a bit part in the Plame investigation, that sooner or later Luskin, Rove's lawyer, would have diligently gone over the facts again, and realized that Rove had forgotten a contact with *Time*'s Cooper, and made sure that Rove corrected his testimony before the grand jury. "I think Patrick Fitzgerald did not indict Karl Rove because there wasn't sufficient evidence," she says. "There simply wasn't enough there, so I think my role in it was insignificant in the end."

She was not prepared for what came next — a media onslaught led by liberal bloggers who felt that Novak had given Rove a "get out of jail free" pass. Rove critics blamed Novak for giving Rove's lawyer information that may have saved him from a perjury charge.

Jane Hamsher of FireDogLake charged that Novak was "a wine-soaked chatterbox" whose first loyalty was to herself.[27] Liberal blogger and media mogul Arianna Huffington opined that Novak had "blurted" out a confidence to source Luskin "like a drunken sailor."[28] In another post, Huffington even suggested that Novak's actions may have greased the wheels for Lenhard, Novak's spouse, whom Bush named a commissioner of the Federal Election Commission.[29] Lenhard's name was initially put forward in July 2003 by Senate Majority Leader Harry Reid (D-NV) to fill a Democratic slot at the FEC.[30] Attorney Rick Hasen, author of a widely read election law blog, challenged Huffington's assertion. He wrote that Lenhard had been considered for a spot at the FEC for 18 months, "long before anyone could have imagined such 'payback.' Huffington's allegation, he added, was "unfortunate and does not appear to be based on reality."[31]

"People who hate Karl Rove were very upset about this," Novak says. "It was kind of ironic to me because I had been as forceful as any other reporter in reporting things about the Bush Administration that needed to be brought to light. Nobody would ever have accused me of taking a fall for the Republicans before."

The experience of being a target of media coverage was eye-opening, she says. It gave her "a renewed appreciation" for what the subjects of news stories endure and "how many errors" and mischaracterizations get into stories. "So many people were writing about this without even calling me.

"The really vicious stuff obviously appeared in the blogs," she says, noting that "one way you get attention for a blog is to be really mean."

Woodward, who had kept secret crucial information about the Plame case for more than a year, got a mild reprimand from *The Post*. Executive Editor Leonard Downie said that Woodward "had made a mistake." Despite his concern about revealing his confidential sources, "we should have had the conversation,'" Downie said. But he added: "I'm concerned that people will get a misimpression about Bob's value to the newspaper and our readers because of this one instance in which he should have told us sooner."[32] Novak's bosses were not so forgiving. Managing editor James Kelly told *The Wall Street Journal* that when he learned of Novak's conduct, he reacted with "displeasure and astonishment."[33] He told *The New York Times* that "I'm taking this seriously. I'm upset and she's upset."[34]

With her editors' agreement, Novak took a leave of absence, something the editors characterized as voluntary. Five months later, Novak decided to leave the magazine. She left, she says, "when it became clear that I didn't have the support [at the magazine] I needed."

As she was mulling her future, Novak contacted longtime CNN journalist Brooks Jackson, who had left mainstream media to found FactCheck.org, which describes itself as "a nonpartisan, nonprofit 'consumer advocate' for voters that aims to reduce the level of deception and confusion in U.S. politics."[35]

"Brooks and I had both covered campaign finance," Novak says, and although she didn't know him well, she'd admired his work, as he did hers. She wanted advice, but Jackson told her he was looking for a deputy director and offered her the job. "At first I didn't know," Novak says. "This was an online-only thing." But she examined it, and thought about what had bothered her about the coverage of her own Plame moment — that often what was written was inaccurate or distorted, or that the reporters had failed to even contact her to get her side of the story. FactCheck does not verify media accounts, she hastens to add. But it is concerned with the accuracy of statements and claims made in the political arena. "It didn't take me long to realize I could have fun there."

One of the reasons FactCheck makes a difference, she says, is that not enough in-depth information is getting to the public. With reporters trying to update the news on a 24/7 basis, she says, it is very hard for mainstream journalists to do the research that could inform the news. FactCheck carries lengthy stories by Novak and others that carefully analyze political ads or statements by politicians, separating fact from fiction. The stories are non-partisan, detailed, and nuanced.

Novak says that she is happy that FactCheck does not evaluate the accuracy of media accounts. "For me, I'd think I'd have a conflict of interest because I know too many people and I like people [in the media] and I don't want to pull my punches to readers." But she also believes that the media's accuracy ought to be scrutinized in a nonpartisan way. "It absolutely needs to be done," she says.

FactCheck.org is a project of the Annenberg Public Policy Center at the University of Pennsylvania. In a cost-cutting move, FactCheck.org shut down its Washington office in 2011, and moved its entire operation to Philadelphia. Novak now is the editorial and communications director of the Center for Responsive Politics, a nonprofit, nonpartisan group that tracks money in U.S. politics and its influence on elections and policy decisions.

Chapter 9

Lady Justice

In her early 60s, Beverley Lumpkin remains striking and stylish, and well-coiffed. She can still turn heads when she enters a room. She has a broadcaster's clear enunciation with just a hint of the Richmond, Virginia, where she grew up, the eldest of seven.

If Lumpkin had been born a man, her life in journalism might have been quite different. But her career was forged during an era when women in the news business were struggling for respect and recognition. While some women, like Joan Connell, profiled earlier in this book, had the happy experience of being mentored by pioneering women editors, women journalists often faced many obstacles.

In 1972, the women of *The New York Times* wrote a thoroughly researched and respectful letter to the publisher and directors of the media company and complained about unequal pay, the lack of advancement, and job disparities at their newspaper. *The Times* had no female vice presidents, national correspondents, editorial board members, national columnists, or drama, film, or television reviewers.[1] The publisher listened, but nothing changed.[2] The women sued, the newspaper fought back, and the protracted litigation resulted in a back pay settlement that averaged out to less than $500 per woman.[3] The *Times* admitted no wrong, but did agree to an affirmative action plan to be monitored by the court.[4] But as late as 1987, men who started out as reporters at *The Times* during the previous five years earned $13,000 more than women who joined the paper during the same period.[5]

In 1984, more than a decade after the women of *The Times* first rose up, Lumpkin joined ABC News. Women also had wrung a settlement out of NBC,[6] but women in the news business still faced discrimination.

Lumpkin had a solid background in investigative work, having spent several years on the staffs of congressional investigative subcommittees. But it took years to be taken seriously at ABC. When she finally landed a permanent job at the network, she discovered that her job duties would not include the investigative work that the man she replaced had done.

In the mid–1980s, a group of women journalists met with ABC news executives[7] "just to bring to managers' attention how badly skewed all our coverage and assignments were," Lumpkin says. The people in charge, she says, were "stunned ... to hear that we had any issues." Women journalists at ABC had put together facts and figures that showed that women were being denied opportunities for advancement, and received less air time than men, and that women in the news division earned 40 percent less than men earned.[8]

"All of these white preppy boys living in their hilltop aeries in the canyons of Manhattan did not know how to hire black people, Latinos, women," Lumpkin says. "They knew how to talk to and hire the people they played squash with." She recalled the struggles of then–ABC News correspondent Carole Simpson to get more opportunities to do stories on poverty. "My God, the executive producers would just say, 'I don't want to hear this depressing stuff about poor people.'"

It's hard not to conclude that Lumpkin's gender had something to do with her career path at ABC. After all, Lumpkin was no green kid. Her life already had taken a few unexpected twists and turns. After her freshman year in college, she dropped out, eloped, and moved to England with her new husband, who was stationed with the Air Force there for three years. When she returned home to Richmond, she worked full time as a paralegal at a local law firm while her husband attended college. The Watergate scandal was in the news, and the *Washington Post* stories fascinated her. She also was learning more about Virginia's unpleasant past. Proofreading her firm's brief in a school segregation case made "the scales [fall] from my eyes," she says. "I had grown up in Richmond and had never much noticed that the schools were segregated or that the black kids a block away from my house didn't go to my school." Learning about the history of school segregation clarified her priorities, she says. "I wanted to make the world a better place."

Her marriage, which had been teetering, didn't last, and she moved to Washington in early 1976. Ultimately she landed a job in the investigations unit of the Federal Election Commission, and then, when that unit was essentially disbanded, she went to Capitol Hill with the House subcommittee investigating the Koreagate scandal. The 1976 scandal focused on attempts by Korean businessman Tongsun Park, with suspected links to the Korean Central Intelligence Agency, to bribe members of Congress, to promote U.S. policies favorable to South Korea.[9] There were a number of ongoing investigations, Lumpkin says, but her subcommittee, chaired by Rep. Donald Fraser,[10] was trying to understand why a U.S. ally had felt the need to bribe elected officials, and "buy influence" with cultural and religious leaders to foster a good relationship with the U.S. "It was one of those times in your life when you work 18-hour days seven days a week and everybody feels that they have a mission," she recalls.

When that inquiry was over, Lumpkin worked on other investigations and landed at the House Ethics Committee. But a new ethics chairman decided to replace all the committee investigators. Lumpkin got some work with a private investigative firm, where the staff used its research skills to help lawyers build their cases. "It wasn't the dirty laundry kind of investigating," she says. "I had a case where I filed Freedom of Information Act requests for our clients who were in the Midwest and didn't really know how to navigate Washington agencies." But the job ended with the 1982 recession.

At this point, Lumpkin was going to school part time to earn her degree and was out of work, collecting unemployment benefits. A House colleague, now working for the ABC news magazine *20/20*, asked her to help the show find the original Watergate grand jurors for a 10-year Watergate retrospective *20/20* was preparing. "Gordon, I don't do missing persons. That's not the kind of investigator I am," was her tart reply. But he reminded her she needed a job. Lumpkin signed a 10-day contract and found "about eight" of the original grand jurors.

Her colleague then asked her to help with a *20/20* investigation on pacemaker fraud. She worked for *20/20* for two years as a "temporary" full-time researcher. In 1984, she applied for a slot as off-air investigative reporter for ABC's Washington bureau, a job that had been filled by a man, Charles Lewis, who also is profiled in this book. As a green, untested 22-year-old, with no investigative experience, Lewis had talked his way into the investigative reporting position. Yet when she was moved into his slot, Lumpkin, a seasoned investigator and now a newly minted college graduate with a 4.0 grade point average, got a surprise.

When she asked the deputy bureau chief John Armstrong, who had hired her, exactly what she'd be doing, he suggested they wait until bureau chief Ed Fouhy returned from vacation.

The first day on her job, knowing that Fouhy was back, she asked for a meeting to discuss her job duties. His answer was, "Well if you don't know that, then maybe we've hired the wrong person."

"I thought that since I was taking Chuck Lewis's job, I was going to be the investigative off-air reporter for the Washington bureau," Lumpkin recalls. Instead, for a year or so into her tenure, Lumpkin was the girl from the network, spending hours in the driveways of newsmakers, waiting for them to emerge, so she could shout a question, and the cameras could get footage of them answering, 'No comment,' or driving away. "[ABC producer] Dean Norland thought he had a fresh new body to just throw out on the street to do stakeouts here, there and everywhere. I didn't get to do a whole lot of investigative stuff for quite some time."

When she did make some headway at the network, her advancement was a bit of a fluke. The media dubbed 1985 "the year of the spy," a period when the FBI made several high-profile arrests, including John Walker, Jr., a retired Navy warrant officer who recruited members of his family to pass on valuable secrets to the Soviets. In November 1985 alone, the FBI arrested CIA translator/intelligence officer Larry Wu-tai Chin, convicted of passing intelligence to China; Ronald Pelton, a National Security Agency communications specialist, convicted of selling secrets to the Soviets; and Navy civilian intelligence analyst Jonathan Jay Pollard, who pleaded guilty to passing along sensitive documents to Israel.[11]

Covering this espionage tsunami required more hands, and Lumpkin was ready. "They started out assigning me to do the reporting and legwork on a lot of those spy cases, and by early 1986, they had decided that was working out pretty well," Lumpkin says. ABC assigned Lumpkin to be the first off-air reporter on the Justice Department beat. She stayed on that beat for the next 17 years.

She loved the beat, but was frustrated by the limits of the job. Neither an on-air correspondent nor a producer, Lumpkin had little control over how her work was presented on television. The network denied her prime time on-camera work. "They decided I just didn't have 'it' whatever 'it' they were looking for," she says of her repeated attempts to become an on-air correspondent who could report stories for the prime-time news programs. (Even when ABC deemed a woman had the right stuff for on-camera reporting, network bosses still fussed over a female reporter's appearance. Former ABC correspondent Lynn Sherr recalls how ABC news head Roone Arledge sent a network vice president to tell her he didn't like the way she dressed.)[12]

"It was never so much that I wanted to see my face in lights, it's that I wanted to be attached to the reporting I was doing." Lumpkin says.

Lumpkin says it was frustrating trying to tutor and feed information to a steady stream of justice on-air correspondents, some of them kind and capable, but many "stupid and arrogant, who take the fruits of your own reporting, mangle it," and then claim all the credit.

Nevertheless, the justice assignment was one she prized and her growing expertise was recognized by her colleagues. "I was sort of the ABC presence on the Justice Department beat," she recalls. "People at ABC had very little understanding or knowledge or appreciation of what I was doing," she says, but her colleagues on the beat respected her expertise. Indeed, in 1997, *Washingtonian Magazine* called Justice Department reporters Lumpkin, Pete Williams of NBC, David Johnson of *The New York Times*, and Ron Ostrow of the *Los Angeles Times* "as good as they get."[13]

Lumpkin started writing a weekly memo about her beat, meant for consumption within the ABC news operation, and an outlet for all the reporting that did not make it on air. "My memos became increasingly chatty or gossipy, or detailed," she says, noting that she'd toss in "whatever was going on and what was coming up" in the department. When ABC started a website, her memo became a "column" posted on the Internet. She discovered that her "blog" was a must read among Justice Department watchers.

Her "electronic columns" took on big issues, such as racial disparities in death penalty cases.[14] They were long, chatty and detailed. They reveal that Lumpkin knew all the players, had access to a lot of sources within law enforcement, and understood the intricacies of the legal system. Whether she was plumbing the looming anxieties of justice officials before John Ashcroft took the reins as attorney general, or explaining an inspector general's report on the government's mishandling of Oklahoma bombing documents that most reporters had missed, Lumpkin's missives were both substantive and sassy. They also reveal her penchant for accuracy. As she noted in a column written in early 2001: "Please do not forget that, despite what the most elite journalists insist on repeating, President Clinton's final infamous clemency grants on Jan. 20 amounted to a total of 177, not 176. There were 141 pardons and 36 commutations. Do not accept less!"[15]

Lumpkin didn't care whether her network bosses and colleagues read it or liked it, what mattered to her was that "everybody on the beat read it." Having the web outlet for her work made her job much more fulfilling.

Whether it was in her memos, or broadcast reporting, Lumpkin felt she had a mission. "I thought it was very important to try and explain some of the very significant things the Justice Department was doing in a way that people could understand," she says. "It's not always easy to explain a complicated legal brief in 50 seconds, or what became 40 seconds or even 30 or 20 seconds, but I would still try to do it. I still thought it mattered that people knew."

Lumpkin also thought it was crucial to confirm the facts before reporting them. After the Oklahoma City bombing in 1995, there were some reports that the suspect had an Arabic last name. Lumpkin kept advising not to report that information. "The head of our investigative unit was pounding on me. He was screaming at me, he was cursing me. Over the phone lines, he was beating me black and blue. But I just kept saying, 'I don't think it's true, or I don't have it, or don't go with it.'" She stuck to her guns and her bosses in Washington later thanked her when Timothy McVeigh emerged as the bombing suspect.

Many of Lumpkin's colleagues were not as cautious. As Adonis Hoffman, a senior associate at the Carnegie Endowment for International Peace, observed shortly after the bombing:

Short shrift was given to the prospect of home-grown terrorists as network anchors and a coterie of experts relied inexorably on America's worst fears to suggest a menacing Arab threat to security in the heartland. As the country became immersed first in the details of the attack, and later in the speculation on who could do such a thing, it became clear that the expected, preferred, and the most likely perpetrators, would be "Islamic fundamentalists" or "radical Arab factions."[16]

The Oklahoma bombing wasn't the only story where reporters made assumptions because what they thought were the facts so aligned with their own world view. The story for which she received the most attention still rankles her because it was picked up by the wire services and misreported. Lumpkin broke the news that someone in the office of Attorney General John Ashcroft ordered blue drapes to cover the huge aluminum Statue of Lady Justice, known around the department as "Minnie Lou," in the agency's Great Hall. She couldn't confirm whether the orders came from Ashcroft directly, and whether he wanted the drapes because he was offended by Lady Justice's exposed breast.[17]

But when the story got picked up by the Associated Press, Lumpkin's nuanced account was thrown out. The AP credited ABC News for reporting that Ashcroft had ordered the drapes. Lumpkin said she spent three days working with network public affairs people to get AP to retract the story, but by then it had a life of its own. One of the reasons that the erroneous story took on a life of its own, Lumpkin says, was that it fit. "The idea that John Ashcroft — everybody thought that he was this blue nose, pompous, ultra-religious guy, the idea that he would order draperies around the statutes comported so perfectly with what people thought they knew, it was just too delicious not to go with that."

Lumpkin covered the Justice Department for nearly two decades, a reporter willing to immerse herself in the difficult details, such as the Foreign Intelligence Surveillance Act, or the FISA law. "For a while I was the only reporter that the justice guys would talk to [about FISA], because they thought I was the only reporter that understood what was going on," she recalls.

She now regrets the move she made in 2003. Weary of breaking in new on-air justice correspondents, and intrigued by the possibilities, Lumpkin took on a newly created beat, covering the Department of Homeland Security. Homeland Security was such a complicated agency, Lumpkin would be the "hub" for covering the new agency. It would be her responsibility to get the stories to the appropriate correspondent. "It sounded brilliant," Lumpkin says. "The problem was nobody in New York ever bought into it."

For two years, Lumpkin worked the beat. She either poured a lot of energy and reporting into stories that never were put on the air, or wound up doing nothing. "I pushed and pushed to do different stories, but the only thing anybody cared about was whether the color code [signifying the threat level] was yellow or green or orange."

Nevertheless, when she was informed in 2005 that she would be laid off, she was shocked. The reason for the layoffs, she was told, was that Washington was cutting its budget and eliminating all the off-air reporters. But Lumpkin feels that some other factors were at work. The only off-air reporters who were laid off at that time were older women. (Lumpkin was then 54.) The year before, another older woman, a producer, was laid off. "They basically got rid of the old girls," she says. She hired a lawyer to get her the best severance benefits possible, but opted not to sue the network, even though she believes she was the victim of sex and age discrimination. "I didn't want to spend the next 10 years of my life in court." She observes that off-air reporters "on all these beats" continue to work for ABC, "but they're younger guys. At the time [she was laid off] I'm sure they were cheaper."

After she was laid off from ABC, Lumpkin again was saved for a time by a Washington scandal, this time the Valerie Plame leak, and the investigation into whether someone in the Bush Administration had revealed the identity of CIA officer Valerie Plame to the media in an attempt to discredit her husband, former ambassador Joseph C. Wilson IV. Wilson had publicly accused the administration of manipulating evidence to make its case for waging war in Iraq.[18] Laid off in July 2005, Lumpkin took a job with CBS in October of that year, helping out with the investigation of I. Lewis "Scooter" Libby, who was convicted of lying about his role in leaking Plame's CIA connection to the media. "Within relative nanoseconds of saying Beverley Lumpkin, ABC News, I was saying Beverley Lumpkin, CBS News," she says.

While she enjoyed the work, it was part-time and lacked health benefits. She took a job as a reporter with the Associated Press. From the start, she says, the AP staff "were just highly skeptical that anyone who came from television could ever measure up." Her brief tenure with the AP, she says, constituted "the worst six months of my entire working life."

The editor who supervised her and edited her copy convinced her that she could neither write nor report. "There was no story I could write that he would not eviscerate. There was no lede [first sentence] that I wrote that he didn't completely maul." Her confidence in shreds, she would spend time with writing coaches, and friends, asking for help. "Look at this, I want to succeed, help me do this," she would ask them. "And they would help me, and I would write something crisp and clear and short. And my editor would take it and he would put in everything but the kitchen sink into the lede and make it sink like a safe. There was nothing I could do that worked."

The editor who supervised her work was demoted, but that didn't change the AP's view of her. She was told that in a month's time, her tenure at the wire service would be over. The last month, she reported to a different editor. "Suddenly, everything I was writing was okay. Suddenly, it didn't need to be rewritten or revamped or anything else. But it was too late," she says, the emotion in her voice still raw.

After more than 20 years as a journalist, Lumpkin was devastated, fearing that her entire career had been a sham.

> If you're even a semi-responsible reporter, you're always feeling guilty. You're always feeling I should have made just one more call, I should have asked just one more question, I should have revised just one more paragraph. It's very easy to make a decent reporter feel insecure and guilty. We always feel we can or should have done better. The most manipulative and evil bosses know that and take advantage of that whether it's television, or the wire, or anywhere else.

Lumpkin worked at AP from November 2006 until May 2007. She spent the "darkest ever" summer job hunting. Fresh from the trauma of her AP experience, she recalled her 23-year tenure at ABC and the fact that she'd never been able to move up the ladder to become either an on-air correspondent or producer, and all the frustrations that came with the job. She acknowledged the pervasive notion that the network brass in New York always felt that they understood the news better than the reporters in Washington. She also realized that "the people who get ahead in television are single-minded and totally focused, and I would say even ruthlessly ambitious." She wasn't cut from that cloth, she says. "You never get ahead if you're a waffler." Nor was she good at ingratiating herself with upper management.

At this point, she decided that she needed to revise her goals. She said to herself, "Journalism is just not working for me. I think I felt very much that I'd been voted off the journalism island."

So she tried to return to the investigative work she'd done on Capitol Hill. Her hill contacts suggested she consider working for the Project on Government Oversight (POGO), a small nonprofit in Washington known for its hard-hitting investigations into corruption, misconduct and conflicts of interest in the federal government.

"The money was stunningly low," Lumpkin says with a laugh. But as an investigator for POGO, she finally got the time to dig deep into an issue and to write lengthy, meaty reports. She also, for the first time, got to express an opinion about her findings. That took some getting used to, she says. But ultimately, she found it "tremendously exhilarating. I used to laugh and say, 'I've kept my opinions to myself for 30 years and now they're all just bursting forth.'"

She also basked in the humanity of the POGO culture. "They bound up my wounds and applied the healing salve and told me how fabulous I was and everything I did was wonderful," she says of POGO executive director Danielle Brian and director of operations Keith Rutter.

Nevertheless, it was hard to give up her hard-news instincts. "Events would happen and there would be a part of my brain that would automatically want to reach for the phone and start making calls. I had no one to report for, no one to report to."

Lumpkin learned that the nonprofit world allows people weekends and nights off. She also gained some insights about journalism. "I did learn to be a spokeswoman for POGO on different matters," making sure that whatever she said was phrased correctly. She would become angry or disheartened when reporters misquoted or misunderstood her. And she was very surprised that reporters would ask her small nonprofit "to do their research for them."

Still, Lumpkin never lost her attraction to the Justice Department. She'd maintained contacts with justice officials. When the Obama Administration came into power in 2009, and after Eric Holder was confirmed as attorney general, she was offered a job in its communications shop. "I said often that these halls are in my DNA," she says. "I have so much love and respect for the institution and for the career people." The Bush years, she says, damaged the institution, and she wanted to be part of the team that would restore the department to the "rule of law."

Lumpkin beams as she gives a tour of the Justice Department "Great Hall" and passes the massive art deco statues, now uncovered, depicting the Spirit of Justice and the Majesty of the Law. Pointing to the murals of Hammurabi and Moses, Lumpkin observes that law-giving "goes all the way back in our Western culture."

It is clear that the law continues to be her passion, and that she continues to believe that getting information to the public about their government is crucial to democracy. Although Lumpkin often finds that as a justice spokesperson, she must be guarded in what she says, she tries "as hard as I can" to avoid giving a routine 'no comment." She always offers to give reporters a Justice Department brief. "Granted I'm saying this to people who are in a hurry or they're writing a damn blog and they only want a 20-second sound bite. I still think it's important to get the word out. I'm Sisyphus. I'm just going to keep pushing that brief up the hill."

When she was a young girl, Lumpkin told her father, a lawyer, that she wanted to be a lawyer when she grew up. He told her, "Beverley, you don't want to be a lady lawyer. Lady lawyers just end up in some drab government office." Lumpkin laughs. "I ended up in drab government offices even without being a lawyer."

Lumpkin remains at the Justice Department. Some of her recent special projects have included assisting with the department's implementation of the administration's Open Government Initiative, and of the Plain Language Act, passed in 2010, that requires all government documents to be written in plain English.

Chapter 10

From *Times* Man to Roadmonkey

Looking for a novel way to jump-start his journalism career, Paul von Zielbauer took a 1,200-mile bike trip through Vietnam and wrote about it. His gamble paid off, ultimately propelling him to *The New York Times*. Nearly a decade later, when he was looking for a way out of *The Times*, it was another trip to Vietnam that gave him his exit strategy.

Von Zielbauer is tall, rangy and muscular, with a shock of dark wavy hair and high cheekbones. He looks more like a graduate student than a veteran *Times* reporter in his early forties. He tells his story in his cluttered apartment at the end of a commercial block in Brooklyn. Growing hungry a couple of hours into the interview, he takes a break to make himself a peanut butter-and-jelly sandwich.

Disillusion was the last thing he expected when he finally made it to *The Times* in 1999. As giddy as a new bridegroom, von Zielbauer went to *The Times* eager to do anything his editors asked. "I felt like I'd been granted access to this legendary place you heard about, and wasn't quite sure it existed. I was now part of this relatively small group of reporters who made it to this paper of record.... It just felt like I'd been admitted to this club that I thought I'd never be admitted to. And I'd pick up the phone and say, 'I'm Paul from *The New York Times*.' What a thrill that was."

With time, that feeling changed. Von Zielbauer makes clear that he cherishes the time he spent at *The Times*, the friendships he made, and the journalism opportunities it offered. Nevertheless, he does not regret leaving. A self-described "regular guy," he was working at the newspaper of the intellectual elite. A Midwesterner and an alumnus of a state college, he did not feel comfortable in the paper's East Coast-centric, prep school environment. He had an independent streak, and chafed at the paper's editor-driven culture. His refusal to curry favor and navigate office politics deprived him of mentors. He wasn't good at jockeying for front-page attention to his work, a way to gain the notice of the top editors. And unlike most reporters, he did not like covering politics.

The Times gave him some opportunities to shine — a posting in Iraq, permission to spend more than a year to investigate the scandal of for-profit health care at New York prisons, a stint covering military trials of soldiers accused of war crimes. But in the pecking order that governs major metropolitan dailies, von Zielbauer feared he would be relegated to the B team.

As in many failed marriages, the early years were good, but with a foretaste of harder times to come. He recalls his first months at the paper "walking on six inches of air" because he was so happy just to be there. Even then, however, he noticed people in the hallways who were clearly unhappy. "You could just tell, it radiated off them. Their misery and lack of joy." It was only later that Zielbauer realized these were journalists who had reached the pinnacle of their profession, but felt trapped. No longer energized or fulfilled by their work, they were unwilling to leave. He recalled that former executive editor Howell Raines had called the paper a "destination employer," and he came to understand why. "People come here basically to work until they're dead," von Zielbauer says.

Von Zielbauer's initiation into journalism had been as circuitous as his ascent to *The Times*. He is the son of ethnic Germans — his father's family is from Hungary and his mother was born in Bavaria — who had left Eastern Europe after World War II, "booted out" by the Russians, he says. His parents came to the U.S. in the mid-1950s as youngsters, and their families ended up in Illinois. He grew up in Aurora, Illinois, and attended Iowa State. His father, who earned a degree from a technical college, was a draftsman who spent most of his career working at the Department of Energy's Fermilab outside Chicago. His mother was a housewife until his parents divorced, when she became a process server in some of the "shittiest parts" of Aurora. As a boy, he dreamed of becoming a professional soccer player. He still loves soccer, but doesn't play because of "multiple surgeries on my left knee." In college, his first major was aeronautical engineering, but he lasted a semester, vanquished by organic chemistry class. So he switched to writing, something he knew he did well. But his true awakening didn't happen until after college, when he and his friend Phil backpacked through Europe. "There's a world out there that doesn't think the way we do, that doesn't drink the same drinks and eat the same food, and believe in the same ways of life."

The trip over and his funds exhausted, von Zielbauer returned home and got work as a technical writer with the consulting arm of Arthur Andersen, then a big five accounting firm. The corporate atmosphere was constricting. "Wearing a tie literally felt like it was choking me," he says. His goal was to save enough money to make his getaway. Two years into the job, with a $4,000 kitty, he was ready.

When he tells this part of his story, he seems to be channeling Jack Kerouac.

> I was only 23 or 24 at the time and filling up journals like crazy. I was writing poetry. I was reading *On the Road* and Henry Miller, Hemingway.... My stepfather gave me a 1983 Jeep Wagoneer with wood paneling on the side that had 180,000 miles on it and I put all my stuff in there, including my bass and my amp and my futon ... and I drove West.... I didn't have a plan, didn't have a guidebook.... I was just sort of out there on my own. I ended up taking most of what you might call the blue highways, the back roads ... got through Texas, Kansas, Oklahoma, ended up in New Mexico and then into the Baja Peninsula in Mexico. Camped on the beach, got a little bored.

He ended up living with Phil, who had settled in Los Angeles, sharing "his crappy $300-a-month studio in this shaky little apartment complex at Franklin and La Brea in Hollywood." His friend had a production job in the film industry, and for a time von Zielbauer supported himself by waiting tables, and analyzing scripts for small production companies. It was not the place he wanted to be. "I didn't like Hollywood. All the palm trees looked sad and polluted and stressed."

After about six months, he made his way to Chicago, hoping to resume a relationship with a girlfriend. The relationship didn't work out, and von Zielbauer found himself without a viable resume. He waited tables, but for a time couldn't find any work. He applied for technical writing positions that he really didn't want, in search of a tolerable steady job with a reliable paycheck. "I went through this brief but powerful humiliation of buying groceries with food stamps," he recalls. "A 24-year-old, able-bodied white guy in America." He felt ashamed for needing the help.

His professional Sahara ended when he started freelancing for *Windy City Sports Magazine*. Rollerblading was in vogue in the early 1990s, and the editors were elated when he produced a thorough feature story comparing various inline skates.

With the help of his *Windy City* editors, he branched out into freelancing for Chicago area suburban weeklies. Hustling to earn a living, von Zielbauer concluded that he probably was not going to become an award-winning poet or short story writer but that he could make a go of being a journalist. When his stack of freelance clips was high enough, he took them to the now defunct but legendary City News Bureau, which served as a wire service for both Chicago dailies, the *Chicago Sun-Times* and the *Chicago* Tribune.[1]

Its alumni included investigative reporter Seymour Hersh, columnist Mike Royko and playwright Ben Hecht, who wrote *The Front Page*.[2] The newspapers relied on City News to cover anything that was missed overnight in the courts, on the police beat, and at city hall. He was hired at $16,000 a year.

Legendary for its motto, "If your mother tells you she loves you, check it out,"[3] City News exposed von Zielbauer to the nuts and bolts of news writing. Working the night shifts, he'd cover cops and prowl the morgue looking for any interesting unclaimed corpses. "If it's a kid, that's a story."

With a year of City News under his belt, von Zielbauer assessed his professional prospects and concluded that he was "behind schedule" and would never catch up if he wanted to make it to the big leagues in journalism. He needed to do something to "shake up" his resume, he concluded. A way opened when his car collided with a cab, and he received a $1,200 settlement. Instead of spending the money on repairs, he bought a ticket to Vietnam. Although the country had been open to tourism since 1989, von Zielbauer knew that to most Americans, it remained a mystery. He also found that the editors he contacted about freelancing from Vietnam were white males who had come of age during the Vietnam War. His premise for the story — going back to Vietnam with a bike, not a gun — appealed to them.

He lined up interest from *Crain's Chicago Business*, the Asian edition of *The Wall Street Journal* and *Men's Fitness Magazine*. Kodak gave him 100 rolls of film, and he found a photographer willing to work for free in the hope that publications would buy his pictures.

Leaving his mother "blubbering at the gate" at O'Hare, he flew to Hanoi, overwhelmed by his first experience in Southeast Asia. "The smell of the mold and mildew on the buildings was so exotic and thrilling and also intimidating." Very few Vietnamese spoke English, particularly in the North. Travel was so new that even *Lonely Planet* was sparse on information for much of the solo trek he was making, cycling from Hanoi to Saigon, formerly the capital of South Vietnam, renamed Ho Chi Minh City after the North Vietnamese routed U.S. forces in 1975.[4]

In Hanoi, he was amazed by the silence of a city where cars remained a rarity. He then headed east to Haiphong, ultimately ending up in Ho Chi Minh City in January 1994. It was a grueling, 1,200-mile, five-month trip. He found himself battling both monsoon rains and loneliness, riding miles through a country where few spoke English, and many stared at this tall, non–Asian cyclist.

Recalling the trek in a 2010 blog post, he wrote that he had fancied himself "a rugged young writer in search of his first foreign dateline." But elation soon gave way to anxiety He wrote: "Sunburned, exhausted and running out of money somewhere between Hanoi and Hai Phong, I had a thought that sank in deeper with every lonely turn of my pedals: I'm no world traveler, but rather a naive imposter; I should have acquiesced to a boring desk job in Chicago, married a pretty Midwestern girl, produced ruddy-cheeked kids and kept things simple."[5] Nevertheless, he persisted and completed the journey. *Crain's* and *The Wall Street Journal* were happy with his pieces. Reuters ran a picture of him cycling into Ho Chi Minh City that made it into the Chicago papers. To commemorate what he'd been through, he got a tattoo. He forked over $2, his rain poncho and a couple of tee-shirts, and a Vietnamese tattoo artist, using only a pushpin, etched Paul's vision of a road-monkey on his left forearm. He had blurted out the word to Phil when they were trekking through Europe. "It was just a funny word that sort of meant something like not giving up your freedom too easily," von Zielbauer says. The tattoo, he says, was there to remind him that if he could do the Vietnam trip, he could take on a lot of other challenges.

When his plane landed in Los Angeles, von Zielbauer opted to stay there for a time and recharge his professional career. He got lucky at the *Orange County Register*. The paper had just lost its reporter who covered the Vietnamese community. Van Zielbauer claimed to be fluent in Vietnamese. On that and the strength of his clips, the *Register* hired him at $40,000 a year. He was elated by the prospect of a daily newspaper gig and a real salary.

He covered two communities, Westminster and Garden Grove, with large Vietnamese populations. He hired a tutor to learn more Vietnamese, and his eagerness as a non–Asian to speak their language earned him a lot of points with the community. But after a year at the *Register*, he was restless. He found that Vietnamese sentiments in Orange County about their former country mirrored the hostility that Cuban exiles in Miami feel about the Castro regime. "Anybody who goes back to the Old Country is a traitor." Every time a Vietnamese doctor decided to return to Vietnam to give free medical care to the people there, there were protests in Little Saigon, he says. "The politics got old."

Also, he was beginning to feel that he needed much more formal training in journalism. Even the basics of journalism ethics eluded him. He recalled telling a colleague that he was going to an interview and planned to ask his subject for free tickets to some event. She was shocked. She told him, "You can't do that!" He extricated himself by claiming to be kidding, but he was thinking, "Why not? I guess I don't understand that.

"I had regretted going to Iowa State instead of a better school. I could have gone to a better one, but my family wasn't real sophisticated" about college he says. To them the process was about "just getting into whatever school you could get into and figuring a way to pay for it. So I just felt undereducated." If you're going to learn journalism, he concluded, the best city to do it in was New York and the best school was the Graduate School of Journalism at Columbia University. West Coast journalism, he says, "was sort of soft, just kind of surf on weekends and get back to your job." But on the East Coast, he says, the reporting is harder, more intense, sharper. "Tough but fair and absolutely to the mat."

He got in, and graduated in May 1996, successfully landing a Fulbright Scholarship on the way. With Germany poised to relax requirements that based the right of citizenship largely on blood ties to Germans, he proposed to study the changing nature of citizenship in that nation.[6]

Von Zielbauer spent 15 months in Europe, not working on his Fulbright proposal. "The Fulbrights are great because there's no deliverable," he says. He spent much of his time becoming fluent in German, traveling and looking for opportunities to freelance. He did some feature pieces for *Newsday,* one on scientology in Germany, another on a controversy over preserving the remains of a Jewish ghetto discovered in Bavaria. And then, at the end of 1996, Slobodan Milosevic tampered with the results of municipal elections in Serbia, prompting massive protests. Only a few years earlier, Milosevic had helped arouse Serbian nationalism that resulted in ethnic cleansing and civil wars throughout Yugoslavia, driving an estimated 800,000 Muslims and Croatians from their homes in Bosnia.[7]

Newsday correspondent Roy Gutman did his ground-breaking reporting on Serbian atrocities during the Balkan wars.[8] It won him a Pulitzer, but also a lot of Serbian resentment. Now the Serbs wouldn't let Gutman back into the country. So von Zielbauer became *Newsday's* point person for the crisis. Using his Fulbright credentials, he was able to get access to the country, claiming he wanted to study Serbian language and culture. He took a train through Czechoslovakia, Hungary, and Austria, and after traveling for 24 hours, ended up in Belgrade. He hung out with Belgrade university students, and wrote about young people outraged about a stolen election who had managed to "get the miners out of the mines and into the streets, and the soccer thugs out of the stadiums, all protesting the government." They were "smart young people who were angry at having their vote stolen engineering all this."

It's clear that his reporting has the mark of someone young enough to be trusted by students, describing the "thick sludge known as Baltic coffee" that keeps the students awake, along with "lots of cigarettes." He describes an organized operation where the psychology students were dispatched to handle propaganda, the archeology majors were doing a newspaper, and the philosophy majors, in army jackets, boots, and knit caps, took over the security detail.[9]

But his coverage challenged the views of *New York Times* correspondent Chris Hedges. Hedges identified "virulent Serb nationalism" as the primary motivation for the student protesters.[10] After *The Times* piece was published, MSN.com, Microsoft's Internet news portal, pulled von Zielbauer's piece because it reflected a different point of view. "I was offended that my story, which was accurate, was basically spiked because some guy with an agenda who happens to work for *The New York Times* was writing falsities. It was offensive to me." (Von Zielbauer was not the only journalist who challenged Hedges on his conclusions about the Serbian students. When they discussed the protests during an online forum sponsored by PBS *NewsHour*, both *Time Magazine's* Central Europe correspondent and a reporter from Serbia's oldest independent magazine disagreed with Hedges about the role of rabid nationalism in the protests.)[11]

When the Fulbright ended, von Zielbauer once again found himself in a familiar predicament. After a new adventure and more clips under his belt, he had to find a job. He moved back to New York, to him the center of the media universe, with hopes of working for *Newsday*. "If you think in terms of a Tolkienesque kind of journey, you're getting close to the place where the ring is."

But *Newsday* wasn't interested. Von Zielbauer turned to his mentor, Columbia Professor Samuel Freedman, who'd been impressed by von Zielbauer's graduate thesis on the rise of alternative comedy in New York City. Freedman called Rex Smith, a former *Newsday* reporter who was editor of the *Albany Times Union*. Smith offered him a job. Assured by his mentor that Albany, the state capital, was in the "orbit" of New York City newspapers, von Zielbauer went upstate, covering transportation and the environment. The transportation beat was a bit of a slog, he says. But he enjoyed writing about the environment at a time when there was both concern and controversy over PCBs in the Hudson River. For decades, until PCBs (polychlorinated biphenyls) were banned in 1976, General Electric Co. had discharged more than a million pounds of the chemical into the Hudson River. But GE questioned whether PCBs were even harmful, state officials had cancelled funds for environmental work in the river, and there were delays in a massive cleanup plan to remove PCBs from Hudson sediment.[12] In the 1990s, many scientists and environmentalists raised concerns about PCB links to cancer, but there was no definitive evidence that PCBs caused cancer in humans.[13] (In 1999, months after von Zielbauer left, the EPA released a report that warned of significantly higher cancer risks from eating fish caught in the Hudson River near Albany.)[14]

George Pataki was governor then, and he had pledged to clean up the Hudson. But he also was an upstate Republican, who didn't want to be perceived as anti-business. While at the *Times Union*, von Zielbauer wrote about state agencies that failed to inform the public about toxic chemicals from manufacturing operations in New York. "I did a few investigative pieces that totally pissed off the Pataki administration and the State Department of Environmental Conservation," he says.

But von Zielbauer was getting impatient. He remembers sitting at his desk, feeling that he'd wasted $30,000 on tuition for Columbia, and that his "gamble" to get to the big leagues had failed. He wondered what his next move would be. To Newark, Milwaukee? "This is not what I had in mind for myself. The whole arc of my career was one in which I envisioned moving forward, not taking lateral moves to slightly larger papers."

But Freedman had not forgotten him. Eventually, he got the call he was waiting for. Joyce Purnick, then metro editor of *The New York Times*, was interested in chatting with him. His initial meeting with Purnick led to a day-long session and several interviews with *Times* editors. By December of 1998, just 15 months after starting at the *Times Union*, he had a job offer. "I started on January 4, 1999, as a metro reporter. I was 32 years old and just totally psyched. I had gotten to the promised land."

Von Zielbauer was hired as an intermediate reporter, one step away from a full-time staff position at the paper. That's a transition that often takes up to three years, but he accomplished it in a record 11 months. In his zeal to get to permanent status, he says, he jettisoned all personal relationships and threw himself into the job.

The honeymoon lasted several years. Working as a general assignment reporter first in New York, then in New Jersey and then Westchester County, he went on to serve as bureau chief in Connecticut. While he found covering the state house boring, he took pride in finding unusual aspects of the state that made good feature stories. (Von Zielbauer found the political aspect of the beat boring at a time when so many political scandals involving the governor and mayors of the state's major cities broke out that it earned the nickname "Corrupticut.")[15]

By 2003, he was assigned to cover prisons, and on that beat he was able to write what he terms his "tour de force," a four-part series on privatized prison health care. "That was *The Times* at its finest, before the cutbacks and the concerns about money and revenue really became acute," he recalls, noting that he spent "more than a year just reporting that story." Von Zielbauer investigated Prison Health Services, a for-profit Tennessee firm that offered low-cost privatized health care to jails throughout upstate New York and the rest of the country. It was the nation's largest provider of jail and prison medical care, and left a trail of abuses in its wake.

The year spent digging was an anxious one. Von Zielbauer says he felt like filmmaker Francis Ford Coppola during the making of *Apocalypse Now,* who felt sure the film would be a disaster and doom his career in Hollywood. "And I kept saying to myself, 'Well, if this story turns out to be terrible, I'll have to quit. I can't do this.'" As it turned out, his fears were misplaced. He wrote a searing series of stories documenting Prison Health Service's callous disregard for the prisoners in its care, many of them in jail awaiting trial for petty offenses. He made the lives of prisoners, the least visible segment of the population, real. Saying that he agreed with the long-held reporters' credo that the role of journalism was to "comfort the afflicted and afflict the comfortable," he had no qualms about assigning blame. This is how he began the series:

> Brian Tetrault was 44 when he was led into a dim county jail cell in upstate New York in 2001, charged with taking some skis and other items from his ex-wife's home. A former nuclear scientist who had struggled with Parkinson's disease, he began to die almost immediately, and state investigators would later discover why: the jail's medical director had cut all but of a few of the 32 pills he needed each day to quell his tremors.[16]

The series was published in 2005. In an editorial, *The Times* called the series "harrowing"[17] and nominated it for a public service Pulitzer. But being immersed in one series for so many months also was a little unsettling. People begin to wonder whether you still work at the paper, he says. And trying to resume regular reporting when you return offers its own challenges. He felt something akin to postpartum depression, he says. "I just can't cover prisons and jails again," he thought. "It's boring. I don't want to do anything."

At that juncture, he volunteered to go to Iraq for the paper. Like soldiers, reporters covering the Iraq conflict could only do it for so long, so papers had to find new recruits to fill their ranks. In March 2006, von Zielbauer, single and childless, was one of five *Times* reporters to volunteer for Iraq duty. The summer of 2006 marked the height of the insurgency, he recalls. "It was a very bloody time and I had no compunction about going."

"It can feel almost routine to read stories about Iraq in the paper," von Zielbauer told the *New York Observer*. "But it occurs to me that there is no more important story in the world right now. We all have questions about what Baghdad feels, smells and sounds like. I want to know that."[18]

But the reality of reporting on the Iraq War was far more mundane. "You're not covering battles. You're covering the Green Zone, from Baghdad," he says. His days were full of interviews and following up on reports of battles, covering the process of the war. Reporters kept to their rooms, close to their computers, so they could update their stories several times each day. "Maybe there's two people in the bureau, maybe there's four, but everyone's under the gun, so no one's really chatty." It was a lonely existence, he says. "You're basically in a sensory isolation tank."

After his posting in Iraq, he covered military justice for *The Times*, traveling to bases to cover war crime trials. He liked being around the military, he says, noting that all the things that made it difficult for him to fit in at *The Times*—his Midwestern background, his ability to be blunt spoken and a "regular guy"—helped him relate to soldiers.

He still smarts at *The Times*' decision to downplay one story he thought deserved much greater attention. When soldiers began to be charged with war crimes, their relatives used the Internet to tap into a groundswell of support. "They were raising money for their sons' defenses and people unrelated to them were coming out of the woodwork to give money to these online funds," he says. He wrote it as a trend story, and the Washington Bureau recommended it be given front-page treatment, he says. But editors in New York thought the movement was too small, despite the fact that his story reported that more than a dozen Web sites supporting the accused soldiers had raised more than $600,000, mostly in small donations.[19]

Not long after, however, *The Times* ran a front-page story about "a very small group" of parents with children in Iraq who had turned against the war, he says. His story was downplayed, he is convinced, "because it was politically to the right of where this editor or the paper is."

The experience gave him another insight into how people got ahead at *The Times*, and what he'd have to do to succeed at the paper. Looking around him, he noticed that other young reporters were being helped up the ladder by mentors, something that wasn't happening to him. He didn't begrudge them their success, but concluded that he was not being groomed to be one of the paper's stars. "I'm not 'most favored reporter' status. Not necessarily disfavored, I'm sort of in the middle."

"You are a guy who plays by his own rules," one editor told him. "I thought to myself, 'I am? Is that the image I have here? Is that my reputation?' She didn't mean it in a bad way," he adds. But he concedes that sometimes he "wasn't with the program," and that he found it difficult to put his passion into stories he did not find compelling. "In a place as political and as super-charged as *The Times*, that probably didn't work for me."

Von Zielbauer says he wasn't into seeking out mentors, finding out what he had to do to succeed at *The Times*. He also wasn't big on figuring out how to get stories that would put him on the front page. "I just wanted to write cool stories that I liked doing," he says. "I didn't want to manipulate that process in order to maximize the return I got. I just kind of wanted people to recognize whatever talent they thought I had or not and respond to that."

Von Zielbauer found an architectural analog for his discontent. In 2007, *The Times* moved out of its location on East 43rd Street, where it had operated for more than 90 years, and into a 52-story office tower on Eighth Avenue designed by Renzo Piano. Many *Times* reporters were glad to move to new digs, but not von Zielbauer. "I liked the fact that everyone was jammed together, that there were papers stacked on papers. It felt like a newsroom." The new building looks splendid on the outside, but from the inside, it looks like an engineering firm, he says. "The desks all faced the same way, no one is looking at each other." It reminded him of an early twentieth century factory sweatshop, he says. All you heard as you walked through the "too big" newsroom were the clicks of computer keys, the warble of phones and the murmur of the heating and cooling system. "That to me is a soul-killing way to run a newspaper."

Even *The Times* own architecture critic, who wrote a glowing review of his new home, conceded that the tower conveyed a "slight whiff of melancholy."[20] Paul Goldberger, then architecture critic for *The New Yorker*, called the new newsroom "a kind of dulled-down, slowed-down, big open space that loses the energy of the old newsroom, but doesn't join it to anything else." The building expressed the news media's lack of a "clear idea" about the future of journalism. "The strange, quiet elegant dullness of that newsroom does seem to me to embody the deer in the headlights," Goldberger said.[21]

Von Zielbauer remembers lunch with a *Times* colleague, and each of them lamenting that newspapering had lost its allure. "Updating a story four times a day for the web, I never got into it," von Zielbauer says. "You didn't get to go into as much depth." Nevertheless, he would have stayed if his editors had honored his request to cover the environment for the paper's metro desk. He would have stayed if he had been able to work at any of the paper's foreign bureaus, in part because of his love of travel and adventure, but also because of the autonomy the job brings. "You're the expert on the story when you're a foreign correspondent," he says. "That's exactly the opposite dynamic ... when your metro editor also lives in New York and thinks ... that he or she knows better what the story is." When an editor is so deeply involved, he says, that relegates the reporter to "widget maker."

Despite his discontent, leaving *The Times* was not an easy choice. He grieved for about six months, he says. "It made me sad to realize that this career that I had worked so hard to achieve is going to end, and end with a denouement of complete uncertainty."

But as he was agonizing over his break with *The Times*, he was toying with the idea of starting his own business. He knew he loved and came alive when exploring new places and traveling. He wanted to share the experience with others in a unique way, and he wanted to find a way for people to combine travel with philanthropy, engaged in short-term projects that did not aspire to dramatically changing people's lives, but that did make tangible improvements in them.

His psychological break with *The Times* came during the summer of 2008, when he returned to Vietnam to scope out the first trip for an adventure-philanthropy business he intended to christen Roadmonkey. "I was committing $1,500 to this idea, going on a work vacation for something that didn't even exist yet," he says. The realization that he was willing to invest so much into his idea was his "holy cow" moment, he says. He knew he must believe in what he was doing. By July 2008, he'd spent $1,000 on a website and had "essentially stopped being any kind of a productive *New York Times* employee."

He was not working under the radar. He let his bosses know what he was doing, and showed his website to Craig Whitney, then *The Times* standards editor. Whitney's only quibble was von Zielbauer's multiple references to himself as a *New York Times* reporter. Von Zielbauer refused to scale back, understanding that his *Times* experience was part of his brand.

But leaving was not easy. The son of twice-divorced parents, von Zielbaurer compared the break with the paper to a divorce. "You don't believe it's quite happening" and there is a mourning period.

Over time, von Zielbauer did develop with more and more certainty a plan for his future, and a clear concept of what Roadmonkey could be. What would make Roadmonkey different was what made him different, his background as a journalist. He would offer his clients an experience they couldn't get elsewhere, the experience of being a foreign correspondent, parachuting into an exotic place, mastering a culture quickly, and learning to live by their wits, ready to change schedules and adapt to new circumstances. "What do foreign correspondents do? They go into places, like I was doing in Serbia. You get there, it's 8 A.M., you don't speak Serbian, you have no fixer, there's this newsworthy event.... You observe, you see which way the wind is blowing, you perceive who's important, you follow your gut instinct." That's the selling point for Roadmonkey, he says. "Travel with me and you learn how to travel like a foreign correspondent."

But the trips are far more challenging than playing out fantasies, they test emotional and physical limits, and require more than a token commitment to the philanthropic aspect of each expedition. Roadmonkey clients tap into their own networks to help raise funds for each project raising the needed resources for each trip.[22]

Von Zielbauer seeks out nonprofits with good track records and a history of accountability and transparency that are based in the area where he's planning an expedition. With the guidance of non-profits in the field, volunteers on Roadmonkey treks take on projects—like building playgrounds—that are doable in less than a week. "There's real happiness to be gained in giving up a part of yourself to someone who needs your help," he says.

Von Zielbauer uses his reporter's instincts to screen those who inquire about Roadmonkey expeditions. The potential consumers of his services must be a hardy lot. On his website, he describes a Roadmonkey as a "curious individual who seeks the unknown often, breaks rules if necessary, tests limits whenever possible and works hard to improve the lives of people in need."

Those who care about their comfort and strict schedules and dislike mud

won't make good Roadmonkeys, he says. But for those who want to be challenged, and to experience a country and culture more authentically, the expeditions can be life-changing. Von Zielbauer feels that each expedition has
changed him as well. He's become more outgoing, more willing to engage
and encourage, becoming a "nicer guy, a little bit more accessible" and more
aware of others' needs.

In November 2008, he used five weeks of vacation to organize and lead
his first Roadmonkey trip, an eight-day cycling trek through northwest Vietnam, and four days of volunteering, building an orphanage for HIV-infected
orphans living near Hanoi.

In his blogs for this and other trips, von Zielbauer's writing takes on a
vitality and energy sometimes missing from his news stories. Settling into
the Hoa Binh Palace Hotel on his Vietnam expedition, he writes:

> After a year and a half of exposure to presidential campaign articles, ads, attacks,
> controversies, bloviations, exaggerations, contradictions, meltdowns, parodies,
> histrionics, hyperbole, lies, spin, spam and what can only be described as the
> American cable news idiotocracy, it sure is nice to be half a world away, walking
> past Hanoi's flooded central lake, into the old quarter, through 1,000-year-old
> fish, meat, fruit and vegetable markets, and over to a little stall where a rosy-
> faced woman ladles her rice-based batter on a steaming drum to make perhaps
> the world's best banh cuon.

In June 2009, Roadmonkey undertook a challenging six-day climb to
the peak of Mount Kilimanjaro in Tanzania, and combined that difficult slog
with a volunteer project to provide clean drinking water and school desks to
children near Dar es Salaam. In September 2009, he officially left the paper.

Interviewed in February 2010, von Zielbauer was still a one-person operation, that morning planning a Roadmonkey event that required him to bake
cookies. "I have to be a CFO [chief financial officer], I have to be a salesman,
I have to be the logistics person, the tour guide. I'm my own tech person. It's
just everything." Roadmonkey, he says, is, in a "personal way," his legacy
much more than his reporting was. "Whatever becomes of it will be largely
because of what I've done or not done."

The split with *The Times* may have been traumatic, but it seems that the
divorce was the right decision. The Roadmonkey website, which looked a
little ragged in the spring of 2010, now has a very professional aura and carries
raves from clients and cites media hits from a dozen publications, including
O, The Oprah Magazine, USA Today and *National Geographic.*

Writing in August 2010, von Zielbauer permitted himself a moment of
triumph: "I admit I feel quite satisfied that, lying on my deathbed, I won't
feel dread and regret for not having pushed life to the maximum."[23]

At the end of 2011, Von Zielbauer reports that Roadmonkey is alive and thriving. He's taken on an equity partner, Heather Rees, who now is Road-monkey director of operations and expeditions. In 2012, he'll be working with a New York City-based marketing firm to market Roadmonkey's travel products "in a more sophisticated way" and to create partnerships with "select brands" that believe in adventure philanthropy. He also reports that without any help from Roadmonkey, "our clients in New York City (who took part in expeditions to Vietnam, Peru, Tanzania, Nicaragua and Patagonia) began meeting for 'flash volunteer projects' and social events. 'This is a hugely encouraging trend," he emailed, and one that is prompting Roadmonkey to plan to hold "multi-media events in Boulder, L.A and the Bay Area, for like-minded adventure philanthropists in those regions."

Chapter 11

The Path Not Taken

Sixty vans. Do you know how many sixty vans is?... It is 120 insulation panels, a left and a right, 60 big clips, 60 air vents, 60 small clips, 240 screws, 240 shots with an air gun, 60 changes of the bit on the tip of the air gun. Sixty times leaning over the engine compartment, gasping as the van moves forward, your weight on your chest bone, struggling to reach into the engine well and insert the insulation panels and the big clip.... Sixty times leaning into the driver's side, taking small steps as the vehicle moves, shoving in screws, bracing left elbow, pulling on the trigger.—*Life on the Line: One Woman's Tale of Work, Sweat and Survival.*[1]

Solange De Santis has always been a risk taker, looking for something beyond the cushy trappings of her high-paid, business journalism jobs, looking for stories that offered more drama and more humanity than earnings reports and the pronouncements of corporate executives.

For that reason, and to the consternation of her upper-middle-class parents, in 1991 De Santis took a job on the assembly line of a General Motors plant in suburban Toronto, Canada.[2] She wanted to learn more about the blue-collar world and the people who inhabited it. Her entry into the plant came at a well-timed moment. The plant where she had applied for a job had taken a year to find a place for her, and in the intervening months, GM announced that it would shut it down in the summer of 1993. She would be able not only to know the life of the plant, but to chronicle its final days.[3]

She became Sally, whose work history hid her university education, and included jobs working in stores and offices. She said she was looking for better pay. She grew to know her colleagues in the Trim 2 department, and to become more adept at the physically demanding job. She ultimately took the story of her 18 months at the plant and transformed it into a well-received book, *Life on the Line: One Woman's Tale of Work, Sweat and Survival.*

The book was an eye-opening experience not only for what she learned about blue-collar workers, but what it taught her about journalism. The whole issue of class, she recalled, "for me was invisible." But she now realized that the reporters she knew were solidly middle class, giving them an insular world view that affected their coverage. The reporters she had worked with in the U.S. and Canada might have had a parent who had worked a blue-collar job, but most "didn't have much of an idea about what it was to—fill in the blank—dig a ditch, build a car, be a plumber." After her experience at the plant, she says, "I certainly saw my fellow journalists in a new light." They suddenly looked "very effete," she says. "We journalists pride ourselves on being earthy people, we're connected with humanity, and we're cool and tell stories of the little people." Journalists may associate themselves "with the underdogs," she concludes, "but a lot of the time we're not really underdogs." When fellow alumni from the Graduate School of Journalism at Columbia University learned about her book, their reaction was: "What a cool thing you have done! As if I had gone on a field trip or something."

But that book didn't end the challenges for De Santis, nor did it offer her a way out of the journalism career that had shaped her life but never had fulfilled her dreams. Indeed, the book complicated her choices even more. At the plant, she met Camille Peters, the taciturn native of Prince Edward Island, whom she would marry, and with whom she would have a daughter.

And the plant's closing meant a return to the business journalism that she had wanted to escape. De Santis always had visions of a very different life in journalism than the one she has lived. "I always have been longing for something that so far I haven't been able to achieve, and that's to write about the arts full time," she says. Then she refines that thought. "I absolutely love telling the stories of people in their communities, whether it's an auto plant, or a church, or a theater—people and their communities."

Looking back, she wonders if coming out of Columbia at 23, she shouldn't have stuck to her guns and insisted on a job covering the arts for a newspaper.

It took sudden unemployment in 2009 to change her career trajectory. Only now, as a single parent in her fifties, with financial responsibilities and living back in the New York metropolitan area, is she mapping a strategy to satisfy her heart, pursuing a career and education path focused on writing about and/or participating in the lively arts.

The way De Santis presents herself to the world is as complex as her life has been. On her web page, she welcomes her readers to the "ongoing drama" of her life.[4] She is bald due to the autoimmune disorder alopecia universalis. But her head is well shaped, and she wears distinctive earrings, giving her a dramatic and yet dignified appearance. Looking at home in an experimental play in Greenwich Village, she is equally credible in her role as the parent of a middle-schooler. Her voice is rich, full, and appealing, as she crescendos into a punch line, or interrupts her own story with a laugh. The "deadline" persona — all business and focus, easily transitions to the more gregarious, outgoing Solange — the person you want to sit next to at a party.

Her journalism career always made some room for non-business writing. She convinced a number of her business employers— including *The Wall Street Journal*— to allow her to write features on the arts. Her mother, Florence Stevenson De Santis, wrote a flourishing syndicated fashion and beauty column for United Features Syndicate that ran in newspapers in the U.S. and Canada. She often took Solange and her brother along on interviews. She remembers tagging along as her mother lunched at Sardi's with actors such as Angela Lansbury and Hal Linden, who made their marks both on Broadway and in television. She was drawn to the glamour, the excitement and the "theatrical" aspect of journalism, the joy of putting together "a wonderful product" and having it run in a publication.

De Santis struck gold when, at age 18, she interviewed Robert Redford for a feature about the costumes for his film *The Candidate*, which was published in the *Montreal Star*.[5] But she never aspired to fashion writing per se, or to follow her mother into the world of syndicated columns.[6]

She wanted to work for a daily newspaper. "I've always loved newspapers and the whole world of newspapers and the people in journalism were interesting and soulful and funny, so put it all together and that's why I was drawn to it," she says.

A new Columbia graduate, she tried for print jobs, but didn't have any luck. She remembers a tryout at the *The Times of Trenton* that was "sort of disastrous because I wasn't good at writing headlines straight out of school."

Through one of her mother's contacts, she found herself talking to NBC Radio News executive Jim Farley. NBC Radio was going to start up a news information service, offering a package of radio news to local stations wanting to switch to an all-news format. "What did I know about radio?" But she had taken a semester course in broadcast writing, and the network needed people. "It was like this big cookie monster. And I guess he [Farley] was looking to hire some young people out of journalism school." NBC was offering to hire her at a salary of $400 a week, in 1976, quite a princely starting pay.

She started out writing broadcast news segments for NBC Radio, followed by a broadcast news job at the Associated Press, writing business news. She finally landed a newspaper job in 1981, when she joined the *Palm Beach Post* as business reporter, part of a tight-knit, three-person department. She enjoyed the work and her "simpatico" relationship with her editor. "I used to write the stories that make people mad," she recalls with a laugh, and her editor would "calm" the ruffled feathers in a small city with what she describes as a "Chamber of Commerce" feeling about its business community.

She could have climbed the ladder at the newspaper, but she did not want a management position. As she looked for reporter openings at larger papers, Reuters came calling. The news service offered her a job as chief financial correspondent for the Los Angeles bureau. De Santis was conflicted, but she reasoned, "It was a good opportunity, a promotion, a step up." She was reluctant to leave newspapers once again for a wire service, but the prospects at newspapers weren't opening up, so she compromised. "It's not 100 percent of what I want, but OK, it's 80 percent."

After she had been based in L.A. through 1986, Reuters offered her a promotion to news editor for Canada in Toronto, Ontario. There she supervised seven reporters and two photographers. It was during her third year in Toronto that De Santis decided to take her first career risk. Reuters generally had a policy of three-year postings, De Santis says, and there was the prospect of a transfer to Sydney, Australia. A native New Yorker, she was not eager to move farther away from her roots. Nor was she eager to move up the executive ladder at Reuters, taking a series of promotions that would increasingly distance her from what she loved best, writing, reporting and "telling stories." She recalls sitting in her living room in Toronto and mulling her future. She realized that she could be earning "well over" $100,000 a year (a huge sum in the late 1980s) and living in exotic world capitals. She looked around her apartment. "It was pretty comfortable. I had a nice car in the back. I got to do pretty much everything I wanted to do." She thought to herself, "How much do I want to buy?" Giving up reporting and writing, she concluded, would depress her much more than forgoing a high income.

Restless, she took an "entrepreneurial flier." NAFTA (the North American Free Trade Agreement) was in the news then, and there was a lot of misunderstanding between Americans and Canadians. "Take health care for example," she says. Canadians thought of Americans as ruthless capitalists who "didn't care about people." Americans tended to believe that Canadians, with their national health insurance system, imposed socialism that afforded no choice to consumers.

She and a Canadian journalist colleague decided to start a bi-national magazine, roughly covering business issues but wide ranging in the topics it would write about. They decided to call it *North America*. They did all the right things, putting together a business plan, and shopping their proposal to established publishers, venture capitalists, and wealthy individuals with a "vested interest" in U.S.-Canadian relations. Everybody thought it was a great idea, she says, but nobody wanted to risk money on it.

After a year or two, she says, the two of them gave up on the idea. But De Santis did not feel like it had been time and money wasted. She told herself,

"Solange, you spent money on a course and the course was what it's like to keep a business going."

Meanwhile, her personal horizons were expanding. "I knew this guy Billy, that I was pretty intimately involved with, who was blue collar, and it was such a different world." It was the relationship with Billy that helped intensify her long-festering curiosity about this gritty, more physical life. She decided to apply for a job at Billy's GM plant, figuring that the worst that could happen was that she would hate the work, or sustain some job injury and opt to drop out.

She was even more intent on taking the job after GM announced its plans to shutter the plant. She recognized that workers coming to terms with a plant closing would have all the elements of a good story. "Here was an auto plant, 3,000 people, and it was closing down. It had been there for 40 years. There had to be a story there." She didn't know quite how she would tell that story — as a magazine article or book — but she knew it was worth going after. But she also felt that whatever the outcome, it would be worth doing. "Even if this isn't anything in terms of a writing project, it will be a remarkable personal experience," she told herself. "You'll get a whole look at a part of society that you don't know at all."

She knew that working at the plant would offer her challenges that her life in journalism no longer was affording her. As she wrote in the introduction to the book:

> The kind of journalism I'd fallen into— mostly routine stories on business and finance — no longer jounced my imagination. I was so bored at the last job I held before the van plant — bond-market reporter for *The Globe and Mail*— that a couple of times, goaded by a trader, I had inserted hidden baseball references into my daily market story....[7]
> I just thought working in an auto-assembly plant that was about to close, next to people facing a job crisis typical of the early 1990s, would be an experience worth recording. The very biggest names in corporate America — IBM, AT&T, General Motors— were laying off thousands of people.... The numbers were so big, that the headlines blurred: thirteen thousand jobs here, ten thousand jobs there. Who were all these people? Each one of those numbers had a face. I needed to meet some of those faces. I needed to know what was happening inside them.[8]

She did not go into the plant to make any political points, she says. At its heart, she says, the book was about "the stories of the people behind the layoffs of the recession of the early 1990s.... I went in as a storyteller, essentially a dramatist."

It was, she discovered, extremely physical work, work that would, after an eight-hour shift, "make you too tired to do anything else." She didn't try to write the book while she was working at the plant, but she kept a journal and detailed notes, and collected plant notices and pamphlets.

The workers in the plant are real, De Santis says, but to protect their privacy she did not use their real names. They did not know she was thinking about writing a book. She called herself Sally, and said that she was a writer, a personal detail that didn't stir much curiosity among the 50-odd colleagues who included the former manager of a bank branch, an Eastern European emigrant, Jamaicans, and a woman who wrote children's books. Nevertheless, because they held blue-collar jobs, she says, they "were sure at a different place in society,"—to a certain extent both invisible and expendable.

When GM closed the plant, she says, "people's lives just were uprooted." She could not predict just how much the experience would affect her. She developed relationships and a sense of camaraderie that made the closing nearly as traumatic for her as it was for some of her co-workers. "Because I'd been there for a fairly good chunk of time I really internalized a lot of this stuff, and was kind of in an upset state myself, and thought, 'Now where do I belong?'"

The plant closing caused a number of dislocations, and some hit close to home. Peters, her boyfriend, put his name in for work at other Canadian plants. He worked for a courier company for a while, a job that combined hard work with low pay. He got a job at the GM plant in Oshawa, Ontario, that lasted for 12 weeks. In 1994, he was called to a plant in London, Ontario, two hours away from Toronto, and worked there until March 1996, and was laid off again. Finally, after working at three plants, and without being called back to work for two years, he took a buyout from GM, and started his own courier business.[9]

She carefully kept all the stories written when the Toronto plant shut down. She was sensitive to the language that reporters routinely used to write about the plant closing, what she called "these people" language. "These people won't ever find a job that pays so well. These people are in a bad way. These people have to find ways to feed their families."

She perceived the remoteness of white-collar middle class professionals, including journalists, to the world of the working class. And she observed that blue-collar workers, when they get any attention from media, are almost exclusively perceived through the lens of business journalism, by people who also cover corporations. "So perhaps half the time you're looking at labor from the corporate top-down financial point of view, as opposed to looking at people as people, which was what I was trying to do [during] my year and a half."

After the plant closed in the spring of 1993, De Santis was out of work for about a year, but just as her unemployment from the plant job was winding down, a friend who was then Toronto bureau chief at *The Wall Street Journal* offered her a job. She resumed her life in full-time journalism in 1994, married Peters in 1995, and a few years later was pregnant with their daughter.

It took a while to get a publisher interested in the book. Canadian publishers considered it a book about workers in an auto plant, and rejected it because "auto workers don't read," De Santis recalls. She praises her agent Jan Whitford for sticking by her and finally finding a home for the book at Random House, where an editor realized that this was not a book about an auto plant, "it was a book about people."

She did the bulk of the writing during her maternity leave. "It was madness, utter madness," she says. "Baby slept, I would write. Baby napped, I would write." Things got even more intense after she went back to work and continued to complete the book. "That was the real insanity. A full-time job, baby, and writing a manuscript. Absolutely nuts. I think I burst into tears one day because of the stress."

If *Life on the Line* was completed under duress, De Santis's writing didn't show it. She opens the book with her very frank assessment of her own comfortable life and career covering businesses. She recounts the annual meetings she's attended, and the announcements of cutbacks she's heard. "It all seemed so easy," she wrote, "sitting in those comfortable hotel meeting rooms, staring at pie charts and graphs, emotion drained from every decision.... There were times," she wrote, "I utterly despised the slick, tie-wearing jerk in front of me, such as the corporate president who pompously declared how the company's most valuable resource was 'its people.' Those were often the same companies that ran pictures of employees in the annual report without mentioning their names."[10]

The book is a vivid, respectful portrayal of individuals who are smart, funny, and exasperating doing very demanding jobs and facing uncertain prospects. She gives her readers a sense of the heat, monotony, stress and physical challenge of working in a plant. De Santis creates a blue-collar world populated by people we grow to know, and with whom we grieve when the plant closes down.

Despite a few negative reviews—the *Los Angeles Times* termed the book a "rambling narrative" that failed to bridge the gap between the writer and her subjects[11]—De Santis was a finalist for Canada's National Business Book Award. She also was praised by *The New York Times,* whose reviewer called the book an "engaging account" and termed her description of her initiation into the job "bone-achingly visceral."[12] (To De Santis's chagrin, the highly positive review ran in the business section, not the books section.) The book also was deemed authentic by those most qualified to know, workers at a GM plant in St. Louis, who read and discussed the book. "They thought it was very accurate," she says, and that the characters seemed true to their own experience.

The book may have been generally well received, but it did not change

De Santis's career prospects. *The Wall Street Journal* expected her to cover financial news, and that was what she did.

Even then, making a mark as a business reporter at *The Journal* wasn't an easy feat to accomplish from north of the border. "You were always competing with a U.S.-based staff.... For every billion-dollar merger we had in Canada, there was a 10-billion merger in the states. For every social trend we had in Canada, the same social trend was occurring in the U.S."

Sometimes big stories did happen in Canada. The Canadian mining firm Bre-X Minerals Ltd. had claimed to have discovered a rich vein of gold in Indonesia, and its glowing predictions drew investors, who put billions of dollars into the company. In 1997, however, the company's gold claims turned out to be fraudulent,[13] a scandal that caused Canada to tighten its investment regulations in 1998. When the scandal got big enough, De Santis found herself displaced by the American staff. When big news broke, De Santis said, "all of a sudden you'd find somebody from New York in your backyard."[14]

She became expert in finding the "quirky" or unusual story. It also offered her a chance to do something she does well, vividly describe people and their predicaments.

She wrote about the Vietnam War's hidden veterans—as many as 40,000 Canadian citizens who left their country to join the U.S. armed services to fight in that war and then discovered that their service wasn't honored by either country.[15]

She traveled to Prince Edward Island with her husband's family to visit Le Village, a French Acadian dinner theater. She describes its plight in one vivid sentence. "Le Village — hotel, pioneer houses, crafts exhibit and shop, restaurant, theater—clings as tenaciously to the edge of the sea as the people who built it hold to the idea of keeping their French-speaking culture alive in a sea of North American English."[16]

She attended a five-day memorial event for the late Canadian pianist Glenn Gould, whose admirers were so intense they reminded one participant of Elvis fans. The only thing missing from the gathering, she wisecracked, "was a séance."[17]

A front-page story mined a lighter vein when she discovered a Canadian bagpipe college. Her story began: "The bagpipe's appeal is difficult to explain. Playing it can be a lonely calling. At a party, nobody asks you to sit down and bang out a song. You wear a skirt. There are the jokes."[18]

But no amount of strategizing could erase other challenges to the job. Her daughter was two years old, and she had a 90-minute commute each way from her home in Milton, Ontario, to *The Journal*'s office in Toronto. She asked if she could work from home two days a week. "They wouldn't hear of it," she says.

She also was hoping the paper might be willing to transfer her to New York City. "I had been in Canada for 13 years, and it was starting to feel like it was time to go home."

That, too, wasn't in the cards.

De Santis cast about for other opportunities. She again opted for free-lancing, and did some corporate speech-writing. In 2000, she happened to see an ad for a part-time reporter with the *Anglican Journal*.

De Santis had chosen the Anglican Church when she married and had gone "looking for a church" for her wedding. The *Journal* is the national news-paper of the Anglican Church of Canada, run by an independent editorial board. Her editor, while a member of the clergy, also had worked at the Halifax *Chronicle Herald*. "He and I just got along like a house afire because Peter [her editor] had journalistic principles." She found, she says, a publication with a staff committed to the journalistic values of accuracy, and willing to report on issues that might occasionally ruffle the Anglican hierarchy. With a 200,000 circulation, it was the "heavy" among religious publications in Canada, she says.[19]

In no way, she says, did she consider her shift from *The Wall Street Journal* to the *Anglican Journal* as transitioning away from journalism. "I wasn't sitting there just taking the bishop's sermon and typing it up. I wasn't doing obits. We did interesting stories and we reported on controversy." She mentioned a series the paper had commissioned, "Sins of the Fathers," which examined the legacy of sexual abuse that had occurred in government-funded Indian residential schools run by the Anglican Church.

De Santis worked at the *Journal* until 2008, when there was an opening in New York City at Episcopal Life Media. De Santis jumped at the chance to take over as editor. "I got the job and this really strong mandate to do jour-nalism, and editorial independence," she recalls. Now divorced from Peters, De Santis moved herself and her daughter to New York. She settled her daugh-ter in a good public school in the metropolitan area, and began her job, in charge of multiple media platforms for the church, including its monthly newspaper, as well as digital news operations.[20]

A year later the picture had changed drastically. When the economic down-turn caused Episcopal Life Media to sharply downsize, her job was eliminated altogether. De Santis found herself a single parent trying to find work in a pro-fession that was imploding. "I really was thinking that this [job] was going to be the end of my career. That I would be at this job for 10 years until retirement, and then I could pursue what I wanted to pursue in music and in theater."

She decided she would not uproot her eleven-year-old daughter, Flo-rence, who was happy at her school. And she determined she would find a new path.

Interviewed just a few days after she became jobless, De Santis said, "I'm really at a crossroads now, and I'm fully aware that this may be it for me in journalism.... Do I want to get out of journalism? No! Not a bit!" she said.

While other reporters contended that journalism's flaws had helped bring about its economic crisis, De Santis disagreed. "Journalism is as useful and as needed as ever," she said, adding that journalism has improved over the years, and that journalists are more educated than they were two generations before. She conceded that the media could be arrogant, but argued: "Of course the profession is arrogant! I'm the writer, the reporter and you mitigate that [arrogance] by trying to be understanding and care."

But she did express grave misgivings about the future. "What concerns me is not so much the death of print, much as I love newspapers, but it's the death of journalism. With everybody having access to the means of production" for news and opinion through the Internet, "the question is, 'who needs us?'"

A follow-up interview seven months later found her in a different and better place. She felt that her resume needed buffing, and was considering taking a course in fundraising. In her search for courses, she happened onto an offering at New York University in educational theater. It was a concept she had never heard of before, she recalls. But she was entranced by the video on the NYU website that discussed working with fourth and fifth graders who had seen the Twin Towers fall on September 11, and helping them create a play to deal with their feelings. The graduate degree drew her, she says, because of the opportunities it offered to work in the arts, perhaps doing education outreach for a nonprofit drama group, or directing plays or staged readings, and because it would also hone her skills as a drama critic.

De Santis has taken out student loans to cover the $40,000 tuition, and hopes that the investment will pay off. She worries about how the insecurity is affecting her daughter, who once confided to her in tears, "I'm afraid we're going to run out of money."

De Santis, while pursuing her studies, continues to do freelance theater reviews. And she's landed news writing gigs. Her degree, she believes, will finally give her the opportunity to immerse herself in the arts, and engage her directly in the act of telling the stories of a community. How that degree leads to a job is not entirely clear, she says. But the hope is that she can direct a theater education program for a nonprofit arts organization, or find a good job as a communications director in the arts field. "At the very least," she says, her graduate degree will "certainly enhance my writing about the arts."

She finds the experience both exhilarating and scary, and she is worried that her 30 years of journalism experience may not accommodate a world with a demand for people highly proficient in digital editing skills. She confides that her "nightmare" is that "basically until I'm 65 and collecting social security, I never get a real job."

But still, she moves on, bartering piano lessons for developing a communications plan for her daughter's music school and revamping its web site. Another accomplishment to put on the resume, she reasons, and another chance to develop more web expertise.

Looking back on her career, De Santis thinks that at age 23, there was a fork in the road, when she could have turned down NBC Radio's offer to do business news. In her fifties, she thinks fate has offered her a second chance. "I'm taking that fork now."

De Santis earned her M.A. in educational theater in May 2011. She now is involved in various theater activities— as judge and dramaturge at the TheatreStarts playwriting competition and doing staged readings in Ontario, Canada. She writes reviews and features for www.theatermania.com and a blog, *Solange on Theater*. She also is editor of *Ecumenical News International*, a news service (www.eni.ch) that covers religion from ecumenical and interfaith points of view.

Chapter 12

Thinking About Journalism

It would be trivializing these deeply personal stories to contend that the experiences they relate are the sum and substance of problems with journalism and why the news business is in such dire economic straits. Still, some themes emerge.

When I was very young, I worked for a weekly newspaper in upstate New York. The entire staff would do "paste up," literally laying down the printed pieces of cold type that would become the publication we sent to readers. I remember that the ad manager, a kindly, ebullient man in his late seventies, would ask us for more "fill" when laying down his ads. That was his way of asking for more stories. To him, they were just the words that lay between the advertisements.

If there is one word that conveys what happened to journalism in the last years of the twentieth century, it is devaluation. Long before the business of journalism was losing value, the owners of major media chains and broadcast outlets were devaluing both journalists and the audience they served. As these profiles demonstrate, the devaluation took many forms, both personal and professional. It is measured by the stories that *Time Magazine* killed for want of space, despite the blood, sweat and tears of the people who wrote them, or the failure of the media to ask probing questions before the U.S. invaded Iraq. It might be sensed in the halls of *The New York Times* where the "B team" reporters carry on, unseen and unhappy, or the way news outlets fired their most senior and experienced employees, heedless of the impact of their loss on the quality of the news. It could be perceived in the people the media largely fail to cover except through stereotypes—the poor, the working class, and racial minorities. It could also be shown by what the media value over fact-based reporting—punditry, and hyperventilating coverage of celebrities.

Whether they left on their own or their jobs were eliminated, the journalists in these pages share many common frustrations. They couldn't innovate, go deep on stories, or make a difference. They found themselves in newsroom cultures that accepted the conventional wisdom rather than challenging it. They were in rigid structures that often made it impossible to make lateral moves to cover the issues they cared about.

Many journalists, editors and media owners were complicit in the public's loss of faith in journalism, and its financial troubles. Technology pushed a tottering institution over the edge.

Journalists were often the victim of devaluation, but many reporters also contributed to its decline. At the same time cognitive psychologist Howard Gardner whom we met in the Introduction was probing the psyches of reporters, longtime author and editor James Fallows was writing *Breaking the News: How the Media Undermine American Democracy*. Fallows wrote a scathing critique of the Washington press corps that faulted the media for elevating bright and snappy commentary over thoughtful fact-finding. Fallows aimed his barbs at everyone from *60 Minutes's* Mike Wallace to *New York Times* columnist Maureen Dowd. He contended that the media fail to serve the American public by emphasizing politics over policy, cynical wisecracks over fact-based analysis, and framing most issues as either a conflict or a horse-race.

Fallows could not yet know how the Internet would affect the news media's profitability, or predict the economic downturn that would affect major sectors of the American economy. But he saw that journalists would to some extent be complicit in their own demise.

By and large, mainstream media's reporting, Fallows wrote, conveys the impression that "public life" is "mainly a depressing spectacle" rather than a component vital to citizen participation in a democracy. Operating under that premise, the only way to entice people to public affairs is to make public policy as interesting as "other entertainment options," Fallows concluded. Fallows warned that the "serious" mainstream media would never be able to compete with "pure entertainment" programs, and its attempt to do so locks the media "into a competition it cannot win.... Worse, it increases the chances of its own eventual extinction. In the long run, people will pay attention to journalism only if they think it tells them something they must know. The less that Americans care about public life, the less they will be interested in journalism of any form."[1]

In short, Fallows's book, which received very good reviews, even from some of those media outlets he had criticized, warned that the media must reform itself and find a way to deliver meaningful information to citizens, or they will simply walk away. (When Fallows took over as editor of *U.S. News and World Report*, the media knives came out. "Fallows is not part of my crowd," then–*Washington Post* executive editor Ben Bradlee told *The New*

Yorker in 1997.[2] Dowd ridiculed Fallows's efforts to gin up publicity for his publication, quoting an unnamed newsmagazine editor who declaimed, "The noble, puritanical Fallows is now just another groveling, pandering, sex-addled newsmagazine hack."[3])

Many reporters, too, simply were too accepting of the conventional wisdom. While the tone of reporting may be cynical, reporters often haven't challenged the assumptions of those in authority, or done independent fact-finding to prove or disprove them. "The heart of journalism should be that you tell people something they don't know. An awful lot of journalism is just repeating stuff that people know in one form or another," says James Steele, an award-winning investigative reporter now at the monthly magazine, *Vanity Fair*.[4]

In his book, Fallows observes that reporters "accept the politicians' guidance on the issues they will cover" but resent being manipulated. Their revenge is to report everything with "attitude and snarl."[5] Or as Scottish journalist Neal Ascherson observes, "We are the most skeptical of professions, but also one of the most passive."[6]

But even those reporters who aspired to the highest ideals of their profession often bucked an uncompromising newsroom culture, driven by unimaginative and timid editors. For generations the culture of many newsrooms has consigned reporters to producing copy, granting editors the power not only over the final version of what gets reported, but also on what constitutes "news" and what is worthy of reporting to begin with. Editors can inspire the best work from reporters, but in the last half of the twentieth century, many exercised power over staffs in ways that stymied good work.

Reporters do not write the headlines for their stories, do not determine whether they run and what prominence they receive, have little control over the length of their reports, or what they look like in their final version. In reporting it's as if you start with an artisanal product, produced by an individual reporter, and then the system does everything it can to make it conform to mass-produced standards.

As H.L. Mencken wrote in 1927: "The journalist can no more see himself realistically than a bishop can see himself realistically.... For one thing, and a most important one, he is probably somewhat in error about his professional status. He remains, for all his dreams, a hired man — the owner downstairs ... is still free to demand his head."[7]

Richard Roth, who appeared in the Introduction, now is senior associate dean for journalism at Northwestern University's Medill School campus in Qatar. But Roth spent years toiling at daily newspapers and was active in the newspaper guild, the labor union for reporters. Writing about his journalism philosophy, he described many of the editors he had worked for as "office-bound 9 to 5-ers ... who mercilessly pillage, plunder and rape reporters' stories."

When he became an editor, he promised himself he would "be unlike every other editor I had known." As editor-in-chief of the *Tribune-Star* in Terre Haute, Indiana, Roth did not hole up in his office and summon reporters to come to see him. Rather, he went to them. As he put it, he "would roam the outfield." He would directly engage with reporters, sitting down and working together on a story, giving them criticism, suggestions and feedback. As he observed, "Reporters had grown used to picking up the newspaper the next morning and seeing how their stories had been changed and never getting an explanation for the changes; the pell-mell pace of publishing a daily newspaper was the accepted explanation for everything."[8]

Roth was a good and caring editor in part because he knew what it meant to be in the trenches. But in the structure that has dominated journalism for decades, it is relatively unusual for a reporter like Roth to ascend to the high ranks of newspaper management. Reporters have very little opportunity to advance in their careers except if they become editors, and even then, the possibility of promotion is not foreordained, says Bruce Shapiro, executive director of the Dart Center for Journalism and Trauma at Columbia University Graduate School of Journalism, which offers training and other support to journalists who cover wars and other disasters. Shapiro, a former reporter who has written about the history of investigative journalism, adds:

> Most editors in most newsrooms come not out of the field but off the copy desk.... The path to reward, the path to influence, the path to shaping the news very often goes to those who have been the most careful, the most conservative, and who have done the least reporting.
> A news business that keeps reporters essentially at the bottom of the pecking order and elevates effective bureaucrats, conservative careful effective bureaucrats ... does create real frustrations and real problems for the people who are the frontline narrators and frontline witnesses and who should be elevated and encouraged in their careers.

Given the management structure at most newspapers, it is not surprising that the culture of the newsroom has not encouraged independent thinking. "Journalism is filled with very, very smart people and yet it is in so many ways an anti-intellectual profession in the United States," says Shapiro.[9]

When I was a new reporter, I worked for an editor who did one-on-one breakfast meetings with his staff. I remember asking him, "Does it bother you that today someone is thinking a new thought that will change the world and we don't know about it?" The editor looked up at me over his eggs and responded tersely, "No."

Shapiro believes this scorn of the intellectual may date back to the "Nineteenth century industrial origins of the news business in which writing about the news gets organized into an assembly line and gets rationalized into factories that produce pieces of paper on which are written pieces of news."

In other countries, there is a different model, he observes. He recalls meeting a journalist from Colombia whose title, roughly translated, was "master of style." Shapiro assumed that meant he edited the paper's lifestyle section. But the reporter told him that the title meant that "he was considered the master reporter, the mentor in the newsroom.... He's the keeper of the newsroom's internal wisdom and practices and ethics." No equivalent of this position exists in most newsrooms, he says.

This anti-intellectualism manifests itself in the increasing tendency of journalists to equate objective reporting with giving equal importance to two sides of an argument, even when the weight of the evidence favors one side over the other. Even questions of fact, supported by the vast majority of scientists, no longer are affirmed by the media, observes Sean Otto in a thoughtful examination of the politicization of science. "Journalistic techniques used to be employed as a means of fact-checking somewhat akin to scientific research," Otto writes. In the past, he observes, reporters would not report a news item unless they got corroboration from several sources. Trying to establish the truth of a story has been replaced by presenting "both sides" of a story. "The first casualty of this approach is journalism's own credibility, and its ability to speak truth to power. If one 'side's' account is untrue and corroboration to determine which story is correct is not pursued, journalism becomes not just a meaningless relayer of information without regard to its reliability, but also weighted toward extreme views."[10]

Despite these systemic limitations on journalism that go back generations, there was for a time a quasi "golden age" for mainstream journalism that allowed many reporters to excel, despite these obstacles. (Many would put an earlier "golden age" at the beginning of the twentieth century, when "muckraking" investigative reporters helped create the climate for the Progressive era. These reporters were, in the words of historian Jessica Dorman, "ubiquitous, urgent, influential."[11]) Some feel this later golden age followed *The Washington Post's* coverage of the Watergate scandal; Steele places it earlier, dating back to the 1960s and the Vietnam War. "We saw a lot of pretty courageous reporting out of the Vietnam War that was calling into question the way government functioned, basically lied to people," Steele says, remarking that in-depth investigative reporting, which surged in the seventies, eighties and nineties, was "quite abnormal," and rare for most of the history of reporting in the United States.

Even then, Steele and his longtime reporting partner Donald Barlett wrote in 2008 that investigative reporters were often constrained by editors in what they could dig into. "Even during these so-called 'golden years' of investigative reporting," they wrote, many subjects remained off limits in some newspapers. While reporting about labor corruption always found a receptive home, corporate malfeasance went largely untouched. Also, an unwritten rule with some editors was that investigative stories had to document illegal acts. This rule existed even though the practices most in need of exposure — ones with the largest impact on ordinary citizens — are usually legal, such as when health insurance companies deny medical treatment, campaign contributions inspire favors, and tax policies get rigged for the benefit of special interests. And investigations that touched on the unsavory practices of advertisers were always off limits, except at publications where the commitment to independent reporting ran deep.[12]

Nevertheless, many of those profiled in this book were drawn to the promise of this quasi "golden age," when journalism seemed to be a worthwhile calling and also an unrivaled way to see the world.

There was a time when Joan Connell could travel the globe and write long, thought-provoking pieces about trends in religion, working for a news service whose clients were medium-sized dailies throughout the country.

There was a time when Bill Walker could be dispatched all over the Western states and write about the new environmental movement and its clash with those who wanted untrammeled development.

There was a time when David Simon could experiment with new formats at *The Baltimore Sun* in order to reveal sides of Baltimore and its underclass that were new to its readers.

This era coincided with a time when print and broadcast news outlets were becoming more competitive with one another, challenged by the specter of media consolidation. Media outlets took chances in an effort to dominate a market. When those chances failed to translate into bigger profits or larger readership, these news outlets by and large shrank their ambitions and pulled back.

Walker's chance to cover the West and write meaningful stories about environmental issues disappeared when *The Denver Post* realized that it wasn't winning its circulation battle with the *Rocky Mountain News*.

The dailies that Newhouse News Service served did not know what to do with Connell's long and thoughtful pieces. "They never had the space back then to run these things in their entirety," Connell recalls.

Simon's attempts to push the envelope on narrative journalism and cover Baltimore's inner city were blocked by his editors, out-of-towners with no local roots, more interested in Pulitzers than innovative, comprehensive local reporting.

The curtailing of big, ambitious journalism goes hand-in-hand with the transition from media owners who believed they had a larger mission than profits to owners who believe their primary and sometimes exclusive duty is to their shareholders. Interviewed in 2010, 15 years after he wrote *Breaking the News*, Fallows, now a national correspondent for *The Atlantic Monthly*, said that the "fundamental problem" that he explored in his book could be boiled down to journalism's change in status. It had once been a "special kind of business" like law, medicine or education, where the profit motive competed with a mission to serve the public good, and where practitioners shared certain norms and values. But the journalism that Fallows wrote about had become simply a business. So network news shows felt compelled to compete for audience with entertainment shows, and infotainment was born. Newspapers, finding themselves in a world where readers had many more options for information, kept looking for new formulas to pump up their audience and be attractive to advertisers, while keeping profitable by cutting staffs.[13]

No one can restore these lost opportunities. But is it possible that the financial implosion that has upended so many individual lives will create the ingredients for a rebirth of mainstream journalism? The answer is a qualified "yes." Shapiro says one sign of hope is the evolution of National Public Radio, now known as NPR, as a "truly mass news source." NPR, which gets some federal support, largely relies on the programming fees local NPR affiliates pay, corporate sponsors, and gifts from foundations and individual contributors.[14] What had been a news organization with a "really modest audience a decade ago," now has a network of stations so expansive "you can drive from Bangor, Maine to Baja, California, and never be out of range of an NPR signal" or far from a community with an NPR station, Shapiro says. The success of NPR and its news programs, he adds, may mean that "the audience for the intelligent and intellectual may be bigger than is often understood."

Nonprofit journalism is flourishing in many venues these days, often offering reporters and editors a way to work more collegially, and to break down the editor-reporter power structure. Economic necessity has fostered collaboration among newspapers, or between broadcast news outlets and new online news operations. Nonprofits, often supported by foundations, please their funders when they extend the reach of their work by partnering with other media outlets, or by making their work available to mainstream print and broadcast outlets. (Some critics are concerned that nonprofits that depend on foundation support may be pressured to tailor their work to an ideological agenda, but nonprofit investigative reporting organizations with long track records, such as the Center for Investigative Journalism or the Center for Public Integrity, show no signs of pulling their punches to satisfy donors. And for-profit publications are vulnerable to pressure on news content from major advertisers.)

ProPublica was founded in 2007 to do in-depth investigative reporting and offer its work for free to various media outlets. It started flush with resources—a commitment of $10 million in annual funding from Marion and Herbert Sandler, philanthropists who ran one of the largest mortgage lenders in California and then sold their business to Wachovia Corporation, earning them billions.[15] And it hit the ground running. Starting operations in 2008, it had won two Pulitzer prizes by 2011. Its most recent prize, for its work exploring abuses by Wall Street bankers, was the first Pulitzer awarded for stories published only online. (*ProPublica's* first Pulitzer, about euthanasia at a New Orleans hospital in the wake of Hurricane Katrina, was published in partnership with *The New York Times Magazine.*[16])

The Texas Tribune, which began operation in 2009, is an online news site funded by nonprofit sponsors whose goal is "ubiquity," meaning that it intends to post its content not only on its own site but at the sites of its distribution partners. As it states on its website: "We want to put robust public interest journalism in the hands of and before the eyes of as many Texans as possible."[17]

Nonprofit journalism centers are springing up throughout the country, helping to fill the void caused by shrinking mainstream media outlets, and a dramatic decline in the number of statehouse and Washington bureaus. At the end of 2011, the iLab at the Investigative Reporting Workshop at American University, which is engaged in developing and tracking new investigative reporting models, reported that 75 nonprofit journalism organizations were up and running, an increase of nearly 25 percent since 2010. These 75 news providers have been sustained with $135 million in financial support and employed 1,300 full-time staffers.[18]

Not all the news was good: Capitol News Connection went out of business after eight years in operation due to a decline in foundation support and the economic troubles of the public radio stations it served. The nonprofit, which offered its broadcasts to public radio stations throughout the country, aimed to give local audiences information about Congress and their elected officials. Its broadcasts had at one time reached 3.1 million listeners.[19]

There even has been a sign of life in for-profit media. AOL , which now calls itself a "leading edge web services company,"[20] has spent millions investing in hyperlocal news sites in communities across the country through Patch.com. The operation hires journalists in each of its communities, equips them with a laptop, digital camera, cell phone, and police scanner, and requires them to publish several times daily — a news story, slide show, or video. For a salary of under $50,000 annually, they work at home and also are required to supervise any freelancers in their area.[21] The jury is still out, however, on whether Patch sites will do much more than report on local sports teams, local restaurants, events, and retailers.

Old-line mainstream media also are finding better ways to monetize their content by erecting paywalls, limiting the access of those who wish to access all their news for free. In 2011, *The New York Times* erected a paywall that had drawn more than 280,000 subscribers within its first three months, signaling that *The Times* will generate welcome new revenue from the experiment.[22] Mid-sized newspapers also are experimenting with ways to charge readers for access to their news stories.

Young people who aspire to journalism are being educated to new realities about their future. Dawkins and Roth see opportunities not at the big-city papers but throughout the country at startups and at smaller news outlets.

New journalists likely will not be tied to one news outlet. They will be much more capable of selling themselves as news creators, starting at a hyper-local website, perhaps setting up a blog and developing expertise on certain issues, coming together to work on a team project at a nonprofit, and then moving on. And their new financial vulnerability may increase the empathy and sensitivity journalists lost when their salaries jumped and they found themselves solidly in the middle class, and at big papers, in the upper middle class.

The journalists profiled in this book went into this field with a sense of mission, and a desire to do good, to have an impact. With niche audiences, will journalists be able to make a difference? Even Steele and his partner Donald Barlett, who have been groundbreaking investigative reporters for more than a generation, have been downsized. The team began at the *Philadelphia Inquirer*, where their exhaustive, multi-part, explanatory journalism about the economic forces that had victimized the middle class touched hundreds of thousands of readers. They went to *Time Magazine*, where their series on corporate welfare and other issues reached an even larger audience. Let go by *Time* in 2006 because the magazine no longer could afford their long-form journalism, the team found a home at *Vanity Fair*, a monthly better known for its coverage of Lindsay Lohan and Lady Gaga than weighty economic and political themes. It's hard to know whether *Vanity Fair* readers "get" Barlett and Steele the way their *Philadelphia Inquirer* readers did.

Steele says that when he and his partner were at the *Inquirer* and wrote the series "America: What Went Wrong?" tracing the influence of Wall Street on public policy and its impact on regular Americans, the stories ran all over the country and then became a book. "We got tremendous reaction wherever it appeared," Steele says, noting that newspapers are "still the most immediate thing in many people's lives, more than blogs, more than web pages."

Barlett and Steele are finding new ways to expand their reach. They are writing a sequel to their series, *What Went Wrong: The Betrayal of the American Dream*. But this time, even before the book is published, they are partnering with Charles Lewis's Investigative Reporting Workshop at American University to produce an interactive website that will create buzz about the project and also will solicit stories for the book.[23]

In 1996, Fallows was a prophet, warning the news media to repent to avoid extinction. But Fallows the prophet lately has become Fallows the optimist. He believes that the same technological revolution that imploded old journalism now is sowing the seeds for a new journalism. Because an individual can reach out to many news sources, those sources no longer can report on the same events and issues in the same way. "The new institutions will have to have something new to bring to people, whether it's more detailed information about their local community or more detailed information about some foreign country they care about or whatever, so I think there'll be a pressure towards a more carefully thought-out journalism." The journalism that survives will be the journalism that stands out, reporting news that does not follow the pack, that provides information that is new or more in-depth, or explores another dimension. And with the implosion of the old media, may have come another positive result: reporters and editors have lost some of their arrogance.

When I was a brand-new reporter, I remember an upstate New York bureau chief for the Associated Press bragging, "If there's an accident and we don't report it, it doesn't happen." Thirty years ago, the mainstream news media were the disseminators of information, and would decide what was news. Activists were supplicants in that world, and they depended on the goodwill of reporters to gain any visibility at all. But things have changed. Fallows observes that in the past people who "were resentful of the assumptions, and the haughtiness from the mainstream press, or maybe [the media's] excessive political bias" didn't have "ways to get those views out, and now there are." Is this the new face of journalism?

In an old Washington mansion near Dupont Circle, now the home of a nonprofit and a foundation, some reporters, looking at bit uncomfortable, speak to a group of environmental and public health activists. It is a sunny morning in late November, and the pinkish walls of the paneled conference room make it look even brighter — a splash of color that seems to make the journalists even more nervous. The reporters are from both NPR and the Center for Public Integrity. Both are longstanding nonprofits with a track record of solid journalism.

The reporters are describing their joint enterprise, "Poisoned Places," an in-depth look at communities across the nation whose residents have suffered for years from environmental degradation caused by the industrial operations in their neighborhoods.

The reporting is multi-faceted — including interactive maps on ambitious websites. It will feature the stories and voices of the victims of these toxins — stories that will be deliberately targeted to show the reach of the problem.

Foundations are in the room, too. "We understand the lifeblood of democracy is a confident, assertive press," said Robert Shull, program officer for Workers' Rights for the Public Welfare Foundation. He said he was happy that his foundation could help "this good work go forward."

Gary Bass, head of the Bauman Foundation, said that the project hit "the sweet spot for Bauman," because of "its good use of interactive data."

The reporters and editors are not there to ask for more money. In a way, their request is more fundamental. They are there to generate buzz for the series, to make it relevant, to ensure that it has an audience that resonates well beyond Washington, D.C. They are asking the activists to help them find more stories, and to get the word out about the series to the communities they worked with.

The Center for Public Integrity starts the ball rolling when one of its reporters, with more than three decades of experience reporting on environmental issues, begins with a story on Corpus Christi, Texas, and how little things had changed since he wrote about the community and its problems in 1991. In the spring of 2011, he submitted a Freedom of Information request for the Environmental Protection Agency's Clean Air Act enforcement watch list. The EPA complied, and within a few months, CPI had a list of about 400 clean air violators.

NPR's contribution was not only its ability to give the story national distribution through its member stations, but also its skill at working with imperfect databases, and finding ways to work with statistics that produce meaningful information.

The goal, the reporters state, is to offer information to citizens in affected communities throughout the country and enable them to take action. They hope the information will also help local reporters to write and produce their own stories about their own communities.

In the past, activists would bring a story to the media, and if the media outlet was big enough, the story would generate public outrage and change. In today's world of fragmented media, even big outlets like NPR rely on activists to spread the word about their stories.

But will this new, slimmed-down journalism serve democracy? Will it provide enough information about local, state and national government to enable citizens to truly participate in the political process?

This question goes unanswered. As a public interest activist and former journalist, every day I fight battles and struggle with issues that cry out for public attention, but rarely receive it. It is difficult to find reporters who want to dig deep to understand regulatory or budget policy. And those who would do so often are overwhelmed by looming deadlines and demands for daily or hourly updating of websites or blogs.

Investigative journalism is well worth retaining and expanding, but so is explanatory journalism, or the simple act of reporting what your member of Congress did, or failed to do, today. It feels as if journalism of the twenty-first century may deliver two kinds of meals—fast-food, from the slimmed-down shadow of your daily newspaper or broadcast news outlet, — if you're lucky to have either — or the gourmet feast of high-quality investigative reporting, reporting that of necessity can only take on a few, high-profile, long-term issues.

But what happens to everything in between? That's the question that all of us who care about journalism struggle with. I am optimistic that a new generation of journalists will develop new ways to do the work of the profession, and that journalism as an institution will continue, likely serving a smaller but more discerning audience. Like Fallows, I have faith that online media will offer diverse information, satisfying the needs of many niche audiences. But will journalism ever again offer us the fact-based information that most of us trust? Will it play a role in providing the information for civilized civic discourse? These questions are more difficult to answer. "The challenge will be bringing collective public attention to any one issue," Fallows says. "It's a problem of democracy as opposed to journalism that we're left with. It's a harder problem."

Chapter Notes

Introduction

1. Celia Viggo, "Tomorrow Is Courier's Last Day," *Buffalo Courier-Express*, September 18, 1982. A.1.

2. Medill Northwestern University, Journalism Faculty, Richard J. Roth, 2010. http://www.medill.northwestern.edu/faculty/journalismfulltime.aspx?id=128741

3. Heather Ann Thompson, "The Lingering Injustice of Attica," *New York Times*, September 8, 2011. http://www.nytimes.com/2011/09/09/opinion/the-lingering-injustice-of-attica.html

4. April Dudash, "SPJ goes international: A student chapter is born in Qatar," *SPJ Works Blog*, June 17, 2010. http://blogs.spjnetwork.org/spjworks/tag/richard-roth/

5. Viggo, "Tomorrow Is Courier's Last Day."

6. "Mark Twain's Little-Known Connection to Buffalo," Buffalo State College, July 14, 2011. http://newsandevents.buffalostate.edu/news/mark-twains-little-known-connection-buffalo

7. Sarah Ellison, *War at the Wall Street Journal: Inside the Struggle to Control an American Business Empire*, (New York: Houghton Mifflin Harcourt Publishing, 2010), 168.

8. Ibid, 190.

9. Tom Rosensteil and Amy Mitchell, "Overview," *The State of the News Media 2011: An Annual Report on American Journalism*, Pew Research Center's Project for Excellence in Journalism. http://stateofthemedia.org.

10. Jeff Gottlieb and Ruben Vives, "Is a City Manager Worth $800,000?" *Los Angeles Times*, July 15, 2010. http://articles.latimes.com/2010/jul/15/local/la-me-bell-salary-20100715

11. Columbia Journalism School news release, "Video posted: Special Pulitzer winners panel, 'Hiding in Plain Sight,'" October 4, 2011. http://www.journalism.columbia.edu/news/539

12. Celia Viggo Wexler, "Walter Reed Scandal: How Mainstream Media Let Us Down," TheNation.com, March 8, 2007. http://www.thenation.com/article/walter-reed-scandal-how-mainstream-media-let-us-down.

13. Commission on Freedom of the Press, *A Free and Responsible Press*, Robert D. Leigh, ed. (Chicago: The University of Chicago Press, 1947), 21.

14. Bill Kovach and Tom Rosenstiel, *The Elements of Journalism*, (New York: Random House, 2007), 7.

15. Howard Gardner, Mihaly Czikszentmihalyi, and William Damon, *Good Work: When Excellence and Ethics Meet*, (New York: Basic Books, 2001), IX–XII.

16. Ibid, 90.

17. Ibid, 128.

18. Ibid, p. 6.

19. Interview with Bill Walker, September 5, 2005.

Chapter 1

1. Bill Walker, "Why I Quit: Confessions of a Burned-out, Fed-up, Pissed-off, Smart-ass Newspaperman," *San Francisco Bay Guardian*, July 18, 1990, 39.

2. Louis Peck, "Anger in the Newsroom," *American Journalism Review*, December 1991. http://67.59.181.208/Article.asp?id=1498

3. Mirta Ojito, "The Long Voyage from Mariel Ends," *New York Times*, January 16, 2005. http://www.nytimes.com/2005/01/16/weekinreview/16ojito.html?scp=2&sq=Mariel%20boatlift%201980&st=cse

4. "The Pulitzer Prizes, 1981 winners and finalists. http://www.pulitzer.org/awards/1981

5. Kent Demaret, "You Got Trouble in Elmore City: That's Spelled with a 't,' Which Rhymes with 'd' and That Stands for Dancing," *People Magazine*, May 19, 1980. http://www.people.com/people/archive/article/0x,,20076503,00.html

6. Bill Walker, "Whole Villages Ravaged by the 'Slim Disease,'" *Sacramento Bee*, December 13, 1987, A1.

7. Bill Walker, "Patterson Sad Farewell to Pair Who Shared Heart," *Sacramento Bee*, March 10, 1989, B1.

8. Jesse McKinley, "Celebrate a Quake? Why Shouldn't We?" *New York Times*, Oct. 17, 2009. http://www.nytimes.com/2009/10/17/us/17celebrate.html

9. Jim Herron Zamora and Henry K. Lee, "Earth First Activists Win Case," *San Francisco Chronicle*, June 11, 2002. http://www.sfgate.com/news/article/Earth-First-activists-win-case-FBI-cops-must-2829885.php

10. Amy Wallace, "Ex-Valdez Leaves San Diego Bay," *Los Angeles Times*, September 13, 1990. http://articles.latimes.com/print/1990-09-13/local/me-135_1_oil-spill

11. Carey Goldberg, "Downsizing Activism: Greenpeace is Cutting Back," *New York Times*, September 16, 1997. http://www.nytimes.com/1997/09/16/us/downsizing-activism-greenpeace-is-cutting-back.html?ref=greenpeace

12. David Shaw, "Alar Panic Shows Power of Media to Trigger Fear," *Los Angeles Times*, September 12, 1994. http://articles.latimes.com/print/1994-09-12/news/mn-37733_1_alar-scare

Chapter 2

1. Justin Van De Kamp, "Flashback TV Ratings: 1987/1988 Season." http://televisionista.blogspot.com/2008/01/flashback-tv-ratings-19871988-season.html

2. Joseph P. Kahn, '60 Minutes' at the 20-Year Milestone," *Boston Globe*, September 24, 1988, living section, 10.

3. Tom Rosensteil and Amy Mitchell, "Overview," *The State of the News Media: An Annual Report on American Journalism*, Pew Research Center's Project for Excellence in Journalism. 2011. http://stateofthemedia.org/2011/overview-2/

4. James Phelan and Robert Pozen, The *Company State: Ralph Nader's Study Group Report on Dupont in Delaware*, (New York: Grossman Publishers, 1973),ix.

5. Ibid, 204.

6. Karen DeYoung and Milton Coleman, "Victim Denounced Policies of Junta," *Washington Post*, September. 22, 1976, A1.

7. Stephen J. Lynton and Lawrence Meyer, "Ex-Chilean Ambassador Killed by Bomb Blast," *Washington Post*, September 22, 1976, A1.

8. Marc Gunther, *The House That Roone Built, The Inside Story of ABC News*, (New York: Little, Brown and Company, 1994), 54.

9. Ibid, 137.

10. "A Talk with Lowell Bergman," PBS *Frontline*, 1999. http://www.pbs.org/wgbh/pages/frontline/smoke/bergman.html

11. William J. Eaton, "Wright Resigns, Urges End to This 'Mindless Cannibalism': Speaker Declares Innocence in Impassioned House Speech," *Los Angeles Times*, June 1, 1989. http://articles.latimes.com/1989-06-01/news/mn-1319_1_select-successor-speaker-jim-wright

12. "Panel Accuses Wright of A 'Scheme To Evade' House Rules on Income," *New York Times*, April 18, 1999, A1.

13. Morley Safer biography, CBS News *60 Minutes* website, July 7, 1998. www.cbsnews.com

14. William Finnegan, "The Secret Keeper: Jules Kroll and the World of Corporate Intelligence," *New Yorker*, October 19, 2009. http://www.newyorker.com/reporting/2009/10/19/091019fa_ fact_finnegan#ixzz1ZYKRJx00.

15. Charles Lewis, "Looking Back at the First Ten Years," *Center for Public Integrity Annual Report*, 2000, 8.

16. "Advisory Board," *Center for Public Integrity Annual Report*, 2000, 4.

17. Charles Lewis, "Looking Back at the First Ten Years," *Center for Public Integrity Annual Report*, 2000, 8.

18. Ibid.

19. "Chronology," *Center for Public Integrity Annual Report*, 2000, 14.

20. "News Conference of the Center for Public Integrity Re: Advisers to Presidential Candidates," Charles Lewis, Chairman and Executive Director, Center for Public Integrity, Federal News Service, February 27, 1992.

21. "Creating a Journalistic Utopia," *New Yorker*, March 25, 1996, 33–36. http://archives.newyorker.com/?i=1996-03-25#folio=032

22. "National Press Club Luncheon Speaker, Charles Lewis, Center for Public Integrity," Federal News Service, April 23, 1996.

23. "29 Are Chosen for Fellowships from the MacArthur Foundation," *New York Times*, June 2, 1998, A16.

24. "News Conference of the Center for Public Integrity Re: Advisers to Presidential Candidates."

25. "2003 George Polk Awards at a Glance." http://www2.brooklyn.liu.edu/polk/polk.html

26. Website of law firm Cuneo Gilbert & LaDuca, LLP. http://cuneolaw.com/lawyers/pamela_gilbert.php

Chapter 3

1. "The Future of Journalism," Testimony of David Simon before the Senate Committee on Commerce Science, and Transportation Subcommittee on Communications, Technology, and the Internet, May 6, 2009.

2. John E. Talmadge, book review, "Bovard of the Post-Dispatch by James W. Markham," *The Journal of Southern History*, Vol. 21, May 2, 1955, 277–278. http://jstor.org/stable/2955146.

3. W. Curtis Riddle and Patrick McGuire, "Reagans Visit Victims of Racism," *Baltimore Sun*, May 4, 1982, D1.

4. David Simon, "Low Marx: UM Tut-Tuts at Grads' Antics," *Baltimore Sun*, May 14, 1982, D1.

5. David Simon, "Lefty Said to Have Asked Delay of Veal Decision," *Baltimore Sun*, March 26, 1983, B1.

6. Bill Free, "Driesell Earns New Contract, Security Option," *Baltimore Sun*, October 28, 1984, 1B.

7. Michael Dresser, "Memories Still Burn Decades after Wreck," *Baltimore Sun,* January

4, 2007. http://articles.baltimoresun.com/2007-01-04/news/0701040101_1_amtrak-robert-booker-crash

8. Keith Harriston, "Judge Acquits Nurse Bolding; Link to P.G. Deaths Called Inadequate," *Washington Post*, June 21, 1988, 01.

9. Chris Spolar, "Baltimore Sun Strike Ends; Workers Accept Pact on 258-to-110 Vote," *Washington Post*, June 7, 1987, 01.

10. David Simon, "The Reporter I : Cops, Killers and Crispy Critters," in *The Culture of Crime*, Craig L. Lamay and Everette E. Dennis, eds. (New Brunswick: Transaction Publishers, 1995), 36. (Originally published in the *Media Studies Journal*, Winter 1992.)

11. David Simon, "Life as a Snitch: Anonymous to the End, 'Possum' Tells Secrets," *Baltimore Sun*, March 16, 1992, A1.

12. Presumably, those four papers would have been *The Washington Post, The New York Times, Los Angeles Times*, and *The Wall Street Journal*.

13. David Simon and Edward Burns, *The Corner: A Year in the Life of an Inner-City Neighborhood*, (New York: Broadway Books, 1998), 540.

14. Margaret Talbot, "Stealing Life: The Crusader behind 'The Wire,'" *New Yorker*, October 22, 2007. http://www.andreaharner.com/archives/2007/11/stealing_life_t.html

15. Laura Vozzella, "Call Me Nosy—Laura Lippman Did, On TV," *Baltimore Sun*, May 17, 2009, 2A.

16. Abigail Pogrebin, "Favorite Son," *Brill's Content*, October 2000, 105.

17. Jim Haner and Timothy B. Wheeler, "Governor Promises City More Money to Fight Lead," *Baltimore Sun*, January 22, 2000, 1.A.

18. Pogrebin, "Favorite Son," 104–105.

19. David Montgomery, "Baltimore Sun's 'Wire' Portrayal Fuels a Hot Debate," *Washington Post*, January 16, 2008. http://www.washingtonpost.com/wp-dyn/content/article/2008/01/ 15/AR2008011503933.html

20. "Another Brick in the Wall," *The Economist*, October 8, 2011. http://www.economist.com/ node/21531479

21. Sharon Waxman, "Sparing No One, a Journalist's Account of War," *New York Times*, June 10, 2004. http://www.nytimes.com/2004/06/10/books/sparing-no-one-a-journalist-s-account-of-war.html

22. "David Simon, Author, Screenwriter, and Producer," John D. and Catherine T. MacArthur Foundation, 2010 MacArthur Fellows, September 2010. http://www.macfound.org/site/ c.lkLXJ8MQKrH/b.6241271/k.8712/David_Simon.htm

23. Dave Walker, "Today in 'Treme': Season 3 Shooting Starts; New Characters Revealed," *Times-Picayune*, October 31, 2011. http://www.nola.com/treme-hbo/index.ssf/2011/10/ today_in_treme_ s3_ shooting_sta.html

Chapter 4

1. Paul Taylor, "Viewed from Rebel Camp, Angola's Outlook No Less Murky," *Washington Post*, January 24, 1993, A20.

2. Jon Thurber, "Wallace Carroll, Persuasive Editor, Among Best of His Era," *Los Angeles Times*, July 30, 2002. http://articles.latimes.com/2002/jul/30/local/me-carroll30

3. "Public Service," The Pulitzer Prizes. http://www.pulitzer.org/bycat/Public-Service

4. William A. Henry III, et al., "Press: The Ten Best Dailies," *Time Magazine*, April 30, 1984. http://www.time.com/time/magazine/article/0,9171,951064-10,00.html

5. Tim Larimer, "The Pulitzer Jinx," *American Journalism Review*, December 1992. http://www.ajr.org/article.asp?id=1413

6. "Backgrounder on the Three Mile Island Accident," U.S. Nuclear Regulatory Commission. http://www.nrc.gov/reading-rm/doc-collections/fact-sheets/3mile-isle.html

7. Paul Taylor, *See How They Run: Electing the President in an Age of Mediocracy*, (New York: Knopf, 1990), 26–27.

8. Paul Taylor, "Outraged' Hart Prepares Rebuttal; Scandal Story Seen as Imperiling Candidacy," *Washington Post*, May 5, 1987, O1.

9. Paul Taylor, "The Coming of the 'We' Decade," *Washington Post*, July 20. 1986, Outlook, P1.

10. Taylor, *See How They Run*, 190–191.

11. Ibid, 5.

12. Ibid, 4.

13. Ibid, 21.

14. Ibid, 4.

15. Ibid, 268–269.

16. Paul Taylor, "In S. Africa, a Life Not Lost," *Washington Post*, August 10, 1992, A1.

17. Paul Taylor, "Viewed from Rebel Camp.

18. Paul Taylor, "Try, The Beloved Country," *Washington Post*, January 27. 1993, C1.

19. Mark Schapiro, "A Reporter Who Quit to Fight for Change: A conversation with Paul Taylor," *Frontline*, October 21. 1996. http://www.pbs.org/wgbh/pages/frontline/shows/press/other/quit.html

Chapter 5

1. Lindsay Kucera, interview via email with Joan Connell, *The AS Review of Western Washington University*, October 11, 2010. http://as.wwu.edu/asreview/bearing-witness-to-tragedy-ethical-reporting-in/.

2. Fact sheet, University of Iowa Writers' Workshop, http://www.uiowa.edu/~iww/about.htm.

3. Carlin Romano, "Wise Men Gone," *Chronicle of Higher Education*, January 24, 2010. http://chronicle.com/article/Wise-Men-Gone-Stephen-Toulmin/63649/

4. Joan Connell, "The Big Business of Babies, Kids by Surrogate: A High-Tech Harvest," *San Jose Mercury News*, November 1, 1986, 1C.

5. Joan Connell, "Young, Muslim & Misunderstood: Devout Teens Must Rely On Their Faith and Each Other To Endure Culture Shock," *San Jose Mercury News*, April 8, 1989, 1C.

6. Mary Frances Coady, "Christ Rises At Taize," *Commonweal*, March 23, 2001, 30.

7. Joan Connell, "God and the Gridiron," Newhouse News Service, *Oregonian*, January 30, 1993, C7.

8. Joan Connell, "Faith and Free Press," Newhouse News Service, *Oregonian*, October 16, 1993, C1.

9. "The Pulitzer Prizes: Beat Reporting. http://www.pulitzer.org/bycat/Beat-Reporting

10. Richard Perez-Pena, "Deborah Howell, One of the First Women to Lead a Big U.S. Newspaper, Dies at 68," *New York Times*, January 4, 2010. http://www.nytimes.com/2010/01/04/business/04howell.html

11. "Our Mission and History," Religion News Service, 2011. http://www.religionnews.com/ index.php?/history

12. "Rwanda: How the genocide happened," BBC News, December 18, 2008. "http://news.bbc.co.uk/ 2/hi/1288230.stm.

13. Joan Connell, "You Be the Editor, The Readers Respond," *San Jose Mercury News*, December 16, 1989, 1C.

14. Joan Connell, "Ethical Compass Needed for Cyberspace Exploration," Newhouse News Service, *Oregonian*, November 10, 1993, D07.

15. Arthur L. Liman, "Hostile Witnesses," *Washington Post Magazine*, August 16, 1998. http://www.washingtonpost.com/wp-srv/national/longterm/irancontra/contra1.htm

16. Linda Kozaryn, "Deck of Cards Helps Troops Identify Regime's Most Wanted," American Forces Press Service, April 12, 2003. http://www.defense.gov/news/newsarticle.aspx?id=29113

17. William Habdas, "Iraq's 55 Most Wanted Cards," iTunes App Store, accessed December 30, 2011. http://itunes.apple.com/us/app/iraq-55-most-wanted-cards/id411906335?mt=8

18. Joan Connell, "Midnight of the Soul: War's Cold Reality Brings Those of Many Religions Together for a Vigil Anchored by Hispanic Faithful," *San Jose Mercury News*, January 19, 1991, 1E.

19. Joan Connell, "An Editor Says Goodbye to a Newspaper, a Community and an Era," *San Jose Mercury News*, August 3, 1991, 10C.

20. Jeremy W. Peters, "Bad News for Liberals May Be Good News for a Liberal Magazine," *New York Times*, November 7, 2010. http://www.nytimes.com/2010/11/08/business/media/08 nation.html

Chapter 6

1. Theodore Iliff, *The Golden Times* (Smithfield, Pennsylvania: RoseDog Books, 2009), 33.

2. Christopher Condon, "Hungary's 50-year Grudge," *Los Angeles Times*, October 29, 2006, M6.

3. David Ignatius, "On the Electronic Barricades: We Encouraged the Students, Then Left Them Holding the Bag," *Washington Post*, July 30, 1989,C5.

4. Thomas B. Rosensteil, "Listening to the World Change on Shortwave." The radio remains one of the globe's leading sources of information. But democratization is forcing broadcasters to re-examine their role." *Los Angeles Times*, September 25, 1990, 2.

5. "On This Day, August 30 1980: Polish Workers Win Trade Union Rights," BBC News. http://news.bbc.co.uk/onthisday/hi/dates/stories/august/30/newsid_4559000/4559293.stm.

6. Cissie Dore Hill, "Archives: Voices of Hope: The Story of Radio Free Europe and Radio Liberty," *Hoover Digest*, 2001, No.4, Hoover Institute, Stanford University. http://www.hoover.org/publications/hoover-digest/article/6270

7. Richard Perez-Pena, "At 25, 'McPaper' Is All Grown Up," *New York Times*, September 17, 2007, C1.

8. "Challenger's Explosion Is Commemorated," *New York Times*, January 29, 1996. A.12.

9. "Girl Rescued After 58 Hours Stuck in Well," *Los Angeles Times*, October 18, 1987, 1.

10. "Berlin Wall Crumbling," *Los Angeles Times*, November 10, 1989, 1.

11. Robert Goldberg, "CNN Winning Electronic War," *Wall Street Journal*, January 21, 1991, A9.

12. Jane Hall, "If CNN Can't Eat the World, Who Can?" *Los Angeles Times*, July 18, 1993, 9.

13. Jim Rutenberg, "CNN Names a Rising Star to Head Its U.S. Network," *New York Times*, February 20, 2002, C8.

14. Lisa de Moraes, "Model-Anchor Quits Headline News," *Washington Post*, March 15, 2002, C1.

15. Ibid.

16. Scripps Howard News Service, "Headline News: Too Much Small Print," *Augusta (GA) Chronicle*, August 20, 2001. http://chronicle.augusta.com/stories/2001/08/20/ent_320071.shtml

17. Rutenberg, "CNN Names A Rising Star to Head Its U.S. Network," C8.

18. Jon Friedman, "CNN Shakeup Hits Programmers," CBS.MarketWatch.com, September 15, 2003. http://www.marketwatch.com/Story/story/print?guid=D9A00012-F0F7-4C50-8346-E9149DF12975

19. Jim Lovel, "Teya Ryan Leaves CNN; Viacom Vet to Replace," *Atlanta Business Chronicle*, September 15, 2003. http://www.bizjournals.com/atlanta/stories/2003/09/15/daily7.html

20. "About Us," IREX web site, accessed December 30, 2011. http://www.irex.org/about-us

21. Christopher Lee, "A Voice at the Heart of the Action," *Washington Post*, January 3, 2003, A17.

22. David Folkenflik, "Critics Says Voice of America Becoming Politicized," *Morning Edition*, NPR, June 17, 2005.

23. Shane Harris, "Voice of America to Move Part of News Division to Hong Kong," *Government Executive*, April 13, 2005. http://www.govexec.com/dailyfed/0405/041305h1.htm

24. Folkenflik, "Critics say Voice of America becoming politicized."

25. Art Levine, "Voice-Over America; You've read about what Kenneth Tomlinson is doing to public TV. What he's already done to the Voice of America is his other scandal." *American Prospect*, September 2005, 11.

26. National Board for Certified Counselors web site, 2011. http://www.nbcc.org/About

27. Ted Iliff, "Chuckles have short life spans in Kabul," August 9, 2010. http://tediliff.com.

Chapter 7

1. Wayne Dawkins, "The Best Year of My Life," *Politics in Color.com*, April 5, 2010. http://www.politicsincolor.com/node/67

2. "The Communications Media, Ironically, Have Failed to Communicate: The Kerner Report Assesses Media Coverage of Riots and Race Relations," *Report of the National Advisory Commission on Civil Disorders* (Washington: U.S. Government Printing Office, 1968)," excerpted from the web site, "History Matters, The U.S. Survey Course on the Web, created by the American Social History Project / Center for Media and Learning (Graduate Center, CUNY) and the Roy Rosenzweig Center for History and New Media (George Mason University), http://historymatters.gmu.edu/d/6553.

3. Wayne Dawkins, "Is the D.C. Press Corps More Diverse, Post-Election?" *The Diversity Factor*, volume 17, Number 3, Summer 2009.

4. Thomas Lueck, "Andrew Cooper, Pioneering Journalist," *New York Times*, January 30, 2002. http://www.nytimes.com/2002/01/30/nyregion/andrew-w-cooper-74-pioneering-journalist.html

5. Wayne Dawkins, "Why Did The City Sun [1984–1996] Matter?" The African American Literature Book Club web site, 2007. http://aalbc.com/reviews/whydidthe_nyc_sun_matter.htm

6. Website for the Philip L. Graham Fund, http://plgrahamfund.org/

7. Dawkins, "The Best Year of My Life."

8. Dennis Hevesi, "Nancy Hicks Maynard Dies at 61; A Groundbreaking Black Journalist," *New York Times*, September 23, 2008. http://www.nytimes.com/2008/09/23/business/media/23maynard.html

9. Wayne Dawkins, "Why Create a Black Alumni Network?" *Black Alumni Newsletter*, July 2010, 3. www.jrn.columbia.edu.alumni/services/ban/

10. *The Journal News: Our History*, July 13, 2006. http:/www.lohud.com/about/co-tjn-history.shtml

11. Wayne Dawkins, "The Police Beat," in *My First Year as a Journalist*, Dianne Selditch, ed. (New York: Walker and Company, 1995), 49–50.

12. Bob Tulini, "Lawnside: Rich and Deep Progress," *Courier-Post*, October. 18, 2006.

13. Wayne Dawkins, "Let's Talk," October 8, 2007, *Spot-on.com*. http://writers.spot-on.com/archives/dawkins/2007/10/dawkins_intro_1001_1.php

14. Brad Bennett, "Black columnists' woes continue: In N.J., Wayne Dawkins is Reassigned to a Reporting position," *NABJ Journal*, volume 13, February 28, 1995, 1.

15. "Bylines," *American Journalism Review*, June 1994. http://www.ajr.org/Article.asp?id=1212

16. Bennett, "Black columnists' woes continue."

17. Brad Bennett, "Dawkins column reinstated: Garden State chapter spearheads efforts," *NABJ Journal*, volume 13, Mach 31, 1995, 1.

18. "Disney Sells Newspapers; Deal Worth $1.65 Billion, *San Francisco Examiner*, April 5, 1997. http://articles.sfgate.com/1997-04-05/news/28571015_1

19. Tim Jones, "Sun-times Owner Adds Gary Paper," *Chicago Tribune*, October 18, 1997. http://articles.chicagotribune.com/1997-10-18/business/9710180189_1_hollinger-interna tional-chicago-based-hollinger-knight-ridder

20. Wayne Dawkins, "Truth Must Be Told About Founder of Blood Bank," *Daily Press*, September 10, 2000, H3.

21. Wayne Dawkins, "A New Face of America Is Emerging," Daily Press, September 19, 1999, H3.

22. "Reinvent Yourself: Essays from Those Who Have Been There and Done That," National Association of Black Journalists, August 2009, 62. http://www.herblowe.com/uploads/4/0/8/5/4085963/reinvent_yourself.pdf

23. "Under a Simple Oak Tree," History, Hampton University web site, 2011. http://www.hamptonu.edu/about/history.cfm

24. "Hampton University, open new school of journalism and communications," Scripps Howard Foundation web site, September 9, 2002. http://www.scripps.com/foundation/news/releases/02sept09.html

25. "Scripps Howard School of Journalism and Communications," Hampton University web site. http://media411.tvjobs.com/cgi-bin/search.cgi?Z=&c=13&k=532 , last updated April 24, 2008.

26. Samieh Shalash, "Tony Brown Leaving as Dean of Hampton University Journalism School," *Daily Press*, May 13, 2009.

27. "PBS Celebrates Black History Month With An Extensive Lineup of Special Programming," press release, PBS web site, January 10, 2008. http://www.pbs.org/aboutpbs/news/20080110_blackhistory.html

28. "Viewers Peek at Politico's Diversity—or Not," *Richard Prince's Journal-isms*, March 21, 2010. http://mije.org/richardprince/viewers-peek-politicos-diversity-mdash-or-not# Politico

29. "Inside TV One," http://tvone.tv/ 2009.

30. Thomas J. Lueck, "Andrew W. Cooper, 74, Pioneering Journalist," *New York Times*, January 30, 2002.

31. "40th Anniversary of Cooper v Power," Saint Francis College news release, May 1, 2007. http://www.sfc.edu/newsDetail.aspx?Channel=/Channels/Admissions/Admissions%20 Content&WorkflowItemID=01aaef56-1148-464f-a938-917abde59ee8

32. James Baron, "Shirley Chisholm, 'Unbossed' Pioneer in Congress, Is Dead at 80," *New York Times*, January 3, 2005. http://www.nytimes.com/2005/01/03/obituaries/03chis holm.html

33. "Reinvent Yourself: Essays from Those Who Have Been There and Done That," 62.

Chapter 8

1. Joseph C. Wilson 4th, "What I didn't Find in Africa," *New York Times*, July 6, 2003. http://www.nytimes.com/2003/07/06/opinion/what-i-didn-t-find-in-africa.html

2. Carol D. Leonnig and Amy Goldstein, "Libby Found Guilty in CIA Leak Case," *Washington Post*, March 7, 2007.

3. "Valerie Plame Wilson: No Ordinary Spy," CBS News, October 21, 2007.

4. "Bush Administration Names Prosecutor in CIA Leak Case," Bloomberg, December 3, 2003. http://www.bloomberg.com/apps/news?pid=21070001&sid=a4JWLHp AgKcM

5. "Thomas B. Edsall and Dan Eggen, "Bush Picks Controversial Nominees for FEC,"

Washington Post, December 17, 2005. http://www.washingtonpost.com/wp-dyn/content/article/2005/12/16/AR2005121601717.html

6. Kevin Stoker, "The Anniston Star," *Encyclopedia of Alabama*, http://encyclopediaofalabama.org/face/Article.isp?id-h-2061

7. "Background Note: Micronesia," U.S. Department of State. http://www.state.gov/r/pa/ei/bgn/1839.htm

8. Debra Puchalla, "The Little Magazine That Could," *American Journalism Review*, March 1997. http://www.ajr.org/Article.asp?id=2261

9. Edward S. Cabot, "1992 in Review: This Was a Great Year for Common Cause Issues," *Common Cause Magazine*, Spring 1993. http://findarticles.com/p/articles/mi_m1554/is_n1_v19/ai_13571849/

10. Neely Tucker, "Final Word on Whitewater Probe Clears Clintons," *Washington Post*, March 21, 2002.

11. Dan Froomkin, "Untangling Whitewater," washingtonpost.com, 2000.

12. Tucker, "Final Word on Whitewater Probe."

13. Ellen Joan Pollock and Viveca Novak, "Capital Secret: There May Be Less to Whitewater Case Than Meets the Eye," *Wall Street Journal*, February 22, 1995.

14. Viveca Novak and Michael Weisskopf, "The Busy Back-door Men," *Time Magazine*, March 31, 1997. http://www.time.com/time/magazine/article/0,9171,986111,00.html

15. "Investigative Reporting Prize," Harvard Kennedy School, Joan Shorenstein Center on the Press, Politics and Public Policy, http://www.hks.harvard.edu/presspol/prizes_lectures/goldsmith_awards/investigative_reporting.html#2003

16. Jesse Oxfield, "A Short History of Perks at Time Inc," *The Daily Beast*, December 12, 2008. http://www.thedailybeast.com/articles/2008/12/12/the-decline-of-perks-at-time-inc.html

17. Nancy Gibbs with Viveca Novak, "Inside 'The Wire,'" *Time Magazine*, December 8, 2003.

18. "Guantanamo Tactics, 'Inside the Wire," Fresh Air, NPR, May 5, 2005.

19. "AP: Sexual Psychology Used in Guantanamo," Associated Press, January 27, 2005. http://www.foxnews.com/story/0,2933,145608,00.html

20. Viveca Novak, "Impure Tactics," *Time Magazine*, February 13, 2005. http://www.time.com/time/magazine/article/0,9171,1027500,00.html

21. Richard Lieby, "The Liberal on Karl Rove's Case," *Washington Post*, December 7, 2005.

22. Viveca Novak, "What Viveca Novak Told Fitzgerald," *Time Magazine*, December 19, 2005. http://www.time.com/time/magazine/article/0,9171,1139820,00.html

23. Matthew Cooper, Massimo Calabresi and John F. Dickerson, "A War on Wilson?" July 17, 2003. http://www.time.com/time/nation/article/0,8599,465270,00.html

24. Novak, "What Viveca Novak Told Fitzgerald."

25. Viveca Novak, "Mr. Fitzgerald Goes to Washington," *Time Magazine*, October 30, 2005. http://www.time.com/time/magazine/article/0,9171,1124306,00.html

26. Viveca Novak, "Woodward Unveiled," *Time Magazine*, 20 Nov. 2005. http://www.time/com/time/magazine/article/0,9171,1132804,00.html

27. Jane Hamsher, "Viveca Novak: Trouble Comes in Threes," *Huffington Post*, December 12, 2005. http://www.huffingtonpost.com/jane-hamsher/viveca-novak-trouble-come_b_12109.html

28. Arianna Huffington, "Plamegate and the Press: When Will Somebody Get Fired?" *Huffington Post* December 13, 2005. http://www.huffingtonpost.com/arianna-huffington/plamegate-and-the-press-w_b_12228.html

29. Arianna Huffington, "Heck of a Job, Viveca?" December 18, 2005. http://www.huffingtonpost.com/arianna-huffington/heck-of-a-job-viveca_b_12504.html

30. Thomas B. Edsall and Dan Eggen, "Bush Picks Controversial Nominees for FEC," *Washington Post*, December 17, 2005. http://www.washingtonpost.com/wp-dyn/content/article/2005/ 12/16/AR2005121601717.html

31. Rick Hasen, "Lenhard FEC Appointment as 'Payback' for Novak Testimony?" Election Law Blog, December 19, 2005. http://electionlawblog.org/?p=4427

32. Howard Kurtz, "Woodward Apologizes to Post for Silence on Role in Leak Case," *Washington Post*, November 17, 2005. http://www.washingtonpost.com/wp-dyn/content/article/2005/11/16/AR2005111601286.html

33. Christopher Cooper and Joe Hagan, "Time Writer Cites Details of Talk with Rove Lawyer," *Wall Street Journal*, December 12, 2005, A4.

34. David Johnston, "Reporter Recounts Talk About C.I.A. Leak," *New York Times*, December 12, 2005. A. 23. http://www.nytimes.com/2005/12/12/politics/12leak.html

35. "About Us" FactCheck.org. http://factcheck.org/about/

Chapter 9

1. Nan Robertson, *The Girls in the Balcony: Women, Men and The New York Times*, (New York: Ballantine Books, 1992) 7–8.

2. Ibid, 157.

3. Ibid, 209–210.

4. Ibid, 207–208.

5. Ibid., 232.

6. Ibid, 209.

7. Carole Simpson, *News Lady*, (Bloomington: Authorhouse, 2010) 114.

8. Lynn Sherr, *Outside the Box: A Memoir*, (Rodale, 2006) 228

9. "South Korea: Spooking Capitol Hill," *Time Magazine*, November 15, 1976. http://www.time.com/time/magazine/article/0,9171,712311,00.html

10. "Investigations: Koreagate on Capitol Hill?" *Time Magazine*, November 29, 1976. http://www.time.com/time/magazine/article/0,9171,914710,00.html

11. "The Year of the Spy." FBI website. http://www.fbi.gov/about-us/history/famous-cases/the-year-of-the-spy/

12. Sherr, *Outside the Box,* 212.

13. Barbara Matusow, "Powers of the Press," *Washingtonian Magazine*, August 1997, 60.

14. Beverley Lumpkin, "Race and the Death Penalty," Halls of Justice: A Weekly Look Inside the Justice Department, ABC News, July 7. http://abcnews.go.com/US/story?id=96513&page=6

15. Beverley Lumpkin, "Halls of Justice: A Weekly Look at the Justice Department," ABC News.com, March 9, 2001

16. Adonis Hoffman, "The Racial Undertones of the Oklahoma Bombing," *Chicago Tribune*, April 28, 1995. http://articles.chicagotribune.com/1995-04-28/news/9504280109_1_arab-americans-oklahoma-bombing-african-americans

17. Chitra Ragavan, "Ashcroft's Way," *U.S. News & World Report*, January 18, 2004. http://www.usnews.com/usnews/news/articles/040126/26ashcroft.htm

18. Carol D. Leonnig and Amy Goldstein, "Libby Found Guilty in CIA Leak Case," *Washington Post*, March 7, 2007. http://www.washingtonpost.com/wp-dyn/content/article/2007/03/06/AR2007030600648.html

Chapter 10

1. "History of the City News Bureau," The Newberry Library collections, 2008. http://mms.newberry.org/html/CityNewsBureau.html

2. "Chicago's City News Service Closes Shop," December 12, 2005, Associated Press. http://archive.newsmax.com/archives/ic/2005/12/12/142111.shtml

3. Ibid.

4. "Ho Chi Minh City," *Encyclopedia Britannica*, accessed December 31, 2011. http://www.britannica.com/EBchecked/topic/268316/Ho-Chi-Minh-City

5. Paul von Zielbauer, "My Story," Mindfood.com, August 19, 2010. http://www.mindfood.com/at-paul-von-zielbauer-my-story.seo

6. '2 German Parties Reach Deal to Relax Law on Citizenship," *New York Times*, October 15, 1998. http://www.nytimes.com/1998/10/15/world/2-german-parties-reach-deal-to-relax-law-on-citizenship.html

7. Tony Barber and Andrew Marshall, "Serbs expelled almost 800,000 Muslims," *The Independent*, September 21, 1994. http://www.independent.co.uk/news/world/europe/serbs-expelled-almost-800000-muslims-1450105.html

8. Sherry Ricchiardi, "Exposing Genocide ... For What?" *American Journalism Review*, June 1993. http://www.ajr.org/article.asp?id=1516

9. Paul Zielbauer, "Strong coffee, Cigarettes, Power daily Struggle to Win Democracy," *Washington Times*, December 17, 1996. A13.

10. Chris Hedges, "Student Foes of Belgrade Leader Embrace Fierce Serb Nationalism," *New York Times*, December 10, 1996. http://www.nytimes.com/1996/12/10/world/student-foes-of-belgrade-leader-embrace-fierce-serb-nationalism.html?pagewanted=all&src=pm

11. "Protests in Serbia," Oneline Newshour Forum, December 11, 1996. http://www.pbs.org/newshour/forum/december96/serbia_12-11.html

12. Elsa Brenner, "Setbacks challenge the Hudson, *New York Times*, July 12, 1998. http://www.nytimes.com/1998/07/12/nyregion/setbacks-challenge-the-hudson.html? page wanted=all&src=pm

13. Paul Zielbauer, "What are PCBs?" *Albany Times-Union*, September 20, 1998, A5.

14. "Human Health Risk Assessment, Mid-Hudson River, Executive Summary, Environmental Protection Agency, December 1999. http://www.epa.gov/hudson/hhra.htm

15. Paul von Zielbauer, "The Nutmeg State Battles the Stigma of Corrupticut," *New York Times*, March 28, 2003, D1.

16. Paul von Zielbauer, "As Health Care in Jails Goes Private, 10 Days Can Be A Death Sentence," *New York Times*, February 27, 2005, A1.

17. "Death Behind Bars," editorial, *New York Times*, March 10, 2005, A26.

18. Gabriel Sherman, "Times Recruits Team for Baghdad Bureau: Its 'Volunteer Army'" *New York Observer*, June 11, 2006. http://www.observer.com/2006/06/times-recruits-team-for-baghdad-bureau-its-volunteer-army/

19. Paul von Zielbauer, "Web Sites Rally Support for G.I.'s in Legal Trouble," *New York Times*, July 22, 2007. http://www.nytimes.com/2007/07/22/world/middleeast/22abuse.html?pagewanted=all

20. Nicolai Ouroussoff, "Pride and Nostalgia Mix in the Times's New Home," *New York Times*, November 20, 2007. http://www.nytimes.com/2007/11/20/arts/design/20time.html?pagewanted=all

21. Bob Garfield, "The News Tower: Transcript," *On The Media*, NPR, May 30, 2008. http://www.onthemedia.org/2008/may/30/the-news-tower/transcript/

22. "How We're Different," Roadmonkey web site. http://www.roadmonkey.net/site/how-were-different.php

23. Von Zielbauer, "My Story."

Chapter 11

1. Solange De Santis, *Life on The Line: One Woman's Tale of Work, Sweat and Survival*, (New York: Anchor Books, 2000), 70–71.

2. Ibid., 15.

3. Ibid, 43.

4. Solange De Santis, "Curtain Up!" 2008. http://solangedesantis.com

5. De Santis, *Life on The Line*, 24.

6. Ibid., 24.

7. Ibid, 8.

8. Ibid. 7.

9. Ibid, 271.

10. Ibid, 9–10.

11. Charles Solomon, "One for the Read; Undercover Reporter at GM Plant Never Shifts Out of First Gear," review of *Life on the Line: One Woman's Tale of Work, Sweat, and Survival,* by Solange De Santis, *Los Angeles Times,* November 17, 1999, 2.

12. Deborah Stead, "How Blue Is Your Collar," review of *Life on the Line: One Woman's Tale of Work, Sweat, and Survival,* by Solange De Santis, *New York Times,* June 13, 1999, 3.7.

13. Mark Heinzl, "Bre-X probe intensifies as tests find little gold, *Wall Street Journal,* May 6, 1997, A.3.

14. Solange De Santis and Mark Heinzl, "Canada Recommends Tougher Rules for Mining Firms After Bre-X Fiasco," *Wall Street Journal,* June 9, 1998, 1.

15. Solange De Santis, "Northern Parallel: Vietnam vets fight for Canada's respect," *Wall Street Journal,* November 17, 1995, A.1.

16. Solange De Santis, "The mobile guide: An Acadian Fete Authentique," *Wall Street Journal,* September 4, 1996, A12.

17. Solange De Santis, "A Glenn Gould Gathering: The Pianist Remembered," *Wall Street Journal,* October 7, 1999, A. 28.

18. Solange De Santis, "Nice Bagpipes, Man, But Don't You Feel A Draft in That Skirt?" *Wall Street Journal,* October 12, 1994. A.1.

19. "Anglican Journal: About Us," *Anglican Journal* web site, 2011. http://www.anglican journal.com/aboutus/history.html

20. "Solange De Santis Named Editor of Episcopal Life Media," Episcopal News Service, September 1, 2008. http://www.ecusa.anglican.org/79425_97484_ENG_HTM.htm

Chapter 12

1. James Fallows, *Breaking the News: How the Media Undermine American Democracy,* (New York: Vintage Books, 1997) 8.

2. Kurt Andersen, "The Outsider," *New Yorker Magazine,* March 31, 1997.

3. Maureen Dowd, "All Tripped Up," *New York Times,* June 28, 1998, 4.1.

4. Author interview with James Steele, July 2010.

5. James Fallows, *Breaking the News,* 178.

6. Neal Ascherson, "A Democracy of Journalists," openDemocracy July 18, 2011. http://www.opendemocracy.net/neal-ascherson/democracy-of-journalists

7. H.L. Mencken, *A Gang of Pecksniffs, and other Comments on Newspaper Publishers, Editors and Reporters,* ed. Theo Lippman, Jr. (New Rochelle: Arlington House Publishers,1975) 129.

8. "Richard J. Roth" Journalism Faculty, Medill Northwestern University website http://www.medill.northwestern.edu/faculty/journalismfulltime.aspx?id=128741.

9. Author interview with Bruce Shapiro, April 2010.

10. Shawn Lawrence Otto, *Fool Me Twice: Fighting the Assault on Science In America,* (New York: Rodale, 2011) 10.

11. Jessica Dorman, "Where Are Muckraking Journalists Today?" Nieman Reports, Summer 2000. http://www.nieman.harvard.edu/reports/article/101937/Where-Are-Muckraking-Journalists-Today.aspx

12. Donald L. Barlett and James B. Steele, "Reporting Is Only Part of the Investigative Story," Nieman Reports, Spring 2008. http://www.nieman.harvard.edu/reportsitem.aspx?id=100077

13. Author interview with James Fallows, August 2010.

14. "About NPR: Public Radio Finances," NPR, http://www.npr.org/about/aboutnpr/publicradiofinances.html

15. Richard Perez-Pena, "Group Plans to Provide Investigative Journalism," *New York Times*, October 15, 2007. http://www.nytimes.com/2007/10/15/business/media/15publica.html

16. Paul Steiger, "A Note on ProPublica's Second Pulitzer Prize," April 18, 2011. http://www.propublica.org/article/a-note-on-propublicas-second-pulitzer-prize/single

17. "Texas Tribune Inc." Community Matters, September 19, 2009. http://communitymatters.biz/2009/09/19/texas-tribune-inc/

18. Charles Lewis, Brittney Butts, and Kate Musselwhite, "A Second Look: The New Journalism Ecosystem," Investigative Reporting Workshop, November 30, 2011. http://investigativereportingworkshop.org/ilab/story/second-look/

19. Melinda Wittstock, "Award-winning Nonprofit Capitol News Connection to Close," CNC News, September 12, 2011.

20. "About AOL," AOL, http://corp.aol.com/about-aol

21. Verne G. Kopytoff, "AOL Bets on Hyperlocal News, Finding Progress Where Many Have Failed," *New York Times*, January 16, 2011. http://www.nytimes.com/2011/01/17/business/media/17local.html?pagewanted=all

22. Ryan Chittum, "The NYT Paywall Is Out of the Gate Fast," *Columbia Journalism Review*, July 22, 2011. http://www.cjr.org/the_audit/the_nyt_paywall_is_out_of_the.php

23. "About This Site," What Went Wrong: The Betrayal of the American Dream, http://americawhatwentwrong.org/about/

Bibliography

Communication on Freedom of the Press. *A Free and Responsible Press: A General report on Mass Communication: Newspapers, Radio, Motion Pictures, Magazines, and Books.* Edited by Robert D. Leigh. Chicago: University of Chicago Press, 1947.

Dawkins, Wayne. *Black Journalists: The NABJ Story.* Merrillville, Indiana: August Press, 1997.

_____. *Rugged Waters: Black Journalists Swim the Mainstream.* Newport News, VA: August Press, 2003.

De Santis, Solange. *Life on The Line: One Woman's Tale of Work, Sweat and Survival,* New York: Anchor Books, 2000.

Ellison, Sarah. *War at the Wall Street Journal: Inside the Struggle to Control an American Business Empire.* New York: Houghton Mifflin Harcourt Publishing, 2010.

Fallows, James. *Breaking the News: How the Media Undermine American Democracy.* New York: Vintage Books, 1997.

Gardner, Howard, Mihaley Csikszentmihalyi and William Damon, *Good Work: When Excellence and Ethics Meet.* New York: Basic Books, 2001.

Gunther, Marc. *The House That Roone Built, The Inside Story of ABC News.* New York: Little, Brown and Company, 1994.

Iliff, Theodore. *The Golden Times.* Pittsburgh, Pennsylvania: RoseDog Books, 2009.

Jones, Alex S. *Losing The News.* New York: Oxford University Press, 2009.

Kovach, Bill and Tom Rosenstiel. *The Elements of Journalism.* New York: Random House, 2007.

Lamay, Craig L. and Everette E. Dennis, ed. *The Culture of Crime.* New Brunswick: Transaction Publishers, 1995.

McChesney, Robert W. and Nichols, John, *The Death and Life of American Journalism.* New York: Nation Books, 2010.

Mencken, H.L. *A Gang of Pecksniffs and other Comments on Newspaper Publishers, Editors and Reporters.* Edited by Theo Lippman, Jr. New Rochelle: Arlington House Publishers, 1975.

Phelan, James and Robert Pozen, *The Company State: Ralph Nader's Study Group Report on Dupont in Delaware,* New York: Grossman Publishers, 1973.

Robertson, Nan. *The Girls in the Balcony: Women, Men and The New York Times.* New York: Ballantine Books, 1992.

Saar, Erik and Viveca Novak. *Inside the Wire: A Military Intelligence Soldier's Eyewitness Account of Life at Guantanamo.* New York: The Penguin Press, 2005.

Selditch, Dianne, ed. *My First Year as a Journalist: Real World Stories from America's Newspaper and Magazine Journalists.* New York: Walker and Company, 1995.

Sherr, Lynn. *Outside the Box: A Memoir.* Rodale, 2006.

Simon, David. *Homicide: A Year on the Killing Streets.* New York: Ballantine Books, 1991.

_____ and Edward Burns. *The Corner: A Year in the Life of an Inner-City Neighborhood.* New York: Broadway Books, 1998.

Simpson, Carole. *News Lady.* Bloomington: Authorhouse, 2010.

Taylor, Paul. *See How They Run: Electing the President in an Age of Mediocracy.* New York: Knopf, 1990.

The Trotter Group. *Black Voices in Commentary.* Newport News, VA: August Press, 2006.

Index